A Future for Presentism

A Future for Presentism

Craig Bourne

CLARENDON PRESS · OXFORD

OXFORD
UNIVERSITY PRESS

Great Clarendon Street, Oxford OX2 6DP

Oxford University Press is a department of the University of Oxford.
It furthers the University's objective of excellence in research, scholarship,
and education by publishing worldwide in

Oxford New York

Auckland Cape Town Dar es Salaam Hong Kong Karachi
Kuala Lumpur Madrid Melbourne Mexico City Nairobi
New Delhi Shanghai Taipei Toronto

With offices in

Argentina Austria Brazil Chile Czech Republic France Greece
Guatemala Hungary Italy Japan Poland Portugal Singapore
South Korea Switzerland Thailand Turkey Ukraine Vietnam

Oxford is a registered trade mark of Oxford University Press
in the UK and in certain other countries

Published in the United States
by Oxford University Press Inc., New York

© Craig Bourne 2006

The moral rights of the authors have been asserted
Database right Oxford University Press (maker)

First published 2006

All rights reserved. No part of this publication may be reproduced,
stored in a retrieval system, or transmitted, in any form or by any means,
without the prior permission in writing of Oxford University Press,
or as expressly permitted by law, or under terms agreed with the appropriate
reprographics rights organization. Enquiries concerning reproduction
outside the scope of the above should be sent to the Rights Department,
Oxford University Press, at the address above

You must not circulate this book in any other binding or cover
and you must impose the same condition on any acquirer

British Library Cataloguing in Publication Data

Data available

Library of Congress Cataloging in Publication Data

Data available

Typeset by Laserwords Private Limited, Chennai, India
Printed in Great Britain by the
MPG Books Group, Bodmin and King's Lynn

ISBN 978-0-19-921280-4 (Hbk)
ISBN 978-0-19-956821-5 (Pbk)

10 9 8 7 6 5 4 3 2 1

For mum, dad, and family

Contents

Preface and Acknowledgements — xi

Introduction — 1
    I What is a theory of time? — 1
    II Initial plausible options for a theory of time — 3
    III What conditions must any adequate philosophical theory of time satisfy? — 14

Part I The Presentist Manifesto — 19

1 When am I? — 21
    I The Present Problem — 21
    II Tensed theories toppled — 24
    III Tensed truth-conditions: token-reflexive or non-token-reflexive, that's not the question — 33

2 A theory of presentism — 39
    I The parameters of the problem — 39
    II A radical response — 40
    III Priorian presentism — 41
    IV Reductive presentism — 47
    V Ersatzer presentism — 52
    VI Branching time for presentists — 61
    VII The advantages of ersatzer presentism — 65

3 Some outstanding problems for presentism met — 70
    Problem 1 McTaggart's argument — 70
        I McTaggart's position — 71
        II McTaggart's argument — 73
        III How ersatzer presentism avoids McTaggart's argument — 76
    Problem 2 A deontic, semantic, and paradoxical need for other times — 78
        I The deontic need — 78
        II The semantic need — 79

	III The paradoxical need	80
	Problem 3 Future contingents, non-contradiction, and the law of excluded middle muddle	82
	Problem 4 Transtemporal relations (I)	95
	I *Earlier than* and defining tenses	96
	II Determinables	98
	III Qualitative relations	98
	Problem 5 Transtemporal relations (II): reference	99
	I Prior, proper names, and presentism	99
	II Rigidity for Russellians	102
	III Who wants to be a Millianaire?	103
	IV Passing the nominal parcel	104
4	Transtemporal relations (III): causation	109
	I Formulating theories of causation within presentism	110
	II The direction of time and causation: the counterfactual connotation of causation	115
	III The direction of time and causation: the means–end connotation of causation	121
	IV Mellor's argument against causal loops	131
	V Presentism and backwards causation	134
Part II Presentism and Relativity		**137**
5	Physics for philosophers	141
	I Basic notions	141
	II Essentials of special relativity	146
	III Minkowski space–time diagrams	151
	IV Minkowski's philosophical conclusions	157
6	The present dialectic in special relativity	160
	I Putnam's thesis	160
	II Stein's antithesis	162
	III Questioning the grounds for adopting Einstein's definition of simultaneity	172
	IV Understanding and defining absolute simultaneity	173
	V The interpretation of the Lorentz transformations	176
	VI The 'conspiracy of silence' objection	179
	VII Simplicity and surplus content	182
	VIII The Present Problem revisited	184

IX	Conclusion	185
7	Becoming inflated	187
I	The Mellor–Rees argument against tense theories	187
II	Can expansion combat such wrinkles?	191
III	Event and creation horizons	197
IV	Bursting the balloon	198
8	All the time in the worlds: Gödel's modal moral	204
I	Gödel's philosophical position on the nature of time	205
II	Establishing part 1 of Gödel's argument	206
III	Part 2 of Gödel's argument	212
IV	Using TNT as ammunition against Gödel's conclusion	213
V	Tenseless time: one way to dispose of TNT safely	214
VI	The essential properties of time	216
VII	Another way to dispose of TNT—although taking great care to do it safely	217

Bibliography 225
Index 239

Preface and Acknowledgements

I got hooked on the philosophy of time as a first year undergraduate in Cambridge after reading Hugh Mellor's *Real Time* and attending his lectures in the Easter Term of 1995–6. That term I was also supervised on time by Jeremy Butterfield, and although we agreed that the tenseless theory was indeed a wonderful thing, I thought presentism was not entirely dead. That thought turned into this book. One reason for thinking presentism was not entirely ruled out as a viable position was that I thought presentism could escape McTaggart's argument. Thinking I was on to something, I remember being a little depressed when Katherine Hawley, who supervised my third year undergraduate coursework on time, pointed me towards Robin Le Poidevin's 1991 book, where I found he had already beaten me to this idea! It was some consolation, though, to see that he thought presentism should be rejected on other grounds. Apart from that contribution, however, and Arthur Prior's work in the 1950s and 1960s, there was virtually no literature on presentism during this time. However, there has been a growing interest in the position in recent years, and I hope this will be seen to be a timely book.

Almost all of the ideas included here were formulated while I was a graduate in Cambridge (M.Phil. 1998–9; Ph.D. 1999–2002).

Chapter 1 was first given as a talk in Cambridge in October 2000, and also read at the Ninth Annual Harvard–MIT Philosophy Conference, March 2001, and the Joint Session of the Mind Association and Aristotelian Society, York University, July 2001. It was first published as 'When am I? A Tense Time for Some Tense Theorists?', *Australasian Journal of Philosophy*, 80 (2002), 359–71.

Chapter 2 was given as talks in Cambridge in July 1999, June 2001, and at the Moral Sciences Club in March 2002 (as 'Between Timid and Timbuktu'), as well as in Leeds in February 2004 (as 'Real Time III: The Presentist Strikes Back'). It was first published as 'A Theory of Presentism', *Canadian Journal of Philosophy*, 36 (2006) 1–24.

Chapter 3 has a rather complex history, but some of Problem 2 was first published in a review of *Time, Tense and Reference*, edited by Q. Smith and A. Jokić, *Mind*, 114 (2005), 747–50; Problem 3 was first published as 'Future Contingents, Non-Contradiction and the Law of Excluded Middle Muddle', *Analysis*, 64 (2004), 122–8, and Problem 5 was first given as a talk in Leeds in June 2005.

My work on Newcomb's problem and backwards causation (Chapter 4, section III) was first read at the Joint Session of the Mind Association and Aristotelian Society, Nottingham University, July 1999. Many thanks to Kate Williams for letting me use some of her work in section II.

My take on special relativity in Chapter 6 was first given in a talk in Cambridge in February 1999.

Chapter 7 was first published as 'Becoming Inflated', *British Journal for the Philosophy of Science*, 55 (2004), 107–19.

Chapter 8 was first given as a talk in Cambridge in February 2000, and has been given, together with work from Chapters 6 and 7, at a workshop on *Time and Existence* at Leeds University, June 2005 (as 'The Present Dialectic in Relativity'), and at Bristol and Reading Universities, February 2006 (as 'All the Time in the Worlds: Gödel's Modal Moral').

Many thanks to those who commented on various parts of this work or who have been generally supportive: Jeremy Butterfield, Oren Goldschmidt, Katherine Hawley, Robin Le Poidevin, Peter Lipton, Joseph Melia, Michael Potter, Peter Smith, various audience members (particularly in Leeds) who have attended my talks and lectures, and those helpful anonymous referees. Special mention must be made of Hugh Mellor, who, despite holding contrary views, has been a good friend and supportive throughout.

Friends who deserve a mention for their contribution to my well-being during the long history of this book are Sarah Boyes, Bee Brooke, Josie Cluer, Paul Dicken, Nora Goldschmidt, Oren Goldschmidt, Clare Jarmy, David Kelnar, Tor Lezemore, Annabelle Ross, James Sharp, Cait Turvey Roe, Kate Williams, my current students from Pembroke and St Catharine's Colleges, and my daft little egg Emily Caddick. Special mention must be made of Marina Frasca-Spada, who has been a constant source of help and encouragement.

I am indebted to St Catharine's College, Cambridge, for appointing me to a Research Fellowship (2002–6), which allowed me to complete this book.

C. P. B.
Cambridge
March 2006

Introduction

I What is a theory of time?

Time plays a central role in our lives and our world-view; it is fundamental to the idea of what it is to be the very beings that we are; it is indispensable to the way we structure our experiences; it is central to our understanding of the world. Its cultural importance, as the linguist David Crystal (2002: 120) notes, is reflected in the multitude of temporal metaphors we employ:

> we *have* time, *find* time, *allow* time ... *take* time, *give* time, *fix* time, and *borrow* time (by living on it). We *need* it, *spend* it, *save* it, *waste* it, *lose* it, *gain* it, *buy* it, *value* it, *make* it *up*, and *play for* it. ... Time *passes, whiles away, flies, runs, drags, hangs (heavily)*, or *stands still*; we can *mark* time and *keep* time. ... We can *make* time. Time can *heal*. And ... we can *kill* it.   (Crystal (2002: 120))

Its ubiquity in everyday thought and conversation, its importance in structuring our day and co-ordinating meetings with others, and the fact that we all take time and need time in quieter moments for contemplation—perhaps even upon time itself: 'Time passes. Listen. Time passes.' (Dylan Thomas, *Under Milk Wood*)—goes someway to explaining why we all feel we can have a say in discussions of it: just as with many matters philosophical, scores of reflective people claim to have some kind of 'philosophy' of time. But some of the metaphors above are taken more seriously than others, at least by analytical philosophers. For although we all feel we have a stake in time, as reflected above in the metaphors of ownership and value, it is the metaphors of measurement and motion that we take seriously and as attempting to capture some fundamental aspect of the world. Why this should be is an interesting question, and perhaps distinguishes the interests that analytical philosophers have in time from those in the continental tradition; but why the metaphors of measurement and motion, as opposed to those of ownership and value, are taken more seriously—that is, why we do *not* think we can find such a thing as time, let alone spend it when we do, but nevertheless think there *is* some literal truth in its flowing—is because the truth behind the latter kind of metaphor *facilitates* what we take to be important in the former. Time is important to us because it allows us and things around us to change, to develop, to cease. That's why we find time to spend it. More to the present point, that's *how* we are able to spend it: it is facilitated through change, and thus one reason why, I think, the metaphors of measurement and motion are taken with more ontological seriousness than the rest. Thus we shouldn't appeal to linguistic usage to determine what is important about time; we should delve deeper to discover what it is that grounds such usage and how it is possible for such metaphors to be manifested.

One way of partitioning off the more serious metaphors, and the reason why those facilitate the others, seems to be that, whereas the metaphors of ownership and value reflect facts about *us* and what we do *with* time, the metaphors of measurement and motion seem to be more about the nature of time *itself*. And since the nature of time is what this book is about, these are what we need to consider. Such platitudes as 'time flows' or 'the past is fixed but the future is open' have, then, to be accounted for in any adequate theory of time, since these platitudes help form, and to a large extent constitute, our *concept* of time. Inevitably, questions arise from the commonplace things that we say and believe, such as 'If the future is mapped out before us, are our actions futile?', questions that require a systematic account to make sense of the things that are said and believed about time, and which gives answers to the questions that arise during the enterprise itself. Anything that attempts to offer something along these lines, I shall call a 'theory of time'.

Before I start presenting my own theory, I shall spend the rest of this introduction setting the scene for it. I shall sketch the most popular theories of time and some of the problems with which they have to deal. Although this book is a defence of presentism, I am much impressed by the tenseless theory of time. For me, this is the theory to beat, the one to match in terms of elegance, transparency, and explanatory power. I shall show that my particular version of presentism can do just that, and that presentism is the only real alternative to the tenseless theory.

II Initial plausible options for a theory of time

There are many different theories of time to be found in the literature, but they each fall into one of two broad categories: the *tenseless* theories, on the one hand; and the *tensed* theories, on the other.

(a) The tenseless theories

According to tenseless theories, all times are equally real, as are all the objects (by which I shall mean things, events, facts) located at them—Plato, for instance, exists as a flesh and blood creature in the same way that we do—and there is no passage of time from future to present to past (hence the label 'tenseless' theory of time). Early versions of this theory were advocated by Russell (1915), Broad (1921), Goodman (1951), Williams (1951), Quine (1960), Smart (1963), and Grünbaum (1967), but more recent defences include Smart (1980), Mellor (1981) and (1998), Oaklander (1984), and Le Poidevin (1991). It can be represented as follows:

(1) **Tenseless theory**: all times are real and time does not flow.

But if times themselves are not past, present, or future, how are they to be located in a temporal sequence; how are they to be ordered? According to the tenseless theory, we should think of objects being *earlier than*, *later than*, or *simultaneous with* each other, and as being located by *dates*. So the event of my birth on 16 November 1976 is later than that of Descartes', but earlier than the date on which this sentence is currently being read. McTaggart (1908) called the ordering of objects in this way the 'B-series'. It is obvious that objects *do not*

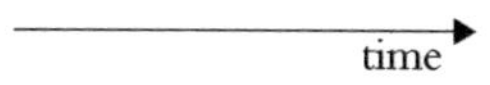

——————→
time

FIG. 0.1. The tenseless theory

change their B-series locations over time: if e is ever earlier than e^*, then e is always earlier than e^*.

Contrast this with locating objects using *tenses*. McTaggart called the sequences of objects ordered in this way the 'A-series'. Since this is to think of time as flowing—as changing from being future, becoming present, and then receding off into the past—the characteristic feature of objects in the A-series is that they *do change* their A-series locations. Following Mellor (1998: 8), we can distinguish the A-scale (the sequences of tenses) from the A-series (the sequences of objects themselves located by these tenses), and we can make an analogous distinction between the B-series and the B-scale.

Now, to say that the tenseless theory does not treat tenses in any ontologically significant, A-*series*, way is not to say that the tenseless theory can dispose of the A-*scale*. This was the mistake that the early defenders of the theory made. For modern defenders of the tenseless theory acknowledge that the *concept* of tense is essential to a proper account of action: it is no good for us to know that the meeting is on the 25th at 3 p.m. unless we know what time it is *now* and when the meeting is, relative to our present time. We can plan for it if it is future, or send apologies if it is past, or run if it is in five minutes; but we can't do anything effective (unless we are lucky) just by knowing its date. But conceding that A-*concepts* are essential in this way is not to say that we need to take tenses with any ontological seriousness. This can be seen clearly in specifying what, for the tenseless theory, makes tensed propositions true. The tenseless 'token-reflexive' truth-conditions account goes as follows:

(TR.1) A token utterance u of 'e is present' is true iff e occurs simultaneously with u

(TR.2) A token utterance u of 'e is past' is true iff e occurs earlier than u

(TR.3) A token utterance u of 'e is future' is true iff e occurs later than u[1]

---

[1] There is some debate over whether the token-reflexive truth-conditions account is the best way to formulate the semantics for the tenseless theory. Smart (1980), for instance, offers what has become known as the 'date' theory. How to choose the best formulation of the truth-conditions for the tenseless theory is not something I shall discuss here, but I refer the reader to Le Poidevin (1998) and Oaklander (2003b) for a detailed discussion of the

We should note here that the right-hand side of the biconditional is not meant to be taken to give the *meaning* of the tensed statement token (as in the early versions of the theory) but rather to be taken as specifying the *truthmaker* for the tensed statement token. These are obviously tenseless facts; and so, if tenseless facts are sufficient to make tensed statements true, tensed facts are not required. Tenses, according to this view, have no ontological role to play in the truthmakers for tensed statements.

Before discussing the tenseless theory further, however, I should say a little more about tenses and sketch some of the rival theories that do take tenses with ontological seriousness.

(b) Tenses

It is standard to represent the tenses, past, present and future, using 'P', 'N', and 'F', respectively. However, it has been controversial whether we should treat 'P', 'N', and 'F' as to be predicated of events and interpreted as referring to the properties, *pastness*, *presentness* and *futurity* of events, written '*Pe*', '*Ne*', and '*Fe*', respectively. For Prior (1968a), Christensen (1976), and Levison (1987) think that many problems for tensed theories of time (which I shan't go into here) originate from thinking of time's flow as a change in the temporal properties of events. Because of this, Prior's aim is to reduce talk about events and changes in events to talk about things and changes in things. In other words, he thinks the problems are caused by an event ontology. But, according to Prior, since, *via* his analysis, we need not be committed to events, but only to things, the problems vanish.

Prior (1968a: 16) considers the following example:

(0.1) My falling out of a punt has receded six years into the past.

This suggests that there is an event (my falling out of a punt) which is itself going through a process of receding into the past, i.e., using metric operators with a unit of one year,

---

relevant considerations, and to Mellor (1998), who proposes the following in response to Smith's (1993: ch. 3) criticisms of the token-reflexive theory: 'Any A-proposition 'P' about any event e is made true at any t by t's being as much earlier or later than e as 'P' says the present is than e' (Mellor (1998: 32–4)).

(0.1*) $(\exists e)(P^6 e \,\&\, e = $ my falling out of a punt$)$.

But Prior says that there is no reason to believe in events: 'events do not exist at all; only *things* exist—events are just what things do and what happens to them' (1996a), and so there is no reason to believe in such an object as *my falling out of a punt*; for (0.1) can be rewritten as

(0.2) It is now six years since it was the case that I am falling out of a punt,

i.e.,

(0.2*) $\mathbf{P}^6(\exists x)(\exists y)(x = $ me $\&$ punt $(y)\,\&\,$ falls out of $(x, y))$

Or, rather, to capture the fact that I still exist whether or not the punt does:

(0.2**) $(\exists x)(x = $ Craig Bourne$)\,\&\,\mathbf{P}^6(\exists x)(\exists y)(x = $ Craig Bourne $\&$ punt $(y)\,\&\,$ falls out of $(x, y))$

This commits us to acknowledging no more than the existence of myself and a punt that *did* exist. In other words, the work done by temporal predicates which appear to name temporal properties, such as 'is past' and 'is future', and noun-phrases which appear to name temporal locations, such as 'the past' and 'the future', is done by replacing them with temporal adverbs, which modify sentences about things and their properties and relations.

Although this analysis involves reducing temporal predicates to temporal adverbs, this is not to say that the debate is merely about language and linguistic tense, any more than, say, nominalism in the theory of properties shows the debate is simply about our use of predicates. The purpose is to establish the ontological commitments of true propositions. Prior claims that the analysis shows that he is committed only to things and the properties they have, will have, and have had, and is not committed to events and the temporal properties of pastness, presentness, and futurity (but see chapter 2: §III, where I show his view is not entirely satisfactory).

But it would be uncomfortable for those who believe in an ontologically significant notion of tense to rest on the elimination of events. For Davidson (1969) claims that we require the existence of events in order to make sense of: (a) action statements ((1967a); (1969:164)); (b) causal statements (1967b); (c) explanation (1969: 165); (d) the mind–body problem (1969: 165), and (e) the logic of adverbial modification (1969: 166). Although I shall deny (b) in Chapter 4, Davidson's treatment of (a) and (e) is for the most part persuasive (but see Casati and Varzi (1996)). And, even though some philosophers (e.g., Horgan (1978)) think that all talk of events can be eliminated in Prior's way, by treating modifiers not as predicates of events but as sentential operators—which does not require quantification over events—the upshot of this research may be that neither a pure event nor a pure thing ontology can do the job of a combined ontology of events and things; we may well require both. Fortunately, those who take tenses with ontological seriousness can remain somewhat neutral on this; for (0.1) need not have been analysed as (0.1*) at all but could be analysed as:

(0.1**) $\mathbf{P}^6(\exists e)(\text{falling out of (me, punt, } e))$

which equally (with (0.2*)) need not commit us to anything which exists in the past, although it does commit us to events (at least events that *did* exist).[2]

Thus, we can treat 'P', 'N', and 'F' as operators on propositions, written '$\mathbf{P}p$', '$\mathbf{N}p$', and '$\mathbf{F}p$', and read 'It was the case that p', 'It is the case that p' and 'It will be the case that p', respectively. And for present purposes it does not matter which interpretation of 'P', 'N', and 'F' is understood since, e.g., 'Pe' can be phrased in terms of '$\mathbf{P}p$' by taking 'p' to be 'e occurs'. What matters is that doing this in no way precludes tensed theorists having events in their ontology, in the way that I've explained.

Both 'Pe' and '$\mathbf{P}p$' correspond to facts, namely the facts that e *is* P, and that *it was the case that p*, respectively. Properties are either relational or non-relational, so P is either meant to locate the event e

---

[2] Strictly speaking, of course, if events are not instantaneous and are treated as changes, the best a presentist can have here is that, at any particular time, only *part* of an event exists concretely. But, using the methods in the following chapters, we can represent changes easily and in this way use all the advantages of event-talk.

in relation to something else, like the present, or locate it in virtue of its just being past. Likewise, '**P**' tells us when '*p*' is true, namely, in this case, when the fact that *p* is past.

More complex tenses can be represented by iteration, as in '*PFe*' and '**FP***p*', but this requires some niceties of interpretation in both cases. For in the case of properties of events, we cannot take '*P*' in '*PFe*' to be predicated of *Fe* since *Fe* is a fact, not an event; yet tenses here were supposed to be properties of events. Thus, we must think of *PF* as a whole to be the tensed property of the event *e*. In the case of operators on present-tensed singular propositions, the outer most operator does not (necessarily) operate on a present-tensed proposition (as in, e.g., **FP***p*). But so long as the inner-most proposition is present-tensed, this is all that matters. From here onwards, I shall represent tenses using the propositional operators.

Either way, the question remains as to whether we should take tenses to be relational or non-relational. In Prior's system of tense logic, tenses locate objects in virtue of their being either past, present, or future *simpliciter*: the propositional operators **P** and **F** are taken as primitive, and are governed by various axioms. However, as Prior notes ((1967: 38–42); (1968c)), it is possible to define the operators by quantifying over times and invoking the *earlier than* relation. Tenses can then locate objects by specifying how much earlier or later objects occur in relation to the present. This is similar to how I shall characterize tenses in this book (see Chapter 2).

One major advantage of this approach is that it enables us to have some common ground between tensed and tenseless theories. As noted above, the tenseless theory uses the 'B-series' relations *earlier than*, *later than*, and *simultaneous with* to order objects in time. This results in the difference between the A- and B-series amounting to this: objects in the B-series are earlier than, later than, or simultaneous with *each other*, whereas objects in the A-series are earlier than, later than or simultaneous with *the present*. Thus calling those relations 'B-series' relations is a misleading way of putting it, since they are relations that can be shared by both A- and B-scales.

This enables us to state the truth-conditions of '**P***p*', '**N***p*', and '**F***p*' essentially as follows (the full story being given in Chapter 2):

'**P**p' is true at a time t iff 'p' is true at some time earlier than t; and

'**N**p' is true at a time t iff 'p' is true at some time simultaneous with t;

'**F**p' is true at a time t iff 'p' is true at some time later than t,

where t for tensed theorists is the present time, but for tenseless theorists is any given time. This goes some way to bypassing issues that once dominated the philosophy of time. For now the real issue is not whether tensed language and concepts can be reduced to tenseless language and concepts, since we've seen that tenseless theorists can quite happily concede that this is not possible, without having to take tenses with ontological seriousness. Nor is the issue one of whether tenses can be defined without invoking the relations of *earlier than* and *later than*, since, as we've seen, these can quite happily be incorporated into the A-scale to define what it is to be past and future. Rather, the fundamental difference between tense and tenseless theories I take to be this: the tenseless theory postulates the B-scale relations (and real *relata*) and no more, whereas the tense theories postulate an ontologically privileged present moment (which changes as time moves on).

In this book, the notions of past and future are defined in terms of the *earlier than* and *later than* relations, respectively. I then go on to define these relations in terms of what I call the 'E-relation', something different from the genuine *earlier than* relation (see Chapter 2). Thus the interesting debate really concerns whether there is something special about the present, not whether one scale is more fundamental than the other—after all, I talk in terms of both and ultimately take none of them as primitive, defining the A-scale notions in terms of something other than B-scale relations. Tooley (1997) also denies that the debate between tensed and tenseless theorists concerns whether the notions of pastness, presentness, and futurity or the notions of earlier, later, and simultaneity should be taken as analytically basic, since his is a tensed theory that defines pastness and futurity in terms of earlier and later. Neither, if we follow Tooley, should the partition be made in terms of whether tensed statements are taken to have tensed or tenseless facts as truthmakers, since these too cut across the different theories, given that Tooley invokes tenseless facts as the truthmakers for tensed statements (but see Chapter 1: §II for criticism of his theory).

Similarly, the debate cannot be formulated in terms of whether tensed statement tokens are taken to have token-reflexive or non-token-reflexive truth-conditions. For this does not partition all tensed theories from all tenseless theories, since tenseless theorists can formulate truth-conditions either way (see n. 1); and although tensed theorists have traditionally given tensed non-token-reflexive truth-conditions for tensed statements, some tensed theorists have put forward tensed token-reflexive truth-conditions for tensed statements (e.g., Lowe (1998)) (see Chapter 1: §III, for discussion and criticism of his position).

Neither can the debate be phrased in terms of whether we should read the existential quantifier in a tensed or tenseless way. The existential quantifier *should* be read tenselessly and *need not* be read any other way. It should be read tenselessly in order for presentists to be saying something non-trivial: if 'exists' means 'presently exists', then to say that only those objects which exist are those that presently exist is to spout an uninteresting truism. A tenseless reading is the only way of giving us common ground between the two sides of the debate; it tells us the substantial respects in which they differ. Neither is a tensed reading necessary to capture tensed existence predicates, such as the tensed existence predicates in '*a* exist*ed* but no longer exists', since this can be captured by:

(0.3) $\mathbf{P}(\exists x)(x = a) \& \sim(\exists x)(x = a),$

where the quantifiers are tenseless.

The debate I am concerned with, then, is purely metaphysical: if one's theory postulates an ontologically significant notion of the present, then that theory is a tensed theory.

(c) *The tensed theories*

Since what characterizes a theory of time as tenseless is the fact that it postulates equally real times but no ontologically significant notion of the present, then, ontologically speaking, there's only *one* way to be a tenseless theorist—the differences among tenseless theorists arise in formulating and filling out this ontological picture. There are, however, *many* ways, ontologically speaking, of being a tensed theorist. There are 7 combinations of the basic tenses that could be taken to exist by tensed theorists: P; N; F; P + N; P + F; N + F; P + N + F. Given that it is just not plausible to believe in the existence of the past, say, without believing in the existence of the present—for where would *we* exist in this picture?—we must believe in some sort of the present in order to have a plausible theory of time. For tensed theorists, this leaves available: N; P + N; N + F; P + N + F. Now, it may be suggested by some verificationists that N + F is a plausible option, something along the lines of: we have no warrant for asserting statements about the past since they cannot be verified, but statements about the present and future are warranted because they could be verified either now or in the future. I shall just assume here that verificationism can be rejected on independent grounds and so shall not discuss it further.

So let's consider one of the more plausible options: P + N + F, that past, present, and future are all real. The *linear* version of this comes in two forms. The first states that past, present, and future are equally real and time's flow amounts to the continual change of the temporal properties of being future, then present, then past. This is the view that McTaggart ((1908); (1927)) explicitly attacks, but which has been advocated in recent times by Lowe (1998). The second states that although past, present, and future are all real, the present is ontologically privileged, and time's flow amounts to the gaining and losing of the property of being present, rather than the swapping of the property of being future with that of being present and that of being past. Neither of these views asserts that temporal becoming is a change in the *existence* of which objects (events, things, facts, times themselves) there are, although one does get the feeling that the past and future objects in the second position do have a shady existence until the spotlight of the present shines upon them. This type of tensed theory can be represented as follows:

(1) **Past + Present + Future..ism**
   Past, present, and future are real and time flows.

```
    ————————★————————▶
        Past Present Future
```

FIG. 0.2. Past, present, and futurism

A slightly different version of this is the 'degree presentism' of Quentin Smith (2002), which states that not only do events have degrees of pastness and futurity, depending on how far away they are from the present, they also have corresponding degrees of reality. Thus, the present has full-blown existence, the recent past has a lesser degree of reality, and the distant past has an even less degree of reality. This can be represented as follows:

(1a) **Degree Presentism**
Not only do tenses come by degrees, but so does reality

```
degree of reality
        ___
       /   \
      /     \
     /       \
    Past  Present  Future
```

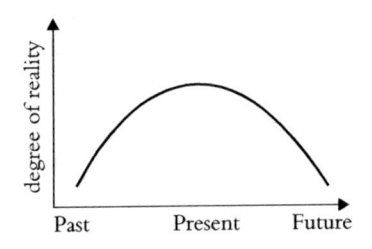

FIG. 0.3. Degree presentism

Unlike these views, some tensed theories hold that there is an ontological *asymmetry* between past and future. Within the P + N + F type of tensed theory, there is the view that past, present, and future objects exist, but that time's flow amounts to the dropping out of existence of the many real future possibilities, that is, as a subset of all those future objects become actual, such as the view of McCall (1994). I shall call this *branching-futurism*. It can be represented as follows:

(2) **Branching-futurism**
Time flows as future branches become actual.

But there is another way of holding an asymmetric view by adopting the P + N option and asserting that only the past and the present exist, and that time's flow amounts to coming into of existence of objects, such as the view associated with Broad (1923) and most recently

FIG. 0.4. Branching-futurism

defended by Tooley (1997). I shall call this position *no-futurism*. It can be represented as follows:

(3) **No-futurism**
   Only the past and present exist.

FIG. 0.5. No-futurism

No-futurism conceives of reality growing, whereas branching-futurism conceives of reality shedding, but both conceive of time's flow as a change in what exists.

The final initially plausible option is to adopt just N: presentism. Like no-futurism and branching-futurism, presentism also conceives of time's flow as a change in existence: only the present exists, the future is that which will come to exist, and the past is that which did exist. But, unlike these asymmetric views, in terms of the concrete reality of the past and the future, presentism treats them symmetrically; they are ontologically on a par: neither exists. It can be represented as follows:

(4) **Presentism**
   Only the present exists.

FIG. 0.6. Presentism

So there is a clear partition between tensed and tenseless theories of time: essentially, tense theorists assert that in some objective, mind-independent, sense or other the present is privileged; whereas tenseless theorists assert that all times are real, no one of which is ontologically privileged. Presentism privileges the present in that it is the only time that exists. The asymmetric views privilege the present in that it is either the only time at which no later times exist (in the case of no-futurism) or is the first time at which time branches (in the case of branching-futurism). Degree presentism privileges the present in being the only time that has full-blown reality. And past + present + futurism privileges the present by its simply being privileged. Or rather, if we follow Lowe (1998: 49), who explicitly rejects any claim to ontological privilege for the present, we might think that the present is just different from the other tenses—although it is hardly as transparent an account of what it is to be present as is given by the other theories. But how are we to choose between these various alternatives for a theory of time? Let me first say a few words about what makes for a good metaphysical theory in general.

III What conditions must any adequate philosophical theory of time satisfy?

There are at least three conditions that we would hope any good philosophical theory to satisfy.

(1) Common sense

Any good theory will accord as far as possible with intuition. 'Intuition' is not meant to be understood as unthinking prejudice, but rather to capture the views of an independent sensible person, where 'independent' means someone whose sensibleness has not been spoiled by a theory that for some reason—it's their own baby, or it makes them quirky and stand out from the crowd—they'd like to defend. For instance, it is all very well denying that morality has any objective basis; but for such a theory not to recognize the difference that any sensible person can see between genocide and parking violations undermines the plausibility of any such theory: *something* has to be said to account for this intuitive difference, even if, ultimately, it is not based in objectivity. Likewise, a theory that says that it is possible to have some knowledge is preferable to one that says that we cannot know anything—at least, a plausible theory would be one that explains the difference between those things we claim to know from those we don't, even if ultimately we can't know anything. We do require intuition in this sense to be respected (in terms of being taken seriously enough to be accounted for) in any good theory.

(2) Explanatory

Error theories are one way in which we can keep hold of and account for common-sense views, and are imperative when we hold that our common-sense views are literally false. In the case of a theory that says our common-sense views *are* correct, it should give us an account of *how* it is possible for intuitive truths to be true, as opposed to just stating that they are. For instance, it's no good to say merely that knowledge *is* possible; we need an account of *how* it is possible.

(3) Transparency

The account itself should be transparent, both with regard to the things postulated, the nature of those things, and any other mechanism involving them. Obscurity should be avoided.

All this carries over to the particular case of a metaphysical theory of time. As already noted, there are certain platitudes that every theory must account for before it even attempts more substantive issues: if it can't account for the platitudinous, what chance has it got as a successful substantive theory? As we've seen from the metaphors of measurements and motion, we say that time 'flows'. We also say that the past is 'fixed' but the future is 'open', and think it is right and proper to hold asymmetric views about the past and the future: we only dread the future, not the past; we remember the past, not the future; we plan for the future, but not the past, and we try to bring about those plans for the future in the way we don't try to bring about things in the past. And we do all of this from the perspective of the present: we do not think we are located at any other time. (Of course, we might think that we have past or future selves; but we do not think that we are one of them.)

Of course, different stories about how to understand these platitudes will vary across the different theories. The point is that any adequate theory should have *something* satisfactory to say about them, or be rejected. The ontologically asymmetric theories appear to have an easy time accounting for the asymmetries reflected in our platitudes: the non-existence of the future and existence of the past, for example, seems to account for our saying that the future is open yet the past is fixed. But whether this in itself accounts for why we cannot remember the future, or dread it, or bring it about, on more careful consideration, is not clear—after all, would the non-existence of the past stop us from remembering it, or encourage us to bring it about that something did happen? There must be some underlying mechanism that better explains such things.

It is instructive to look to the tenseless theory for how it explains things like this, for it encounters the other side of the coin, namely explaining why we cannot 'remember' the future if it does exist, as well as accounting for all the other asymmetries reflected in the platitudes. The tenseless theory says that time does not flow, but it accounts for our *saying* that it does by showing how we can account for the illusion that it does. Both this and the asymmetry issues can be accounted for by invoking *causation*: although there is no ontological difference between earlier and later times, the reason why we say that the past is fixed and the future open is because we cannot causally affect earlier times than now, but can causally affect later times than now, and so on. Similarly, time appears to flow because of the causal mechanism associated with perception. According to Mellor's (1998) account, we perceive an event e which then leaves a memory trace in us. When we perceive another event f later than e, we perceive that e is earlier than f because at the time of perceiving f, we also remember e. Thus, it is the causal mechanism underlying how such perceptual information is acquired which explains why we only perceive past and present events, but not the future.

Good as theories along these lines are, we should not take them to prove too much. Falk (2003: 215), for instance, draws the moral from his tenseless account of our experience of time's flow that '[tense] with all its whoosh and whiz is a subjective accretion, a form of egocentric appearance'. But such accounts should not be taken to favour the tenseless theory. For despite the fact that tenseless theorists are usually lumbered with this problem because they say we experience tense in a tenseless world, tensed theorists *also* need to say something—just saying that time is tensed doesn't in itself give tensed theorists a story about our *perception* of tense. Suppose we follow Falk in saying that we need to change our perceptual information in order to keep track of changes in our environment, and that this continual change of information amounts to our experience of time's passage. Since all this account relies on is the notion of change, a notion that both tense and tenseless theorists employ, both can happily adopt it. The metaphysical issue of what this underlying change in the environment amounts to is entirely independent of such an account. Of course, it might be argued that real tense becomes superfluous in such an account, and so the tenseless package is better. But this holds only if there are no other reasons for adopting the tensed package. And if there are other reasons (see Chapter 2, §VII(c); Chapter 4, §V), then the choice between the tensed and tenseless package will not rest on a theory of the perception of time's flow.

The causal account is also invoked to explain why we only dread the future, but not the past. Although Spinoza should be credited with first raising such issues (see Cockburn (1997) and (1998)), Prior (1959) asks why it is, for instance, that we dread tomorrow's trip to the dentist, but are so thankful afterwards that it is over. This seems unaccountable on the tenseless theory, for, according to it, that trip to the dentist always has been and always will be on that particular day; its B-series location does not change. Yet these are the only temporal facts the tenseless theory allows. But surely we are not thanking goodness that the trip is on that particular day—after all, we knew that before we went, and certainly weren't thanking anything then! Prior reasons that what explains this cannot be that the event has a particular date, but must be because the event is *past*, and thus the tensed theories are to be preferred. But the correct response is rather that it is the *belief* that it is past (and not happening now) that explains why we are relieved (see MacBeath (1983)). Furthermore, this must be the case for both tensed and tenseless theorists: the fact that it is past cannot make me relieved unless I believe it. But this story leaves it open what makes such beliefs true; it is left open whether we should be tensed or tenseless theorists in light of these considerations. Nevertheless, there is still a question about why we feel relief when we believe that something is past, but dread when we believe something is future. It must be that there is a causal story, such that our *memory* of the pain and our present experience of no pain results in relief. And that's why we don't feel relieved *before* the pain. So, again, the causal story is central to explaining our perceptions and emotions concerning temporal matters.

But such appeals to causation will only work if causation itself runs from earlier to later. And, of course, the success of appeals to causation for presentists relies on them being able to make sense of causal relations between past and present objects. These matters are addressed in Chapter 4.

The question now is: if all of these theories can account for the platitudes so far mentioned, then how do we go about choosing between them? I say that what really separates the good theories from the bad is the fact that we do everything from the perspective of the present: we do not think we are located at any other time. The profound significance of this simple point will become apparent in Chapter 1.

PART I
The Presentist Manifesto

1
When am I?

Is there anything more certain than the knowledge we have that we are present? It would be a scandal if our best theory of time could not guarantee such knowledge; yet I shall show that none of the theories of time described in the last chapter can guarantee it, apart from presentism and the tenseless theory. The rest, then, must be rejected.

I The Present Problem

As noted in the last chapter, there is a clear partition between tensed and tenseless theories of time: essentially, tense theorists assert that in some objective, mind-independent, sense or other, the present is privileged; whereas tenseless theorists assert that all times are real, no one of which is ontologically privileged.

Many tense theorists hold that more than one time is real, yet one among them is privileged, namely the present. This, however, raises the question of how *we* can know that we are present and not past (or future). I shall call this the *Present Problem*:

> Given that we do know we are present, and that it is absurd to doubt it, any adequate theory of time must find a way to guarantee such knowledge.

There is a seemingly obvious solution to the Present Problem: we should treat the terms 'present' and 'now' as indexical terms: my use of 'now' at any given time simply picks out the time at which it is used; consequently, my *now* is guaranteed to be present, since it is merely the time at which I am: *sum ergo sum nunc*. How could I be anywhere else?

The advantages for the indexical account of 'present' (echoing Lewis (1986: 93) with his indexical theory of actuality) can be put as follows. Suppose that one time alone is the privileged present. It is still true that one time alone is ours, is this one, is the one at which we are. What a remarkable bit of luck for us if the very time at which we are is the one that is the privileged present! Out of all the people there are in the past, present, and future, the great majority live at times that lack privileged presentness, but we are the select few. But what reason could we ever have to think it was so? How could we ever know? Past groats buy no fewer past leeches, and so forth. And yet we *do* know for certain that the time at which we are is the time at which we are. How could this be knowledge that we are the select few?

Here we should distinguish two questions, based on the different uses of 'present': the *indexical* use above; and the *referential* use, which treats 'present' as referring to the privileged time of the tensed theory. Call this privileged time *present* (and similarly call the times earlier than and later than it *past* and *future*, respectively), leaving the indexical sense of 'present' unstarred, i.e., the sense in which we have unproblematic acquaintance with our surroundings. The first question can then be stated as: in the indexical sense, is it possible to doubt that we are present, i.e., doubt that we are when we are? Of course not! Consider Mellor (1981: 53):

[J]udging my experience to be present is much like my judging it to be painless. On the one hand, the judgement is not one I have to make...But on the other hand, if I do make it, I am bound to be right, just as when I judge my experience to be painless. The presence of experience...is something of which one's awareness is infallible.

...No matter who I am or whenever I judge my experience to be present, that judgement will be true.   (Mellor (1981: 53))

This lends support to the indexical analysis of presentness, for it explains why our own presentness is something we could not be mistaken about (barring severe pathological mental disorders). Nevertheless, we could perfectly well know *this*, i.e., that we are when we are, even if we were *past*, i.e., even if our time were not the time on which the badge of privilege has been conferred. So the indexical analysis itself will not solve the Present Problem, which can be restated as follows:

> *The Present Problem*
> Although we know by immediate acquaintance which time is our own, how can we know that our time is *present*?

Some might not think this is much of a problem and claim that we have immediate acquaintance with what it is to be in the *present*, something different from what it is to be *past*. But, again appealing to Lewis (1986: 93) in his analogous discussion in the possible worlds debate of knowing that we are absolutely actual rather than merely possible:

> Adams [(1974)] ... says that [we] can account for the certainty of our knowledge of our own actuality by maintaining that we are as immediately acquainted with our own absolute actuality as we are with our thoughts, feelings and sensations. But I reply that if Adams and I and all the other actual people really have this immediate acquaintance with absolute actuality, wouldn't my elder sister have had it too, if only I'd had an elder sister? So there she is, unactualised, off in some other world getting fooled by the very same evidence that is supposed to be giving me my knowledge. (Lewis (1986: 93))

And, similarly, if such a tense theorist and I and all the other present people really have an immediate acquaintance with the *present*, didn't Plato have it too? So there he is, off at some other time in the *past* getting fooled by the very same evidence that is supposed to be giving me my knowledge of being *present*. Thus although subjective experience, as Mellor notes above, is an infallible guide to 'presentness', it is not an infallible guide to *presentness*, for, if it were, then Plato's experience would have to be qualitatively different from our own; yet it is clear that there is no identifiable difference, nothing that we can call a manifestation of such an experience. For what is it to experience *presentness* over and above what it is to experience 'presentness'? On the other hand, if there is something that it is like to experience *presentness*, then for want of a characterization of it, we can never be sure that we are presently manifesting it.

Thus, I say, and shall argue for this in more detail below, that the only way a pluralist about times (by which I mean someone who holds that more than one time is real) can solve this problem is by first denying that any times *are* *present*, and thus something we can be mistaken about. And this is precisely what tenseless theorists do. According to tenseless theorists, our time is not ontologically privileged, but is one among a plurality of equally real times; that is, they deny the assumption that there is a difference *in kind* between our time and other times; the only sense of 'present' they recognize is the indexical sense. And it is with these two features that they solve the Present Problem.

But this is not the only solution to the Present Problem: it arises only if we start from the position of pluralism. Consider presentism, which denies the existence of real past and future times. It is clear that presentism also solves the Present Problem, not due to any distinct phenomenological experience, but simply because if we only initially invoke the existence of our present time as the one real time, we could not help being *present*, since *ex hypothesi* it is not possible for us to be anywhere else: *I am, therefore I am present.*

Thus there are two types of theory that can solve the Present Problem: the tenseless theory and presentism. I shall now go on to show that any theory that invokes many real times, yet says one among them is privileged, cannot satisfactorily answer the Present Problem, and should therefore be rejected.

II Tensed theories toppled

It should be noted that not all theories which call themselves 'presentist' are immune to the sceptical challenge. For Quentin Smith's (2002) 'degree presentism', discussed in the introduction (§II(c)), isn't immune. But this is unsurprising since degree presentism does not count as a genuine variety of presentism anyway, despite its name. For degree presentism is the view that not only are there degrees of pastness and futurity from the present, but that *reality* reduces in degrees the further it is from the present, which has full-blown reality. So other times other than the present do exist; it's just that they are less real. Now, regardless of any of its other problems, it raises the question: consider those people who have a shady existence until they gain the full-blown property of being *present*; how do we know that we are not in this impoverished state of having shady existence, either as *future* people who are yet to be promoted to such a privileged position, or as those *past* people with whom the full-blown *present* has lost favour?

What about the other tensed positions? I'll now show in detail how the no-futurism of Tooley (1997) and the branching-futurism of McCall (1994) cannot adequately meet the Present Problem, in order to illustrate the general point that pluralist tensed theories are in trouble.

(a) Why there's no future in Tooley's no-futurism

Tooley defends what I have called *no-futurism*: the past and present are real, but the future is not. According to Tooley's version of no-futurism, reality grows as more and more *tenseless* facts come into existence and remain in existence. In other words, the moment that is the ontologically privileged moment, the *present* moment, the moment at the cutting edge of reality, continually changes in the ceaseless tide of becoming, leaving behind (equally real) shadows of our present selves.

Tooley's theory is a hybrid of the tenseless and tensed theories. For Tooley agrees with the tenseless theory that it is tenseless facts that make tensed beliefs true. Thus, when I now believe that I am presently writing, my belief is not made true by the fact that when I believe it, my time of writing is *present*, but is made true by the fact that my believing it is simultaneous with my writing. We can say, then, that what I believe (that I am now/presently writing) is true when I believe it. Similarly, when Plato, back in 365 BCE, believes that he is now/presently teaching Aristotle, his belief is not made true by the fact that when he believed it his time was *present*, but is made true by the fact that he believed it when he was teaching Aristotle. Thus, we can say that what Plato believed then of himself (namely, that I am teaching Aristotle) was true when he believed it.

But Tooley's theory differs from the tenseless theory in that, according to his theory, there is a time (the *present*) at the cutting edge of reality at which tenseless facts come into existence and remain in existence. Specifically, according to Tooley:

> The present, at a given time, consists of those states of affairs that are actual as of that time, and which are such that there are no later states of affairs that are actual as of that time. (Tooley (1997: 196))

Initially, this appears to be an attractive definition of what it is to be *present* at any given time, and Tooley's theory is ingenious at avoiding many problems associated with traditional tensed theories. But, ultimately, I do not think it will work. Specifically, it falls foul of the Present Problem: what is there in Tooley's theory to guarantee the link between this definition of being *present* and the tenseless truth-conditions offered for tensed statements, a link required to avoid the possibility that *our* 'present' and *the* *present* could peel apart?

Since it is *tenseless* facts that make our beliefs true, whether we are in fact *present* or not is not something to which we can have (or need) access; it makes absolutely no difference to us whether our time is *present* or not! At least, we can have true *tensed* beliefs that we are present, because these are made true by *tenseless* facts, but our *tensed* belief that we are *present* would have to be made true by the fact that our time is also *present*, i.e., that it is the only time at which no later times exist. Yet *nothing* has been said so far to guarantee the link between believing that we are *present* and that time actually being *present*. This, then, raises the question of how we can know that our time is *present*, for we would have all the same beliefs (about, for example, whom we are presently teaching, whom we have just taught, and whom we are planning to teach) even if we were *past*—Plato, after all, back in 365 BCE, believes truly that he is teaching Aristotle, and it makes no difference to him that he is *past*! How are *we* not in the same position, according to no-futurism? So here am I, a no-futurist, convinced that my present time is *present*. But wasn't I just as convinced yesterday, when I went through these arguments then? So, there am I as I was yesterday, as real as I am now, believing that I am *present*, and thinking pretty much the same things then about my previous selves as I think today. Yet I know now that my earlier self is mistaken; so how do I know that I now am not?

Suppose we try the following strategy to guarantee such a link. Suppose we say that *when* we believe (truly) that event *e* is present (i.e., occurs simultaneously with our belief), it is also true that *e* is *present*, i.e., that as of that time when e occurs, only that time and earlier times exist. This obvious response leads to contradiction. For suppose events, $^Ne_1,\ldots,^Ne_n$, occurring now are *present*. This renders earlier events, $^Pe_1,\ldots,^Pe_n$, as *past*. But if Plato believes (truly), in 365 BCE, that events, $^Pe_1,\ldots,^Pe_n$, are present (i.e., occur simultaneously with his belief), then, according to this proposal, $^Pe_1,\ldots,^Pe_n$ must also be *present* *when* he believes it, i.e., in 365 BCE. But this a plain contradiction: under these conditions, events $^Pe_1,\ldots,^Pe_n$ would be both *past* and *present*. Furthermore, the position that I have just forced is clearly one successful interpretation of McTaggart's argument, of which I shall offer a fuller discussion in Chapter 3. (Note that it does not help to relativize the *present* to a time, since this reduces to the tenseless theory.)

The objection here might be that this is unfair: what *is* true is that Plato's belief *was* true *when* he believ*ed* it, i.e., that when he believed it, his present *was* the ontologically privileged *present* moment. But, however much we italicize such tenses, this does not help the theory here under consideration. For no-futurism asserts the reality of more than just the present moment, and this must amount to the following claim (if it amounts to anything intelligible), namely

(B1) 'There exists (not located now, but located in the *past*) a time when Plato believ*es* that his (then) present teaching of Aristotle at t is *present*'

i.e.,

(B2) $(\exists t)$(It was the case that: Plato believ*es* that: t is *present*)

And in this, I claim, Plato is mistaken, for *ex hypothesi* t is not *present* since t is *past*. (Note that it cannot be said that Plato believed that he *taught* Aristotle, since this would be to ascribe him a past-tensed belief in 365 BCE, and that is not what he had then; hence the reason for keeping his beliefs present-tensed within the scope of a past-tensed operator.)

Of course, some tense theorists may insist that this isn't the case, and that it grossly misrepresents the tensed position. They say:

(B3) It *was* the case that: Plato believ*es* that: t is *present*, i.e.,

(B4) It was the case that: (∃t)(Plato believes that: t is *present*)

and that Plato's belief *was* true when t was *present*, so Plato is not mistaken about anything after all.[1] I find this account perfectly acceptable as a way to avoid being mistaken. And just as well, since this is not the view I am criticizing, but promoting as the only alternative to the tenseless theory. For (B4) is a *presentist* story about how to treat statements about the past, and I have no argument with them; far from it: this is the very reason I think presentism is the only tenable tensed position as regards solving the Present Problem. Those tense theorists who are pluralists, however, cannot avail themselves of this solution, for (B4) states that Plato *believed* that t *was* *present* (which presumably it was when he believed it), but no longer believes any such thing, since he does not exist. Pluralist tense theorists, on the other hand, state at least that past and present times are equally real, i.e., all exist. But this is unintelligible unless it means that there exists a time located in the *past* when Plato *believes* that that time *is* *present*. For to say there *was* a time when Plato *existed*, and still help yourself to the notion of the past and present being *equally real*, is to have had your cake while still eating it, and I cannot make head nor tail of that.

In short we can say the following. No-futurists *can* say that *when* the time *was* *present* (i.e., later than which no other times existed), Plato's belief *was* true, and he is not mistaken about anything. But this ignores the fact that Plato's time is *not always* *present*. Yet, if there is a real tenseless fact (which there is, according to Tooley's theory), the constituents of which are Plato, Aristotle, and a teaching relation of some sort, then Plato will *continue* to believe that his (then) time is *present*, and in this he is mistaken. This is bad news: even the stopped clock is right twice a day. And since there is nothing

---

[1] Some might complain that this is a tenseless reading of the existential quantifier. It is: the existential quantifier ranges over all that exists. For, as I explained in the introduction, presentists require the tenseless reading, otherwise their thesis that only what is present exists is trivial. And if it were restricted to what presently exists, no-futurists could not assert the real existence of the past as well as the present. Maybe they could have two quantifiers, one present-tensed, one past-tensed. Fine, but I'd simply restate the problem as: how can any given no-futurist be sure that it is the present-tensed quantifier that ranges over them and not the past-tensed quantifier?

in our experience to tell us whether this extra fact holds (that our present is also *present*), the very possibility that the two notions peel apart with no-futurism (a link guaranteed by presentism and the tenseless theory) consequently lands us with scepticism about whether our present is *present*.

Tooley's theory, then, cannot satisfy all the requirements of an adequate theory of time. His conception of a tensed theory does not play any role in ascribing tensed statements and beliefs truth-values, and because tensed statements and beliefs have been divorced from the tensed aspect of the world in this way, it leaves open the sceptical challenge posed by the Present Problem, something that cannot satisfactorily be dealt with by no-futurism on pain of contradiction.

(i) A possible response Suppose we swallow the conclusion that we are most probably *past*, and that there is a *real* process of temporal becoming occurring somewhere in the future (i.e., somewhere in the *present*) that only the privileged few get to experience (not that even they can tell!). What is wrong with this? After all, we have learned from special relativity that all may not be as it seems with time, and that there just are certain limits on what we can know about time.[2]

It is clear that any no-futurist that is motivated to adopt no-futurism on the basis of human concerns and experiences cannot accept this possibility—that is, that we are mistaken in taking the processes that lead them to believe in the flow of time, such as our perception of change, as showing anything about where we are in time—since this would undermine their motivation. For although no-futurism may be thought to do these jobs on the assumption that we are *present*, the fact that we cannot guarantee that we *are* *present*, together with the fact that we would have all the same accounting to do anyway if we were *past*, shows that the theory cannot account for what it set out to achieve, since it isn't the unreality of the *future* that accounts for our experiences, etc., if we are *past* people, so it can't be what accounts for our experience, etc., even if we are *present* people. The unreality of the *future* would therefore be redundant.

[2] I shall discuss the Present Problem in the context of special relativity in Ch. 6.

Tooley (1997: 379–80), however, is explicit that he is not interested in motivations from experience: his version of no-futurism is motivated by his account of causation (see his chapters 3 and 4). It is open, then, for Tooley to accept these results as just another one of those things we have discovered about time. But, first, we should question whether our experiences can be so neatly divorced from issues of causation. Since a tenseless fact is a tenseless fact regardless of whether there are later facts than it or not, *past* people would believe and experience all the same things if we supposed them to be *present*. That is, their causal beliefs and their causal interactions at that time would be no different if that time happened to be *present*. Thus, this casts doubt on the claim that an adequate account of causation has anything to do with the existence or non-existence of later times, and thus casts doubt on whether Tooley's argument from causation is sound. The option is not open to argue that these people would not experience or believe the same things because they are *past*, since then it would not be intelligible to claim that the world grows by the accretion of *equally existent tenseless facts*. Tooley cannot have it both ways.

It seems to me that the very possibility that we could be *past* should not lead us to wonder whether we are, but rather to reject any view that allows for it as conceptually misconceived. Nevertheless, if Tooley were to take my sceptical conclusions as just another one of those discoveries about time, then that would be one more weird and wonderful fact about time that he cannot know but the presentist can, and this must surely be counted as a massive disadvantage of his theory.

(b) McCall's branching model dropped

McCall's (1994) theory states that whereas there is only one (actual) past and present, there are many equally real possible future 'branches', and time's flow amounts to the dropping off of these branches as one of them becomes actual. So whereas Tooley conceives of reality growing, McCall conceives of reality shedding, but both conceive of time's flow as a change in what exists. The *present*, in McCall's theory, is distinguished as the point at which these future branches become actual.

WHEN AM I? 31

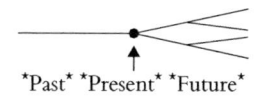

Past *Present* *Future*

FIG. 1.1. Branching-futurism

McCall's conception is represented in Fig. 1.1. McCall argues that this model has many explanatory virtues, such as accounting for 'the direction and flow of time, the nature of scientific laws, the interpretation of quantum mechanics [in its account of quantum non-locality], the definition of probability, counterfactual semantics, and the notions of identity, essential properties, deliberation, decision, and freewill' (McCall (1994: preface)). He argues that these features give us good reason to think that it is the correct model of the universe however implausible it may appear at first sight. Nevertheless, there is an objection that such theories must address. But, in meeting this objection, I say McCall's model still fails to meet the Present Problem in a most disturbing way.

Smart (1949) argues that in order to make sense of tensed theories of time, such as those of McCall and Tooley, higher dimensions of time must be invoked, for changes of temporal properties in events are themselves changes *in* time and therefore require a meta-time in which this change can take place. And specifically against McCall, in his (1980), Smart argues that because the shape of the tree structure is different at different times:

This seems to imply a proliferation not only of branches of the shrub but also a proliferation of shrubs. After all a given shrub either has or has not branches on a certain lower part... of its trunk. A single space–time universe surely either has branches before *t* or it does not have branches before *t*. We must suppose therefore a vast multiplicity of universes, one for each value of *t*. Think of a universe with branches after *t* but none before *t* as a card with a shrub drawn on it. Then McCall's picture suggests... that there is a super-universe which is like a pack of continuum-many cards, one above the other, cards higher in the pack portraying a longer unbranched 'trunk' than those lower in the pack. (Smart (1980: 7))

Furthermore, this argument applies *mutatis mutandis* to no-futurism (such as Tooley's): there must be 'a whole array of universes so that "later" ones have more content than "earlier" ones' (10). So, Smart concludes: '[I]n order to makes sense of a dubious notion of pure becoming we end up by postulating a bloated universe' (10).

Now, although Smart's argument is one from the excessive ontological commitments of such theories, we can extend his argument and raise sceptical worries concerning *our* place in this deck of cards. Presumably, we would prefer (now) to be on the top card of the deck, but if all cards are real, and consequently, all individuals on each card are as real as each other, how can we guarantee we've been dealt such a lucky hand and are located where we hope we are?

We needn't, however, concern ourselves with spelling out this worry, for McCall does have an ace up his sleeve. For this problem only arises once the commitment to higher dimensions of time has been established. But this is something tense theorists need not concede, for, as McCall notes (1994: 10, 31) a change of temporal properties is not something that itself takes place *in* time, but is rather precisely what time's flow *consists in*. This response seems to avoid Smart's objection from bloated ontological commitments. Nevertheless, this response in no way addresses the Present Problem, which could be rephrased as: although we may grant that there is only one card in McCall's deck, what guarantee have we that we are located at the first node of the shrub drawn on this card?

Similar arguments can be made *mutatis mutandis* against McCall's theory in regard to the status of *past* people as were made against Tooley's, so I shall not spell them out here. More worrying considerations that affect McCall's theory concern those equally real *future* people. Again, there is nothing to rule out the possibility that we might be them, precariously perched on one of the branches; and disturbingly so, since they (i.e., *we*!) may drop out of existence at any moment as soon as one of the other branches becomes actual. Suppose we shift Fig. 1.1 back in time, and are located in the *future*. See Fig. 1.2.

According to this view, we will drop out of existence as soon as someone (possibly one of our past selves) in our past, that is to say, in the *present*, decides on a course of action that conflicts with what happens along our branch. This is clearly absurd. We're not *future* people, let alone *possible* *future* people who, in the history of the world, never will become (became?) actualized. But could we ever know? I see no way the theory can rule out the unsettling possibility

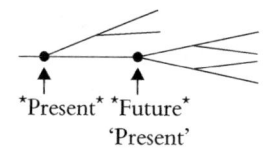

FIG. 1.2. Present Problem for branching-futurism

that we may drop out of existence. It won't do for McCall simply to stick a 'you are here' arrow on his diagrams (e.g., pages 3, 4 and 63). And even if we were *future* people with the *present* moment somewhere in our distant past, we would still have all the same things to account for. But since our present is not *the* *present*, such things cannot be accounted for in terms of branches in our future dropping off as they become actualized. But if branches do not need to drop off to account for our experiences, etc., then why do they need to drop off at the *present*? And, furthermore, it is difficult to see how the dropping off of branches does account for our experience of the flow of time anyway, given that for McCall, too, it is tenseless facts that make our tensed statements and beliefs either true or false, consequently separating the tensed aspect of the world from our tensed beliefs.

III Tensed truth-conditions: token-reflexive or non-token-reflexive, that's not the question

It might be thought that the problems encountered by pluralist tense theorists could be avoided by giving the correct account of truth-conditions for tensed statements. Tooley and McCall adopt tenseless truth-conditions for tensed statements and it might be thought that the arguments above show that this is where the problem lies. But I shall now show that this is an independent issue.

Mellor (1981: 101) thinks that tensed theories of time must supply tensed truth-conditions for tensed statements. Furthermore, he thinks that these truth-conditions must be non-token reflexive, as follows:

(NTR.1) Any token of '*e* is present' is true iff *e* is *present*
(NTR.2) Any token of '*e* is past' is true iff *e* is *past*
(NTR.3) Any token of '*e* is future' is true iff *e* is *future*

Mellor then argues that such accounts have incredible consequences, and should therefore be rejected. Because tensed tokens are made true, according to these tensed theories, by tensed facts, all tokens of '*e* is past' are made true by the same tensed fact, namely that *e* is *past*, all tokens of '*e* is present' are made true by the same tensed fact, namely that *e* is *present*, and all tokens of '*e* is future' are made true be the same tensed fact, namely that *e* is *future*. That is, the truth of various tensed statements depends on the tensed facts alone regardless of when the statements are tokened. But, if tokens do change their truth-values, then according to Le Poidevin (1991):

> This makes nonsense of tensed assertion. ... [For] if we say 'It is raining', we only rule out dryness for the time of the utterance, not for the indefinite past or future. But if that very utterance is capable of becoming false, then we must interpret it as ruling out dryness at all other times. This means that we could never be in a position to make any tensed assertions, nor to believe any made by anyone else. This is clearly absurd.   (Le Poidevin (1991: 55))

Tensed theorists wishing to adopt the non-token-reflexive account should in response distinguish between truth-at-a-time and truth *simpliciter*.[3] This allows them to say that 'Plato is being born' is true at that time *t*, although false at the *present* time, i.e., false *simpliciter*. This is intuitively obvious and solves the problem with tensed assertion, since although such assertions change their strict truth-value, if they ever were true at *t*, they remain true-at-*t*, which is the relevant time people should believe them, act upon them, etc.

This solution alleviates the sting of Mellor's objection. According to the non-token-reflexive accounts, if the token 'The Queen is dead' is said earlier than the Queen's death, then it is false until the Queen's death becomes *present*, in which case that very token becomes true. But that tokens change truth-value is untenable, according to Mellor, because 'No one thinks, for example, that my death will posthumously verify every premature announcement of it!' (1998: 78–9). However, the distinction between truth and truth-at-a-time

---

[3] I take my cue here from Adams (1974) in his analogous distinction in the possible worlds debate between truth *simpliciter* and truth-at-a-world.

above makes the position palatable, because it allows us to keep hold of the idea that the token if once true will always remain true, i.e., will remain true-at-that-time for all time, and yet according to *present* fact, is false, i.e., false *simpliciter*.

This is a plausible account that gives an explanation of the conflicting intuitions. However, it will not help avoid the absurdity involved in holding a tensed position that asserts the existence of more than the present moment. For if *past* times are as real as the *present* time, then at *past* time t a speaker's utterance of 'e is present' is made false by the fact that e is *past*. So we have a case of the Present Problem: the speaker is mistaken in thinking that e is *present*. The solution offered here is to distinguish truth *simpliciter* from truth-at-a-time. But surely we do not want to concede so much and admit that although something could be true-for-us-at-a-time it could in an absolute sense be false *due solely to the fact that our present is not *present**? But then either we fall into contradiction by guaranteeing that our present is *present* (as explained in II above), or we simply relativize truth to a time, and it has collapsed into the tenseless position.

Presentism, however, can adopt this non-token-reflexive account. For presentists could construct times from certain sets of propositions, namely the conjunctions of all those present-tensed propositions that we would say were true at that time. This gives presentists the guarantee that they are not mistaken about which time is *present*, for from the fact that only one time has a concrete realization, together with the fact that the time in which we live is not a set of propositions, but concrete, we can derive the conclusion that our time is *present*. This allows presentists the warrant for thinking that their statements about the present are true *simpliciter*, rather than merely true-for-them-at-that-time.[4]

---

[4] Of course, the success of this response depends on how presentism is to be understood: if there is no such thing as the past, then there is no such thing as a past token to have a truth-value. But if times are some sort of construction from present-tensed propositions, an ersatz theory of past (and future) times becomes possible, according to which propositions can be true-at-a-time as well as true/false *simpliciter*, in the same way that propositions can be true-at-a-world as well as true/false *simpliciter* according to ersatz theories in the possible worlds debate. This is indeed how I develop presentism in Ch. 2.

An alternative to the non-token-reflexive theory is the tensed token-reflexive account of truth-conditions, such as offered by Lowe (e.g., in his (1998: 45)). This account runs as follows. As we saw in the introduction (§II(a)), the tenseless token-reflexive account holds:

(TR.1) A token utterance *u* of '*e* is present' is true iff *e* occurs simultaneously with *u*.

Here the 'is' is tenseless. However, tensed theorists such as Lowe suggest we read the 'is' as present-tensed. We then get something along the following lines:

(TTR.1) An utterance *u* of '*e* is present' is *now* true iff *u* is *now* simultaneous with *e*

And for completeness we must add:

(TTR.2) An utterance *u* of '*e* is present' *was* true iff *u* *was* simultaneous with *e*

(TTR.3) An utterance *u* of '*e* is present' *will be* true iff *u* *will be* simultaneous with *e*.

This theory has the advantage over the non-token-reflexive account that the truth of tensed tokens depends to some extent on when it is tokened, and so avoids the objections that Le Poidevin and Mellor raise against the non-token-reflexive theory: if 'The Queen is (presently) dead' is tokened before the Queen's death, and is therefore false, it will not become true when the Queen dies, but will remain false.

This account, however, is still subject to the Present Problem depending on how the tenses are to be interpreted. For if '*was*' and '*will be*' mean 'is true at a moment of *past* time' and 'is true at a moment of *future* time', respectively, then anyone at these times tokening '*e* is present', although not mistaken about whether *e* is occurring *then*, are certainly mistaken in believing that their 'present' indexes the *present* (on pain of contradiction). Again, however, this account is perfectly acceptable for a presentist who prefers to give token-reflexive truth-conditions for tensed statements, for the same reasons as are given above.

In sum, it does not matter which of these accounts tense theorists adopt; rather, the issue is whether the tensed theory in question asserts the existence of more than one real time. Or, rather, the issue is *where* in time the tense theorist locates the truthmakers for the tensed statements, for if they are located anywhere in time other than the present, scepticism about where *we* are located immediately arises.

Of course, some reject the notion of truthmakers altogether. But it is hard to establish what such people actually believe when they reject the truthmaker story other than the platitudes that everyone believes about time; that is, it is hard to see how they can make a real distinction between the tensed and tenseless views. For, as discussed in the introduction (§II(a)), most now agree that tensed statements cannot be reduced in *meaning* to tenseless statements: both sides agree that tense is irreducible in this sense. Thus, unless a difference between tensed and tenseless views is located at the level of the *factual* by invoking truthmakers of some sort, it is hard to see how tensed and tenseless theories can be peeled apart. But since Tooley and McCall and many other tense theorists do already accept the truthmaker story, I need not concern myself here with arguing for the stronger contention that the truthmaker theory is a necessary presupposition of a substantive tensed–tenseless debate, and thus something that should be accepted by all who take the debate seriously. So my argument is essentially of the conditional kind: *if* you buy the truthmaker story, which you should, then you must be careful to satisfy the minimal requirement that any adequate theory of time should, namely to satisfactorily answer the Present Problem.

This still leaves tense theorists with quite a bit of scope. They may still assert differences between past, present, and future, for instance that statements about the past and present are true but that statements about the future are neither true nor false (or all false, depending on taste) either because there are *no* facts to make them true, or because there is, as of the *present*, no *unique* set of facts about what will happen, just many sets of facts about possible futures. The problem, of course, is that an account needs to be given of the nature of the facts which makes true statements true: what, on this view, makes it true to say 'The First World War *did* happen'? The most transparent option is to say that the First World War is located in the *past*. On a tenseless interpretation, this is unproblematic for tenseless theorists. On a tensed interpretation, I have shown this option lands tense theorists in trouble with the Present Problem. Presentism is the only tensed theory to survive. A satisfactory account of truthmakers for past-tensed statements, however, is yet to be given by presentists. But this is something I shall do in the next chapter.

2
A theory of presentism

I The parameters of the problem

Most of us would want to say that it is true that Socrates taught Plato. According to realists about past facts,[1] this is made true by the fact that there is, located in the past, i.e., earlier than now, at least one real event that is the teaching of Plato by Socrates. Presentists, however, in denying that past events and facts exist (on a tenseless reading of 'exist' as already explained) cannot appeal to such facts to make their past-tensed statements true. So what is a presentist to do?

There are at least three conditions that would ideally be met in a satisfactory solution to this problem:

(a) it must preserve our views about which statements are true and which false;
(b) it must be transparent what the truthmakers are for those statements;
(c) it must accommodate the truth-value links between various times.

I justified the need for these conditions in the introduction: §III. Condition (c) is the requirement that if p is a true present-tensed proposition, then just in virtue of our concept of tense there are links between the truths which hold at other times, which have to be accommodated and explained. For instance, if p is a true present-tensed

---

[1] All tenseless theorists are realists about the past, but, as we've seen, tensed theorists needn't be, although some are, e.g., Broad (1923); Gale (1968); Schlesinger (1980); Smith (1993); McCall (1994), and Tooley (1997).

proposition, then in the future it should be a truth that *it was the case that p*.

I shall survey two different families of proposals for the presentist's truthmakers, recent examples of each being advocated by Craig (2003) and Ludlow (1999), and show that they fail at least one of these three conditions. This is not entirely negative, for it shows us what an adequate solution to the problem would look like. I go on to show where presentists can find suitable objects that satisfy these conditions, and in this way give a clear statement of presentism, something that is lacking in the literature.

(a) A note on truthmakers

The truth of our statements depends on the way the world is: contingent truths require truthmakers. Everyone should agree with this. What people disagree about is what truthmakers are. But so long as we all agree that truths depend *in some way* on the contents of the world (whether they are states of affairs, as in Armstrong's work (e.g., his (1997)) or particulars, as in Lewis's (2003)), then that is enough to generate the concerns of this chapter. For ease, then, I shall talk throughout of facts and their constituents as truthmakers, but those sympathetic to particulars as truthmakers can make the relevant changes.

II A radical response

Some deny that future contingents have a truth-value and reject the principle of bivalence for future contingents (see Chapter 3 for a detailed discussion of future contingent statements). For example, Broad reasons as follows:

> Today, when I make the judgement [that tomorrow it will be wet], there is no such fact as the wetness of tomorrow and there is no such fact as the fineness of tomorrow. For these facts can neither of them begin to be until tomorrow begins to be. (Broad (1923: 73))

The reason why the principle of bivalence fails on this account is that there simply *are* no truthmakers for future-tensed propositions; indeed, the very non-existence of the future is taken to consist in the fact that there are no truthmakers. But if the non-existence of the future consists in the fact that there are no truthmakers, then, so the argument goes, presentists should by parity of reasoning treat the past in the same way and also deny that past-tensed propositions have determinate truth-values. This view can, indeed, be found in Prior ((1957: 44 f.); (1967: 151 f.)). (One could also imagine a Russellian alternative whereby past-tensed statements are all false because there are no objects that satisfy the existential claims.)

The advantages of this view are few. It is certainly transparent what the truthmakers for past-tensed statements are: there aren't any! And at least it is honest and conservative: it accepts the need for obvious truthmakers for true statements, and says they cannot be had.

But it is unsatisfactory: ideally, we would want it to be a consequence of any theory that it is true that Socrates taught Plato; indeed, this condition is so stable that if the radical response were the only solution presentism could offer, it wouldn't be off the wall to reject the presentist thesis entirely because of it. Furthermore, it is not clear on this view how we are to distinguish false (or neither true nor false) statements about the past that once were true, from those that are plain false. What, for example, grounds the truth that those statements *were* true? Put slightly differently, the truth-value links are not preserved according to this view. Suppose p is true at t. Then at t, we want it to be the case that it will be the case at a later time t^* that it was the case that p is true. But this doesn't hold because at t^*, p must be neither true nor false (or plain false).

Furthermore, suppose we take truthmakers to be past facts. There aren't any according to presentism; therefore, 'Socrates taught Plato' is neither true nor false (or false). It follows that we cannot *know* that Socrates taught Plato, even though there are strong causal traces that Socrates taught Plato, we are warranted in believing it, and we all do believe it. Odd indeed!

III Priorian presentism

Given that we just do take there to be true past-tensed statements, these will require truthmakers. It isn't good enough to adopt the radical response. After all, the tenseless theory doesn't have to, and that's a theory presentism should aspire to at least match. But where in the presentist's world are the truthmakers to be found? An obvious response is to say that since only the present exists, these truthmakers are to be found *in* the present. But what sort of truthmakers could these be?

Suppose we take our cue again from Prior, and use the propositional tense operators, **P**, **N**, and **F** (read 'It was the case that', 'It is (now) the case that', and 'It will be the case that', respectively), to pick up the tense of an interior tensed proposition. However complex the tense of the initial proposition, it can be analysed as a basic present-tensed interior proposition together with the appropriate iteration of the tense operators. Since the interior proposition is always present-tensed, there is a redundancy in the use of the operator **N** to signify the present tense. This leaves only the **F** and **P** operators as non-superfluous; we can always drop **N** when it appears outside the scope of **P** or **F**. Because of this, Prior held a 'redundancy theory of the present' (Prior (1957: 9–10); (1967: 8–10, 14–15); (1968b); (1968e)): everything that is presently true, is true *simpliciter*; **N** is superfluous in the same way as 'It is true that' is redundant according to the redundancy theory of truth. Indeed, he says 'reality consists in the absence of a qualifying prefix' (1970).[2] However, this is not to say

---

[2] However, it has been argued (Kamp (1971); McArthur (1976)) that **N** is only redundant if it appears outside the scope of the tense operators; it can have a drastic effect if it occurs within the scope of another temporal modifier. Kamp considers the following kinds of idiom,

(i) It was then true that there would be an earthquake (**PF**p),
(ii) It was then true that there would *now* be an earthquake (**PFN**p),

and

(iii) It was then true that there will be an earthquake (**PNF**p).

For Kamp, (i) implies that the earthquake could be at any time, (ii) implies that it is present, and (iii) implies that it is future; hence **N** is non-redundant. That is, although all agree that **N**p ≡ p, **NP**p ≡ **P**p and **NF**p ≡ **F**p, Kamp does not accept, e.g., that **PN**p ≡ **P**p, whereas if **N** were redundant, we would.

However, Prior (1968e) acknowledges that the idiomatic 'now' is non-redundant here in the sense that 'you cannot *just* erase it from a sentence and leave the sense of the whole the same', but argues that 'you can, however, erase it and get something with the same sense by altering the rest of the sentence somewhat' (106). That is, although he agrees that tense logic (such as Kamp's) *can* adequately incorporate such idioms, he does not think it *must* do (*pace* Tooley (1997: 166)) that we should not think of it as being there for, according to Prior:

'Socrates taught Plato' (**P**p)

means

'It is *now* the case that Socrates taught Plato' (**NP**p),

where p is the proposition that Socrates is teaching Plato. This has to be correct because it is a *present* truth that Socrates taught Plato. Thus, the tacit presence of an **N** outside the scope of all other operators implies that *all* tensed propositions *are* present-tensed; that is, implies, e.g., that the proposition that **FP**p *is* the proposition that **NFP**p; and the first stage of the presentist agenda to reduce past- and future-tensed propositions to present-tensed propositions is easily and naturally achieved.

But the essential question is: what *makes* such truths true? What are the constituents of the facts that make them true? Prior denies that these questions need answering: for Prior, there *is* nothing more to say about the nature of time than is said by a perspicuous tense logic (e.g., Prior (1996a: 45)). Nevertheless, I (with others, e.g., Smith (1987: 188–91); Tooley (1997: 166–7); Le Poidevin (1998: 38–9)) feel more needs to be said, especially since the issue of truthmaking is independent of the theory of truth: truthmaking arises just as much for deflationary theories of truth as it does for the correspondence theory (cf. Lewis (2001); and P. Smith (2003)). Thus, even if Prior adopts a

---

so; for, if we prefer, we can eliminate the idiomatic 'now' using a suitable paraphrase of the original sentence, thereby enabling us to keep the redundancy theory of the present. Prior's (1968e) paraphrase is rather long-winded. An easier way of establishing when p occurs, whilst keeping **N** redundant, is to introduce metric tense operators (Prior (1967: 95–111), (1968d); McArthur (1976: 5–7)) which indicate not just that something was the case, as **P** does, but when it was the case. For example, if the basic unit of time is an hour, 'Socrates was sitting three hours ago' can be written '$\mathbf{P}^3 p$'. Using this,

$\mathbf{P}^n \mathbf{F}^m p \Rightarrow p$ is present, when $n = m$;
$\mathbf{P}^n \mathbf{F}^m p \Rightarrow p$ is past, when $n > m$;
and $\mathbf{P}^n \mathbf{F}^m p \Rightarrow p$ is future, when $n < m$.

But, as we shall see in Chapter 3: problem 3, there are cases where **N** can be interpreted as not being redundant, even when it appears outside the scope of other tense operators.

deflationary theory of *truth* (and the present) this will not help him avoid the issue of *truthmaking*; he still needs to say more.

But if we press for an ontology, Prior is ultimately left in an uncomfortable position on one of the prongs of a dilemma. For, given his doctrine that propositions are themselves 'logical constructions' out of the objects they are about (Prior (1971: ch. 1)), *how* is it possible for the proposition that Socrates taught Plato to be true? Which particulars can be invoked as the constituents of such a fact? Not Socrates or Plato—they don't exist. Nor can we invoke a present past-Socrates—what a mysterious object that would be! The alternative is to invoke the primitive present fact that Socrates taught Plato. But without being able to say how this fact is structured (for its constituents are certainly not Socrates or Plato), this move is far from satisfactory. Thus either option leaves us with an obscure ontology.

We might think that these are just problems peculiar to Prior's position and of which later presentists must surely have said something satisfactory. But it appears not. Craig (2003) carries on in the same vein. He claims that reference to past objects is possible, since 'the proper name "Socrates" expresses an individual essence of Socrates rather than denotes nonconnotatively the actual object Socrates and so does not require Socrates to exist in order for the name to refer' (395). This move, following Plantinga's work on proper names (e.g., Plantinga (1974: 71–81; 137–44; 149–63)), would allow propositions like *Socrates taught Plato* to be about Socrates and Plato because 'Socrates' and 'Plato' express the essences of Socrates and Plato, and thus refer to them. Now, this sounds incomprehensible to those who subscribe to the view that in order for genuine reference to an object to take place, the object must exist: for, according to this view, if Socrates does not exist, 'Socrates' does not refer. But Craig is at pains to draw a distinction between what he calls 'reference' and 'correspondence' (394). Correspondence is a relation between world and word and thus requires an object to fall under a name; but reference, we are told, doesn't, since it has 'to do with how terms serve to pick out individuals' (395), something which, it is claimed, doesn't require the existence of the individual. But, even if we concede this, it hardly addresses the question of which objects *are* required for *truthmaking*, a quite separate issue. If it isn't the concrete object that figures in truthmaking, is it the 'individual essences' expressed by the proper names, essences of objects which exist even though the concrete objects themselves don't? No, for Craig only uses individual essences to argue for the possibility of 'reference' to past objects, not in order to spell out the truthmakers for past-tensed propositions. So what are we left with? For Craig, what makes the proposition that *Socrates taught Plato* true is the 'tensed fact' (400) that Socrates taught Plato. End of story. And quite literally so, because nothing more is said about this fact. It certainly cannot have Socrates and Plato as constituents (regardless of whether 'reference' can be made to them), since it is a *present* fact that Socrates taught Plato and, presently, they don't exist. And it is no good complaining that they *did* exist, because we want to know what *does exist* to make the proposition true now. (Note that this is not the unjustifiable requirement that what makes propositions true at a particular time must also be *located* at that time; since what makes the proposition that *Socrates taught Plato* true now, according to the tenseless view, is a fact located in the past, and this seems an entirely reasonable view. The requirement is rather that there *be* something in existence to make the proposition true; so this cannot be something involving Socrates and Plato, for the presentist, regardless of whether they *did* exist.) We are simply not told what the constituents of these facts are or how they are structured. It seems that no real progress has been made on this issue with this version of presentism since Prior's work.

But the view that the present contains within it all of the facts required to make past-, present-, and future-tensed propositions true creates another, less obvious, concern. We can represent times as sets of present-tensed propositions. Suppose p is a true present-tensed proposition. Now, merely from considering the truth-value links which must hold across times, the following set of true present-tensed propositions must also hold of that time: $\{p, \mathbf{FP}p, \mathbf{PF}p, ...\}$.[3] But

---

[3] I am here assuming the truth-value links generated in linear time. Those who don't accept that p also generates $\mathbf{PF}p$ (because they hold that the future branches, say) would still want to hold that p generates $\mathbf{FP}p$ and the truth-value links associated with it. My point is that this version of presentism cannot even guarantee that these truth-value links are preserved.

what guarantees that a later time preserves these links? Given the present time represented by $\{p, \mathbf{FP}p, \mathbf{PF}p, \dots\}$, there must be a later time represented by $\{\mathbf{P}p, \mathbf{PFP}p, \mathbf{PPF}p, \dots\}$. But how can a Priorian presentist even guarantee this, let alone explain it? Of course, **PFP**p must hold in the future, if p holds presently: every adequate theory of time must have this as a consequence or be rejected. But there is no mechanism in this version of presentism to guarantee it. It is no good just appealing to the tense logic and then interpreting this in a deflationary way, since, as noted above, this semantic issue does not address the ontological issues at stake. The ontology, at least as far as Craig is concerned, is such that the present time is comprised of certain tensed facts, including those about what will happen and what has happened. We can add that all times are contingent and distinct entities. But then it follows, if we take the Humean stance, that the truth-value link cannot be guaranteed by any *necessary* connections between such times, or the tensed facts of which they are comprised (at least at the ontological level of tensed facts, if not the semantic level of tense logic). Furthermore, for that matter, there cannot be *any* transtemporal relations to link times together on this view: other times don't exist; and it is hard to see how the ontological content of the present time can in itself legislate how other distinct entities, other times, can be comprised. Yet somehow it must. For if the content of the present time does not legislate this, what, according to this view, does? And it must because it is incredible to think that there could be missing tensed facts from, or additional tensed facts in, various times. The truth-value links have somehow to be a feature of how the facts are structured (as they are on the tenseless theory of time, for example, and as they are on the view I present below). But because no mechanism is in place to preserve the truth-value links and the possibility of a violation of them is opened up, this version of presentism should be rejected.[4]

---

[4] The versions of presentism proposed by Bigelow (1996) and Craig (1997), which also pack all of their proposed truthmakers for past- and future-tensed statements into the present, are subject to such criticisms. See Oaklander (2002) for specific criticisms of these versions of presentism, and Oaklander (2003a) for criticisms of Craig's later (2000a), (2000b) attempts at defending presentism.

IV Reductive presentism

A second shot at the thought that the present itself can supply all of the required truthmakers is the reductive version of presentism. Ludlow (1999: ch. 9) is a recent substantial work on time that proposes this view, and Le Poidevin (1991) (a tenseless theorist) recognizes this option:

> What makes a certain statement about the past true...is the evidence that at present exists.... This is possible in virtue of the fact that there are present facts which derive their character from causal connection with past states of affairs, and which determine (at least to some extent) the character of the future [37] ... [T]his is essential to the...[presentist's] position. (Le Poidevin (1991: 38))

And:

> The extent to which the principle of bivalence is violated by statements about the past or future depends, for [the presentist], upon how much causal determinism he is prepared to allow. In a fully deterministic universe...all future- and past-tensed statements have a determinate truth-value, as this is guaranteed by present fact. But in an indeterministic universe...many statements about the future must for [presentism] lack a truth-value. (Le Poidevin (1991: 38))

Although it is obvious from the above discussion that, *contra* Le Poidevin, this story is not 'essential to the [presentist's] position', it is a position that has been held for a variety of reasons. Łukasiewicz (1970: 127–8), for example, writes:

> If, of the future, only that part is real today which is causally determined by the present time...then also, of the past, only that part is real which is still alive today in its effects. Facts whose effects are wholly exhausted, so that even an omniscient mind could not infer them from facts happening today, belong to the realm of possibilities. We cannot say of them that they were but only that they were possible. And this is as well. In the life of each of us there occur grievous times of suffering and even more grievous times of guilt. We should be glad to wipe out these times not only from our memories but from reality. Now we are at liberty to believe that when all the consequences of those fatal times are exhausted, even if this happened only after our death,

then they too will be erased from the world of reality and pass over to the domain of possibility.   (Łukasiewicz (1970: 127–8))

But apart from ignoring the virtues of taking responsibility for, and learning from, one's past actions, Łukasiewicz forgets that our past glories will also be wiped out on this view. In any case, we cannot gauge the truth of a theory from how emotionally comforting it is.

Nevertheless, there are more respectable sounding reasons for holding this position, such as Wheeler's (1978: 41) view that the two-slit experiment in quantum physics vindicates this conception. He writes:

> Does this result mean that present choice influences past dynamics, in contravention of every principle of causality? Or does it mean, calculate pedantically and don't ask questions? Neither; the lesson presents itself rather as this, that the past has no existence except as it is recorded in the present. (Wheeler (1978: 41))

And Stein (1968: 23) remarks that quantum mechanics 'suggests the notion of a progressively increasing physical uncertainty (or "indeterminism") of the past: a kind of fading of the world's memory', something in the spirit of reductive presentism.

It is not, however, a position which has been fully endorsed by any serious philosopher, although, of course, Dummett has played with this view for years. Ludlow (1999: 162) claims that although this position is not 'an inevitable consequence of the A-theory', it is 'a possible avenue of investigation'. So, although this is only a tentative endorsement, it is important to briefly show how just a short walk down this supposed avenue reveals it to be more of a *cul-de-sac*.

There are two broad categories of theories of laws of nature, which I shall label 'Humean' and 'non-Humean'. Consider the Humean theory, which states that laws consist in nothing more than: whenever there is an F, there is a G, i.e., $(\forall x)(Fx \supset Gx)$. The first issue to address here is the 'whenever' quantifier. If it just ranges over times that exist (i.e., the present time!), then any present conjunction of F with G will constitute a law, which is unsatisfactory. But, more damagingly, if it is restricted to times that exist (the present time), then laws cannot do the job for which they were intended. For, according to this account, they do not extend beyond the present, and thus cannot determine the truth-values of statements about the past and the future. We should, then, take it that 'whenever' ranges over present times as well as those that *have* existed and *will* exist. The problem now is: what makes it true that all Fs *are*, *have been*, and *will be* Gs? For there is nothing we could appeal to in the present. We certainly can't appeal to deterministic laws of nature to ground what has happened and what will happen, since this just lands us in a circle, for the whole problem was to find something in the present that could ground what that law is. And the present state of the universe by itself cannot determine what has happened and what will happen because the present state of the universe is compatible with infinitely many different mutually contradictory pasts and futures: it is only the state of the universe at a given time *together with deterministic laws of nature* which can determine what has happened and what will happen. But there is nothing in the reductive presentist's world which can ground such a law. It is not as if the law can be seen as an extra ingredient in the present, which can help determine one course of history over another, for remember that we are talking about the Humean conception of law, and according to this conception, there is nothing more, ontologically speaking, to a law over and above what does actually happen. This leads us to consider an alternative option, namely to appeal to primitive facts: things just *did* and *will* occur in this sort of regularity. But this then renders the excursion into reductive presentism entirely redundant if we adopt primitive facts: we may as well be Priorian presentists. Thus, a Humean account of laws will not give reductive presentists what they would hope for.

What about non-Humean accounts? Suppose we thought that laws of nature are some kind of necessary connection between universals. According to Armstrong, the law that Fs are Gs is some sort of necessitation relation N between the universals F-ness and G-ness. $N(F, G)$ is a contingent nomic necessity that may not hold across all possible worlds, but if it actually holds, then $N(F, G) \Rightarrow (\forall x)(Fx \supset Gx)$. For various reasons, Armstrong (1983: 86–99) argues that $N(F, G)$ is a first-order relational universal that is instantiated by particular states of affairs Fa and Ga. Furthermore, according to Armstrong's Principle of Instantiation (e.g., (1983: 82)) universals must be instantiated in order to exist. It follows that, given that there are only present states of affairs in the reductive presentist's world, any instantiation of a law can only take place in, and be true of, the present. Thus such laws of nature cannot tell us about what happens at other times, and thus cannot ground determinate truth-values for past- or future-tensed statements. (This is particularly problematic given Armstrong's view that the necessitation relation does not supervene on the state of the world, and can change in what it relates from world to world. For even if $N(F, G)$ holds of the present time, there is nothing to say it will hold across all past and future times. Yet that was what the reductive presentist hoped the necessitation—although it is hard to see how we can still call it 'necessitation' given these considerations—would guarantee.)

This well-known and well-worked-out non-Humean theory was worth mentioning in order to illustrate the general problem with which reductive presentists have to deal: *how* can the laws reach beyond the present? There are, of course, non-Humean accounts that argue that laws can exist without being so instantiated (e.g., Tooley (1977); Mellor (1980)). But a presentist who appealed to these accounts of laws of nature would either have to find something in the present to ground these laws—and it's difficult to see what this could be—or they must appeal to facts outside the present, in which case they've conceded that not all of the truthmakers can be found *in* the present, which was their initial contention. The notion of determinism will not help the presentist on the issue of securing determinateness of truth-value.

Needless to say, reductive presentism cannot have determinate truth-values in an indeterministic world. Yet, even in an indeterministic world, we still want to say that at least past-tensed statements have *determinate* truth-values. We want to say that it is either true or false that a certain brontosaurus had two plants for breakfast, regardless of whether there are any traces of this fact in the present, and regardless of whether the present state of the universe and the laws of nature can determine this fact. To confuse determinateness with determinism is an offence. Reductive presentism thus violates condition (a) of section I.

Furthermore, reductive presentism, however much it initially seems to, *doesn't* in fact meet the truth-value links problem. First, consider

Russell's hypothesis (1921: 159–60): what is to say that the world has not just come into existence complete with fossil records, memories, and other such causal traces? Russell intended this to illustrate the limitations of our knowledge, but pre-theoretically, it seems like a genuine possibility for how the world could be. Suppose it is true, then reductive presentism gives the wrong answers, for it states that certain past-tensed statements are true when they shouldn't be. Of course, nobody thinks that hypothesis is true; but Russell's hypothesis doesn't have to be actually true to cause trouble; that it is true that it is possible is enough to show that reductive presentism has a problem accounting for truth-value links. And we couldn't rule out Russell's hypothesis by appealing to actual laws of nature that wouldn't allow for such a complex environment in such a short space of time, for, as I have argued above, the grounding of those very laws is called into question on the reductive view. That is, in a nutshell, truth-value links are supposedly underpinned by causal links: present facts are effects of previous causes and themselves causes of later effects. But this relies on what it is in the present that grounds this causal link: for it to be true that a given fact is an effect of a previous cause, we need the present fact that it *is* the effect of a previous cause to make this true, since without this fact there is nothing to link the supposed 'effect' to anything that came before, or the supposed 'cause' to anything that comes after. (And we certainly need this, given the many different pasts and futures compatible with the present state of the universe.) But what sort of fact could this be? Taking it as a primitive present fact lumbers us with the Priorian presentist's facts and all their attendant problems. We are no better off after all.

We now have an appreciation of what any successful version of presentism must hope to achieve, and the pitfalls it must avoid. The version of presentism I am about to propose meets these conditions. It also meets the challenges that some (e.g., Oaklander (2002); (2003a)) throw down for presentism to tackle, namely how presentists can help themselves to the notion of *earlier than* without having to invoke real *relata*, and how presentism can distinguish the past from the future. It should also be attractive to those who see close analogies between time and modality, and who prefer ersatz theories of possible worlds (such as Adams's (1974)) over genuine modal realism (such as Lewis's (1986)), for the position I shall defend is essentially this: all of us should agree that Socrates taught Plato, i.e., that the proposition that *Socrates is teaching Plato* was, at some time, true. This, to most people, is so obvious as to not be worth stating. So I ask them to keep this in mind during the more technical exposition of the position which is about to follow. For I say we should take the 'i.e.' seriously; that is, that *what makes it true* that Socrates taught Plato is the existence of a proposition that states this is the case for some time in the past, where a time is a set of propositions that states the other truths about what happens at that time. For obvious reasons, I shall call this position 'ersatzer presentism'.

V Ersatzer presentism[5]

(a) An improvement over Prior's presentism: e-*propositions and* u-*propositions*

I go some way with Prior ((1967: 79–82); (1968c: 124–8)) in constructing times from certain sets of present-tensed propositions.[6]

---

[5] My ersatzer account was mentioned in Bourne (2002) with a promissory note that the full-blown account would be forthcoming. Due to some unfortunate encounters with certain referees, this was delayed somewhat until the publication of Bourne (2006). The account which follows differs from that given originally in my 'A Defence of Presentism' (University of Cambridge: Ph.D. diss., 2002) only in being formulated in terms of objectual rather than substitutional quantification and in including an account of *de re* occurrences of tenses. Others who have endorsed the ersatz approach include Crisp (2003) and Markosian (2004). Lewis (1986: 204) also briefly mentions the possibility of holding some kind of ersatz position concerning time. His reason for dismissing it is that 'No man...believes that he has no future; still less does anyone believe that he has no past'. This is ambiguous. On one reading, it is plain false: no presentist believes they have a future in the sense of real times that exist later than now. On the other reading, it is true but harmless, for presentists (can) believe that there *will* be more times to come, even though there *are* no real times later than our present time (see §V(d)).

[6] For the purposes of this book, I'll take propositions to be primitive abstract objects. However, this is not to say that nothing more can be said about them: they are entities capable of being either true or false, entities to which we can have attitudes (such as beliefs, desires, hopes, and fears), and they are capable of representing states of affairs. Being abstract entities, they raise the understandable question of how we come to grasp them. But I think this worry is misguided: we grasp the proposition that snow is white, for example, not *via* some mysterious interaction with an abstract object, but by having been acquainted with

However, my account differs in important respects. According to Prior, the present moment should be equated with the conjunction of all those propositions which are presently true, i.e., true *simpliciter*; and generalizing, he equates any time with a conjunction of all those present-tensed propositions which would be true at that time.

My conception differs, first, in that I distinguish present-tensed propositions that contain either **P** or **F** operators, which I shall call 'embedded propositions' (*e*-propositions), from those that do not, which I shall call 'unembedded propositions' (*u*-propositions). (Compare, for example, the *e*-proposition: It is now the case that it was the case that Socrates is sitting (i.e., **NP**p), with the *u*-proposition: It is now the case that Socrates is sitting (i.e., **N**p), or simply: Socrates is sitting (i.e., p).)

As we have seen, Priorian presentism required the present to be equated with *e*-propositions in order for the present to supply all of the truths we believe there are, but that it was rather mysterious what the truthmakers were for these propositions, and neither could it account for the truth-value links between the different times. The theory to be developed avoids these difficulties.

(b) Defining times, and the E-*relation*

I propose we construct times using maximally consistent sets of *u*-propositions, which intuitively we can see as those *u*-propositions that

---

white snow, or at least white things and snowy things. Of course, there may be propositions concerning things of which we have never been acquainted; but, in that case, we do not understand them. The main problem, however, is not with understanding propositions, but with how they manage to *represent* how things are. This is a notoriously difficult issue and requires a much lengthier discussion than I can give here. My short answer is this: as Lewis (1986: ch. 3) famously argues, a certain amount of 'magic' is required in order for propositions, taken as *sui generis* entities, to represent the world. This is something which it would be nice to avoid—it doesn't quite fit with my 'transparency' condition. There are, of course, a number of potential 'non-magical' avenues to take, but all I wish to do here is present the big picture and hope that there is a way to fill in this particular detail. However, even if there is not, it is still not a fatal blow to ersatzer presentism. For Lewis (1991: 35–8) himself acknowledges van Inwagen's (1986: 207–10) point that there is a certain amount of magic in the Lewisian account of representation. This cannot be resolved here, but see Divers (2002: 275–92) for more discussion. Furthermore, if tenseless theorists won't allow the presentist such accounts of representation, then the presentist is at liberty to force them into an uncomfortable position concerning how representation is possible in the modal case. Will such tenseless theorists be prepared to swallow genuine modal realism?

are true at that time. These propositions I take to give a complete, maximally specific, description of what is true at that time. But more needs to be added: they, at least, need to be ordered by an 'earlier than' relation (what I shall call an 'E-relation'), in order for the ersatz time series to be structurally similar to a real time series, so it can be taken to be a sufficient substitute. That is, we can introduce the ordered triple $<\mathbf{T}, E, t>$, where $\mathbf{T}$ is a set, E is a relation on $\mathbf{T}$, and $t \in \mathbf{T}$.[7] Intuitively, $\mathbf{T}$ is the set of times, E is the 'earlier than' relation, and t is a particular time. Times I take to be more than sets of present-tensed propositions: first, they consist of sets of u-propositions; second, they also contain a 'date'. That is, I take times (at least for the time being) to be ordered pairs of the form $t = <\mu, n \in \mathbb{R}>$, where μ is a set of u-propositions and $n \in \mathbb{R}$ is the date. Times can now be defined as those ordered pairs of the form $t = <\mu, n \in \mathbb{R}>$ that are members of the set of sets of ordered pairs of the form $t = <\mu, n \in \mathbb{R}>$ that are E-related. Actual times are those times that are members of the set of times that are *actually* E-related. (What this amounts to is explained below.)

Defining times in the way I have done requires us to alter our terminology slightly. Lewis (1986: 140) has complained that ersatzism concerning possible worlds commits us to saying that since worlds are, say, sets of propositions, the concrete object that we are part of—'the world', speaking with the vulgar—cannot be said to be a world. Similarly, since, according to ersatzer presentism, times are abstract objects, the present time is not something we inhabit. But rather than introduce a new term, or typescript, for what I am calling 'times', I prefer to keep this useful terminology. The only differences it makes are that we must be said to inhabit the concrete realization of the present time, and that ersatzer presentism is the view not that only one time exists but that only one time has a concrete realization. This is a mere nominal difference, equivalent to saying that presentists do not believe in any times other than the present; and all is as it should be.

The E-relation is not the genuine *earlier than* relation since it does not relate spatio-temporal objects, but it does *represent* the *earlier than* relation in the way it relates times. The properties of the E-relation

---

[7] À la Kripke (1963). cf. also McArthur (1976).

match whatever we take to be the properties of the genuine *earlier than* relation. This allows presentists to have a time series related by 'earlier than' without being committed to the existence of real, or rather concretely realized, *relata*, something anathema to presentism. Ersatzer presentism thus bypasses the problems that other presentists get into when they do not take such relations as basic, and try to define them in terms of tenses (see, e.g., Oaklander (2002); Mellor (2003: 236–7)).

Various metrical and topological features of time can be represented in the structure of the abstract objects. For example, if we take time to be linear, the E-relation will have the properties of being irreflexive, asymmetric, and transitive; if it is circular, it will be an equivalence relation; if time is continuous, the times are assigned real numbers as dates; if discrete, then only those times that have dates $n \in \mathbb{Z}$ will have realizations; if it is infinite in both directions from the present, then the dates will have the standard order type of infinite time ($\omega^* + \omega$); if time is circular then the dates will be of the form of a periodic function (for some period with value P, $t(x + P) = t(x)$), and so on.

But, despite the fact that these properties of time can be represented in this way, presentism has a very good reason for adopting a *branching* topology; that is, where the E-relation is a one–many relation in the direction from the present to future (the direction in which the dates increase in magnitude), but only a one–one relation in the direction from the present to the past (the direction in which the dates decrease in magnitude). The reason is simple: we all need a way of distinguishing the past from the future. Because presentism treats the past and the future as ontologically on a par, in the sense that it denies that there are any concrete truthmakers located there, the branching-structure of times is an obvious way in which presentism can differentiate between past and future. Furthermore, it accounts for the platitude that the past is 'fixed' and the future is 'open', something that any good theory of time should. Thus, if we follow my proposal, presentism does have at its disposal means for distinguishing the past from the future.[8]

---

[8] It seems to me that it is also a position which is forced on ersatzer presentism. For if we had a linear time, then it would be a mystery why the concrete world would conform

(c) Truth-conditions, truthmakers, truth-at-a-time, and truth simpliciter

I also distinguish truth-at-a-time from truth *simpliciter*.[9] Truth *simpliciter* is an absolute, not time-relative, notion, whereas truth-at-a-time is time-relative: all propositions at a time are true relative to it, but only those propositions which are true at the present time are true *simpliciter*. So, where the propositions involved are any atomic propositions, be they from propositional or predicate calculi, we have:

> (2.1) 'Socrates is sitting' is true-at-a-time iff there is a time, i.e., E-related order pair $<\mu, n \in \mathbb{R}>$ such that μ includes the u-proposition that Socrates is sitting, i.e., 'p' is true-at-a-time $<\mathbf{T}, E, <\mu, n \in \mathbb{R}>>$ iff $p \in \mu$.

And similarly

> (2.2) '$\sim p$' is true-at-a-time $<\mathbf{T}, E, <\mu, n \in \mathbb{R}>>$ iff $p \notin \mu$.[10]
> (2.3) '$p\&q$' is true-at-a-time $<\mathbf{T}, E, <\mu, n \in \mathbb{R}>>$ iff $p, q \in \mu$.

Whereas:

> (2.4) 'Socrates is sitting' is true *simpliciter* iff Socrates (i.e., an actual, concrete, flesh and blood Socrates) is presently sitting.

Furthermore, it is not only present-tensed u-propositions that can be true *simpliciter*; past-tensed propositions can be too. The difference is that whereas present-tensed u-propositions are made true *simpliciter* iff corresponding actual concrete facts are presently realized, past-tensed propositions are made true *simpliciter* by something entirely different.

---

to what the future times represent as happening. With branching time, on the other hand, all possible futures are represented and accessible from each node on a particular branch, so whichever time gets realized next will be represented somewhere on one of the future branches accessible from it. This allows us to bypass the problem of matching what the abstract structure says with how the concrete world is without the need for necessary links between them. All possibilities are represented, so the next time is bound to be represented on some branch.

[9] I take my cue here from Adams (1974) in his analogous discussion of truth *simpliciter* and truth-at-a-world in the possible worlds debate.

[10] I use this truth-condition since μ is defined as a set of u-propositions that is true at that time, thus it is not the case that '$\sim p$' is true iff 'p' is false, since p does not even appear in that time if 'p' is false at that time.

I propose that we treat past- and future-tenses as indicating where our present's corresponding time is in relation to the others. Since these propositions are really about how times are ordered, we have the following truth-condition:

(2.5) '**P**p' is true *simpliciter* iff p is a member of a set μ of u-propositions that is the first element of an order pair $<\mu, n_i \in \mathbb{R}>$ actually E-related to the presently realized ordered pair $<v, n_j \in \mathbb{R}>$, where v is the set of u-propositions that is true *simpliciter*, and $n_i < n_j$.[11]

Note that the 'actual' here is not superfluous: it has a technical use. Since time has a branching structure, then time *actually* has a branching structure and all possible times on each of these branches are *in some sense* of 'actual' actually E-related. Yet I require only *some* times as truthmakers for past- and future-tensed statements, namely those that correspond to what we would ordinarily want to call the actual history of the world. Thus, when I use the phrase 'actually E-related' I mean that there is a time which is E-related to the time that is true *simpliciter*, i.e., that is actually concretely realized. This grounds which E-related branch we should use for finding truthmakers for past-tensed statements, since only one E-related branch is accessible from the concretely realized time in the direction towards the past.

In short we have the following story about truthmakers:

1. What makes u-propositions true *simpliciter* are actually realized concrete facts.
2. What makes past-tensed propositions true *simpliciter* are actually E-related ordered pairs of u-propositions and dates.
3. What makes 'p' true-at-time-t is the fact that $p \in \mu$, where $t = <\mu, n \in \mathbb{R}>$.

It now remains to complete the story by dealing with quantification. First, as I've noted, presentists should read the existential quantifier tenselessly. I also take it that the quantifiers should be read in the

---

[11] Thus Russell's hypothesis is harmless to ersatzer presentism. The E-relation simply does not hold if the world has just come into existence; so no past-tensed propositions are true, as required.

standard objectual way. Thus, '(∃x)Fx' is true *simpliciter* iff there is at least one object in the domain of quantification that is F; and '(∀x)Fx' is true *simpliciter* iff all objects in the domain of quantification are F. Despite being read tenselessly, '(∃x)Fx' might change truth value from time to time because of the continually changing concrete facts and subsequent change in the domain of quantification. Thus:

(2.6) '**P**(∀x)Fx' is true at <**T**, E, t> (and is true *simpliciter* iff the set of propositions at t is true *simpliciter*) iff (∀x)Fx is a member of some μ element of a time earlier than t (understood in the ersatz way), where '(∀x)Fx' is true-at-a-time <**T**, E, <μ, n ∈ ℝ>> iff (∀x)Fx ∈ μ.

(2.7) '**P**(∃x)Fx' is true at <**T**, E, t> (and is true *simpliciter* iff the set of propositions at t is true *simpliciter*) iff (∃x)Fx is a member of some μ element of a time earlier than t (understood in the ersatz way), where '(∃x)Fx' is true-at-a-time <**T**, E, <μ, n ∈ ℝ>> iff (∃x)Fx ∈ μ.

Dealing with *de dicto* occurrences of tenses in quantified sentences is, then, relatively straightforward. But how should we understand *de re* occurrences of tenses in quantified sentences, i.e., where the operators fall *within* the scope of a quantifier, such as in '(∃x)**P**Gx'? This cannot be taken by presentists to mean that 'Something's exemplification of G has pastness', as Smith (1998b) interprets it, since that either means that x has a present past-ugliness, which is as metaphysically dubious a property as we saw the present past-Socrates individual was in §III, or it means that there is an exemplification which is past, which, although perfectly acceptable to the tenseless theory, is something unavailable to presentism. But presentists should not just bite the bullet here and conclude that this just shows that *de re* occurrences of tenses are, therefore, illegitimate. For *de re* tense ascriptions are important to capture, and it would be a failing if presentism lacked the resources to be able to express them. What we need to do, then, is consider such cases, and see what presentists should say in order to accommodate them. Consider the following example.

(2.8) Walter's horse had wings

On the quantified *de dicto* reading, this amounts to

(2.9) $\mathbf{P}(\exists x)(x = \text{Walter's horse} \ \& \ \text{has wings}\,(x))$

For (2.9) to be true, it just has to be true at some time in the past that Walter's horse—that is, any horse that Walter owns at that time—has wings. This is perfectly compatible with Walter's present horse not just not having any wings, but not ever having had any wings; indeed it is prefectly compatible with Walter not now having any horse. To capture the thought that it is Walter's present horse that had wings, we need the *de re* form

(2.10) $(\exists x)(x = \text{Walter's horse} \ \& \ \mathbf{P}(\text{has wings}\,(x)))$

(Note that '**P**', here, remains as a sentential operator operating on an open sentence. It need not be treated as operating on the predicate, creating a complex predicate, as Smith (1998b) does.) The question for presentists is: what makes this *de re* form true? The first stage of filling this out is to notice that it must be that if (2.10) is true, then

(2.11) $\mathbf{P}(\exists x)(\text{has wings}\,(x))$

is true. Note that (2.9) need not be true if (2.10) is, since Walter might not have owned the horse when it had wings; and if it were, say, a magical horse, it might not even have been a horse when it had wings. What matters is that the horse we are talking about in (2.10) is appropriately connected to the winged-creature (or winged-creatures) that we are talking about in (2.11), such that we would call them the same creature. What exactly the relation between them has to be in order for there to be identity over time is a controversial philosophical question in its own right. But whatever conditions we impose on the situation in order for it to be the correct kind of connection, such as whether we need to rule out the existence of equally good candidates, and so on, the fundamental connection underlying identity over time will be of an appropriate *causal* kind. So, in order for (2.10) to be true, it must be, first, that (2.11) is true and, second, that there is an appropriate causal connection between the fact that there was a winged-creature and the fact that there is a horse (belonging to Walter), such that we would say it was the same creature. *De re* forms, then, are not as problematic for presentism as is sometimes made out. Of course, the success of this strategy depends on whether presentism

(d) The future

An interesting question that arises for ersatzer presentism is accounting for future-tense propositions. Can the sentence 'It will be the case that p' be true *simpliciter*? According to this theory,

> (2.12) '**F**p' is true *simpliciter* iff p is a member of a set μ of u-propositions that is the first element of an order pair $<\mu, n_i \in \mathbb{R}>$ actually E-related to the presently realized ordered pair $<\nu, n_j \in \mathbb{R}>$, where ν is the set of u-propositions that is true *simpliciter*, and $n_i > n_j$.

However, '**F**p' is neither determinately true *simpliciter* nor determinately false *simpliciter*, given the branching structure, when p is contingent. Furthermore, consider the truth-conditions for future-tensed quantified statements:

> (2.13) '**F**$(\forall x)Fx$' is true at $<\mathbf{T}, E, t>$ (and is true *simpliciter* iff the set of propositions at t is true *simpliciter*) iff $(\forall x)Fx$ is a member of some μ element of a time later than t (understood in the ersatz way), where '$(\forall x)Fx$' is true-at-a-time $<\mathbf{T}, E, <\mu, n \in \mathbb{R}>>$ iff $(\forall x)Fx \in \mu$.
>
> (2.14) '**F**$(\exists x)Fx$' is true at $<\mathbf{T}, E, t>$ (and is true *simpliciter* iff the set of propositions at t is true *simpliciter*) iff $(\exists x)Fx$ is a member of some μ element of a time later than t (understood in the ersatz way), where '$(\exists x)Fx$' is true-at-a-time $<\mathbf{T}, E, <\mu, n \in \mathbb{R}>>$ iff $(\exists x)Fx \in \mu$.

Given the branching future, '**F**$(\forall x)Fx$' is only true *simpliciter* when '$(\forall x)Fx$' is true at all times later than the present, i.e., on all possible branches. And '**F**$(\exists x)Fx$' is only false *simpliciter* when '$(\exists x)Fx$' is true at no time later than the present, i.e., on no possible branches. That they have determinate truth-values only in these extreme circumstances, however, must only really be treated as a consequence of the branching view, not a criticism of it. But I should discuss here Lewis's (1986: 207–8) argument against branching time, since it is based on a common misconception of it. Lewis writes:

The trouble with branching exactly is that it conflicts with our ordinary presupposition that we have a single future. If two futures are equally mine, one with a sea fight tomorrow and one without, it is nonsense to wonder which way it will be—it will be both ways—and yet I do wonder. The theory of branching suits those who think this wondering makes sense only if reconstrued: you have leave to wonder about the sea fight, provided that really you wonder not about what tomorrow will bring but about what today predetermines.   (Lewis (1986: 207–8))

Lewis is wrong, however, to conclude that a branching future commits one to holding 'it will be both ways'. He is confusing the fact that there *are* many future branches to be realized as of the present time, with the fact that only one of them *will* be realized. After all, that is the only way to make sense of the claim that future contingent statements have indeterminate truth-values—if it will be both ways, then both of the statements are true (see Chapter 3 for a detailed discussion of future contingents). But, according to the branching view, future contingents are presently indeterminate precisely because only *one* branch of the possible branches *will* get realized, but that there *is* no branch in particular that is presently that branch. Thus it makes good sense to wonder now which of the unrealized branches will become *the* future. Thus branching does not conflict with our ordinary presupposition that we *will have* a single future, although it does conflict with the idea that we *have* a single future. The former presupposition is something we surely do not want to reject—it is close to being a platitude. But it is far from clear that the latter presupposition has such a status, and arguably is contrary to most people's common-sense view of the future: many people think, in a clear-headed way, that *pace* Lewis, we don't *have* a single future, but we *will* have one. And, moreover, this has nothing to do with what is 'predetermined': as already noted above (§IV), *determinism* is neither here nor there on the issue of the *determinateness* of the future. Lewis's argument is thus far from compelling.

VI Branching time for presentists

It just remains to fill out the story concerning the branching structure and show how ersatzer presentism can account for the truth-value

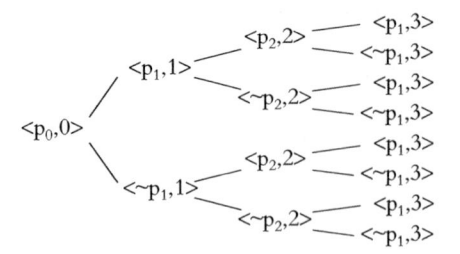

```
          <p₂,2> ─── <p₁,3>
  <p₁,1>         ─── <~p₁,3>
        ╲  <~p₂,2>── <p₁,3>
<p₀,0>              ── <~p₁,3>
        ╲  <p₂,2> ─── <p₁,3>
  <~p₁,1>        ─── <~p₁,3>
           <~p₂,2>── <p₁,3>
                   ── <~p₁,3>
```

FIG. 2.1. Branching time

links between times. Consider Fig. 2.1. At the present, there is only one past accessible to it and no unique future. The set-up is such that all possible futures are represented and accessible from each node on a particular branch, so whichever time gets realized next will be represented somewhere on one of the future branches accessible from it: the branching structure gives us completeness.

(a) A problem with truth-value links?

But a problem arises. Suppose that p_0 is true *simpliciter*, i.e., that time t_0 is presently realized. Now suppose that the proposition p_1 is made true *simpliciter* next. What guarantee have we that it is p_1 at t_1 that has been realized rather than, say, p_1 at t_3? If there is nothing to constrain which time is realized, it seems that we are committed to saying that the concrete facts that have just 'become' realize all of these times equally. But if this is the case, then there are branches according to which

$$<<p_1, 1>, <p_0, 0>>$$

is the history of the world, whereas others represent that

$$<<p_1, 3>, <p_2, 2>, <p_1, 1>, <p_0, 0>>$$

is, whereas according to others

$$<<p_1, 3>, <\sim p_2, 2>, <\sim p_1, 1>, <p_0, 0>>$$

is, and if p_1 is true *simpliciter*, it seems that there is nothing to choose between these options. Something needs to be done to preserve the truth-value links.

The problem here arises because of the sparseness of the concrete present: it is not sufficiently rich to determine everything that needs to be determined in order to defend a plausible view of time. But this is no great news; that's exactly what I have been arguing so far, and precisely the reason for invoking more than the concrete present facts as truthmakers for tensed statements. This was, after all, what confined the previous versions of presentism to an implausible position. But once we remember that ersatzer presentists have more artillery at their disposal, this problem has an obvious solution. For, according to the theory here proposed, the sets of propositions follow the *ordering* of the dates; so although the content of the proposition p_1 is the same wherever it occurs as a member of a time, it is also associated with a date. This allows us to say that when p_0 is realized at time 0, the next set to be realized must be a set that is indexed by 1 (or whatever number sequence or metric we choose to be appropriate), and so on. This is no more mysterious than holding that 2 January follows 1 January, something that all sides accept. So there is a natural way of specifying which time it is that has been realized. The truth-value links remain intact.

(b) A further problem with truth-value links for branching-time presentists?
However, there is another potential objection. Suppose that it is $<p_1, 1>$ that is realized after $<p_0, 0>$, rather than, say, $<p_1, 3>$, due to the fact that $<p_1, 1>$ is indexed by 1 and $<p_1, 3>$ is indexed by 3, and 1 is the least available number greater than 0. Now suppose that proposition p_2 is made true *simpliciter* by the next concrete facts to 'become'. What guarantee have we that it is the p_2-set in the history

$$<<p_2, 2>, <p_1, 1>, <p_0, 0>>$$

that is realized, rather than the p_2-set in the history

$$<<p_2, 2>, <\sim p_1, 1>, <p_0, 0>>?$$

Indeed, since there is nothing in the present to determine which one is realized (both p_2-sets are, after all, indexed by 2), it seems that we are committed to saying that both have equal claim to have been realized, and our truth-value links again break down.

This objection again relies on there not being enough in the present to determine which of the sets is realized. But, again, this is not the theory that I am putting forward; there *are* more facts available to determine which p_2-set is realized. For once we have in place the fact that it is $<p_1, 1>$ that is realized after $<p_0, 0>$, there is a fact of the matter as to which branch has been realized, namely the $<<p_1, 1>, <p_0, 0>>$ history rather than the $<<\sim p_1, 1><p_0, 0>>$ history. It follows that it must be the p_2-set accessible from the $<p_1, 1>$ that is the next to be realized, since it is a fact that that branch is realized and not the $<\sim p_1, 1>$ branch.

This can be represented formally, rather than diagrammatically, by adding an accessibility relation defined over times, and adding a 'positional' element to times. Times are now ordered triples of the form $<\mu, n \in \mathbb{R}, \sigma>$, where σ is the position of the time in the branching structure, something given by specifying the sequence of times along its past. For discrete time, this can be achieved simply by including the last time realized as the third element (since this time will specify its past, and so on). Thus, for the case of discrete branching time, time $n+1$ has the form $t_{n+1} = <\mu, n+1, t_n>$, where $t_n = <v, n, t_{n-1}>$, and so on. The accessibility relation R for $<\mathbf{T}, E, t, R>$ can be defined as follows: for all times, t_{n+1} is accessible to t_n iff t_n is a member of t_{n+1}, i.e.,

$$(\forall t)(R(t_{n+1}, t_n) \equiv t_n \in t_{n+1})$$

We can also generalize to continuous time. The reason that we must say something slightly different for continuous time is that there is no 'next available date' or 'last time realized' to be the positional element. But all that needs to be said to constrain the order of realization is first to say that the order of realization must follow the order of the real numbers as given by the *greater than* relation. Second, it may not be possible to specify a particular time as the positional element of a time, but it *is* possible to specify the position using the *sequence* of times leading up to that time (which I represent as '$\sigma_{<a}$'), and then represent times as follows:

$$t_a = <\mu, a \in \mathbb{R}, \sigma_{<a}>$$

So generalizing to include continuous time, the accessibility relation R for $<\mathbf{T}, E, t, R>$ can now be defined as follows: for all times, t_b is accessible to t_a iff t_a is included in the third element of t_b, i.e.,

$(\forall t)(R(t_b, t_a) \equiv ((t_a \subset \sigma_{<b}) \& (t_b = <v, b \in \mathbb{R}, \sigma_{<b}>)))$.

(c) Tying up loose branches: one last objection met

Now that the metaphysics and semantics have been given for ersatzer presentism, I should answer one possible objection: *why* is it that a certain atomic proposition p appears in a given E-related time if not because *it was the case that* p? But if this is the explanation, if this is how the story ultimately bottoms out, then how is ersatzer presentism any better off than Priorian presentism?

There are a few things to say in response. First, whether a given proposition appears in a time is simply a brute fact. Or rather, since all possible sets of propositions appear on the branches, it is a necessary truth that such propositions appear in some of the times, and it is a brute fact that one of them gets realized. This is no objection since it is no more mysterious than concrete facts being realized at the times they are according to tenseless theorists. The real bite of the question may be thought to come from explaining why the various times are E-related. But on reflection it is more of a toothless suck than a vicious bite. For, according to ersatzer presentism, what makes 'It was the case that p' true is an actually E-related ordered triple, whereas according to the tenseless theory, what makes it true is an actually *earlier than*-related concrete fact. Now to ask why these ordered triples are actually E-related is about as fair as asking why the concrete facts are actually *earlier than*-related in the tenseless theory, i.e., not at all—they just *are*. In this sense, then, all theories take it as a brute fact that it was the case that p; the advantage over Priorian presentism is that these other theories have an account of what this fact looks like, be it an E-related abstract structure or an *earlier than*-related concrete one.

VII The advantages of ersatzer presentism

Ersatzer presentism, then, can meet the three conditions that any satisfactory account of time should: it allows us to state truths about the past; it wears its ontological commitments on its sleeve, and it ensures that truth-value links are preserved. It also seems to me that it satisfies the demands of common sense in that it accommodates the platitudes held concerning time. Of course, the ontology of abstract objects that is invoked in order to accommodate them is not part of our common-sense view, but that can hardly be taken as a criticism of the theory, for neither is it part of our common-sense view that the past must be composed of concrete objects, as the tenseless theory says. Common sense only extends so far as the platitudinous claims and has no more to say about the underlying mechanism that accommodates them than it does in physical theories which aim to accommodate our common-sense experience of the world by invoking uncommon objects. In science, the underlying physical explanation may need to be very complex; but so long as it accommodates the common-sense experience, that is all it is required to do to satisfy the demands of common sense. The same goes for philosophy. Ersatzer presentism may be a complex story, but it satisfies the platitudinous demands of common sense beautifully. There are three further advantages.

(a) The tensed–tenseless debate is a substantial debate

It is often argued that there is no substance to the tensed–tenseless debate—that once we recognize the confusion over tensed and tenseless readings of various quantifiers and copulas, the tenseless theorist's 'does exist in the past' is not substantially different from the tense theorist's 'existed'—they are the same theory under different descriptions. This charge certainly cannot be levelled against ersatzer presentism. According to ersatzer presentism, the constituents of past and future times are not spatio-temporally or causally related objects, unlike past and future times according to the tenseless theory. The constituents of ersatz past and future times are propositions, numbers, and sets, and so can only have those relations that can hold between propositions, numbers, and sets. These conceptions of past and future times are so radically different that it would stretch the meaning of the word 'same' to claim that they are essentially the same theory under different descriptions! Unlike the tenseless theory, according to ersatzer presentism, there really is no time like the present.

(b) Indiscernibility and time without change

Le Poidevin (1991: §3.3, §3.5) (and see also Butterfield (1984a)) thinks that the possibility of indiscernible times and time without change cause fundamental problems for so-called 'propositional theories of time'. For instance, Prior's construction of times from conjunctions of present-tensed propositions results in his not being able to account for time without change, for such a period would consist of times where the conjunctions of propositions were identical. This argument amounts to saying that Fig. 2.2 represents a possibility which Prior cannot allow for. That is, defenders of the possibility of time without change assume that there can be times where $(t_2) \neq (t_3)$ yet where the conjunction of propositions remains the same.[12]

But, first, it is not clear whether time without change *is* possible independently of the theory under consideration; whether, that is, the possibility of time without change *must* be a feature of any satisfactory theory, or whether it is merely a novelty of some theories and 'possible' only in the sense that a particular system allows for it. It is not clear, then, whether this is an objection or merely a consequence of constructing times from propositions.

Second, whether propositional theories of time can allow for time without change depends on whether times are maximal conjunctions of present-tensed propositions *only*, the very reason why Prior has problems. For, in order to be a substantial claim, the argument from time without change must assume that $(t_2) \neq (t_3)$, but, ironically, this is the argument's very downfall since we do then have a way of

p&~q	p&q	p&q	~p&q
(t_1)	(t_2)	(t_3)	(t_4)

Time →

FIG. 2.2. Time without change

---

[12] Newton-Smith (1980: 24) takes the possibility of time without change to mean something different, namely a period where there are no changes at all—not even of the passage of time itself. Thus, I assume that he would say different dates constitute a change, in which case we do not have time without change. Be this as it may, the possibility with which Newton-Smith is concerned is no attack on propositional theories, for whether change—including change of time!—can cease to take place altogether can be discussed independently of whether we hold a propositional theory or not, if, indeed, this thesis can be made sense of at all.

distinguishing (t_2) and (t_3), namely by including that date within the time, as in the ersatz theory presented above.

The problem comes in giving a metaphysical interpretation of a change of date without a corresponding change in the present-tensed propositions at those dates. But this is as much of a problem for ersatzer presentists as it is for those who believe in concrete times: whatever reason they have for postulating such periods of time must equally be reasons for ersatz theorists doing the same (see Shoemaker (1969), for example, for reasons we might give for postulating such a period). Thus ersatzer presentism can allow for time without change if anyone can. And time without change is just a special case of the more general problem of how propositional theories can distinguish times whose conjunction of present-tensed propositions is indiscernible from another. Including dates within the time will distinguish them.

(c) Ontological parsimony

The third advantage is that many have complained that there is no good motivation for becoming a tense theorist, let alone a presentist. Tooley (1997: 250) argues that before we do commit ourselves to a tensed theory, there is a 'need for metaphysical argument'. Here I claim the argument in favour of ersatzer presentism over its rivals is *ontological parsimony*. The tenseless theory, for instance, postulates appropriately related past and future concrete objects as truthmakers for various tensed statements; but this is something ersatzer presentism can discard. Neither does ersatzer presentism postulate mysterious facts *in* the present to make past-tensed statements true. Indeed, the discussion indicates that a theory that just rests solely on concretely realized present facts will not adequately account for all the truths we need. So the appeal to more objects other than concretely realized present facts is the necessary concession presentism must make to be viable. But it is still a highly attractive theory if you *already* believe in abstract objects (propositions, numbers, and sets), which many of us do. Thus it isn't so much an issue of quantitative versus qualitative parsimony (see Bacon (1995: 87); Lewis (1973b: 87) for this distinction). The argument is that ersatzer presentism is *quantitively* more parsimonious than the tenseless theory; that is, the set of objects that ersatzer presentism postulates is a proper subset of those objects that the tenseless theory postulates. But quantitative savings are still significant: everyone agrees that one *can* have too much of a good thing. Thus, if you prefer ontologically economical theories without having to live on a shoestring, then ersatzer presentism is the theory to adopt.

3

Some outstanding problems for presentism met

Now that the positive theory has been presented, I'd like to pick up on a few issues on which I could not elaborate for fear of losing the bigger picture, as well as develop some new issues. In doing this, I shall introduce the problem of transtemporal relations, but I shall leave the important case of causation to be dealt with in its own right in the next chapter. This chapter, then, will tackle the following issues:

(1) McTaggart's argument
(2) A deontic, semantic, and paradoxical need for other times
(3) Future contingents, non-contradiction, and the law of excluded middle muddle
(4) Transtemporal relations (I)
(5) Transtemporal relations (II): reference

Problem 1 MCTAGGART'S ARGUMENT

McTaggart's argument is something that has for many been the deciding factor in whether or not to adopt a tensed or tenseless position. Traditionally, it has been the tenseless theorists that have wielded McTaggart's argument in support of their view because they claim that it shows that there is a contradiction in the very notion of the flow of time, or, as Mellor puts it: 'What disproves all [tensed theories] is a contradiction inherent in their concept of change' (1998: 70). On this interpretation of the situation, then, McTaggart's argument poses a serious threat to all tensed theories.

I shall show that this is an incorrect assessment of the situation: presentism is not subject to McTaggart's argument. First we should consider McTaggart's position in general.

I McTaggart's position

McTaggart's position is that both A- and B-series are essential to our concept of time, but that the A-series is more fundamental since the B-series is dependent upon it: temporal relations are given by time's flow. Time involves change, and if the B-series is to constitute time, it must involve change. But as there is nothing in the B-series which can change—a poker hot at time t_1 and cold at t_2 is, always has, and always will be hot at t_1 and cold at t_2—it is inadequate by itself to constitute time. As Ayer (1973: 16) puts it, '[Tense theorists] feel that the river of time has somehow been turned into a stagnant pond'. For an account to be adequate it must have characteristics corresponding to pastness, presentness, and futurity, and change them as time flows. In other words, according to McTaggart, time requires an A-series. However, as he argues, there is a contradiction in the A-series. Therefore, since the B-series alone is inadequate to constitute time, and the A-series is contradictory, McTaggart concludes that time itself must be unreal.

This is a radical conclusion and the history of the debate consists largely in various responses to McTaggart's position. Tenseless theorists argue that the B-series has the machinery to supply a complete description of reality, including an adequate account of change, and therefore that McTaggart's contradiction argument shows only that *tense* is unreal (Mellor (1981)). Russell (1903: §442), for instance, holds that change is nothing more than an object's having incompatible properties at different times. But, as McTaggart points out, this as stated does not adequately characterize the difference between variation of properties across time, which is change, and variation of properties across space, which is not change.

Note that to resolve this particular issue we need not worry too much, interesting though it may be in itself, over distinguishing genuine change, which involves the variation of intrinsic properties of an object over time, from 'Cambridge' change, which does not. Take my becoming an uncle, for instance, or my becoming famous. Neither of these involves an intrinsic change in me; rather the first involves a change in other family members, and the second involves a change in the state of knowledge of others. But, in both cases, a genuine change does occur to something, and so the question is still: what is the difference between change and spatial variation?

Obviously, it is not good enough simply to say that temporal variations are *by definition* changes, since this just cries out for an explanation as to why we have a special term for temporal variations and what the difference is between spatial and temporal variations it is meant to indicate. The proper answer is that changes are those things which are brought about by *causation* (Le Poidevin (1991: ch. 8); Mellor (1998: ch. 10.6)). Causation brings about the poker being cold at t_2 after being hot at t_1 in the way it doesn't when the poker is hot at one end and cold at the other. So McTaggart is right to say that we need more than the bare B-series to account for change; but his solution was incorrect: the more that is needed is causation, not a moving present.

I agree with the tenseless theorists, then, that they can offer a perfectly good account of change. Moreover, this should be taken as a welcome result for presentists, since it gives them at least one way (independently of the tensed–tenseless issue) of distinguishing time from space (see Chapter 5: §IV for another way of distinguishing time from space). This is useful for presentism, since there need no longer be a worry that if no such difference between time and space can be found, then presentists about time should be 'presentists' about space (although, as we shall see in Chapter 6, this unwelcome result is embraced by some).

For these reasons, I distance myself from Ayer's comment about how tense theorists feel about the tenseless theory. Many tense theorists, however, accept the rest of McTaggart's position but respond to McTaggart's contradiction argument by denying that there is a contradiction in the notion of tense. I, however, accept that McTaggart shows that there is a contradiction in the position that he considers: my view is that it does not affect my version of *presentism*.

II McTaggart's argument

According to tense theorists, objects (i.e., facts, events, times, whatever) change their tenses in that they are future, become present, and then past. Now, it is not possible for an object to be past without its having been present and future.[1] Similarly, it is not possible for an object to be future without its becoming present and past. Thus all objects in the A-series have all three tenses.

McTaggart ((1908), (1927)) uses this to argue that since all objects in the A-series have all three tenses, and that these tenses are incompatible with one another, that, therefore, there is a contradiction in the A-series. Thus, nothing in reality has tenses. He writes:

> Thus our ... statement about M—that it is present, will be past, and has been future—means that M is present at a moment of present time, past at some moment of future time, and future at some moment of past time. But every moment, like every event, is both past, present and future ... [But] if M is present, there is no moment of past time at which it is past. But the moments of future time, in which it is past, are equally moments of past time, in which it cannot be past. Again, that M is future and will be present and past means that M is future at a moment of present time, and present and past at different moments of future time. In that case it cannot be present or past at any moments of past time. But all the moments of future time, in which M will be present or past, are equally moments of past time. And thus again we get a contradiction.   (McTaggart (1927) in Le Poidevin and MacBeath (1993: 33))

There have been many tense theory responses to McTaggart's argument, but they generally fall into two types: (a) those that appeal to higher-order levels; and (b) those that invoke the notion of succession.

(a) Type 1 response: appeal to higher-order levels

The first type invokes higher-order levels in which the contradiction at the lower level can be resolved, either (i) by introducing ever

---

[1] Although this could be debated. It is particularly pressing given the discussion of special relativity in Ch. 6, where Stein argues that an event e_1 can be in the past of an event e_2 without it ever having been in the present of e_2. But I reject Stein's position, and so shall assume that all objects in the A-series have all three tenses.

more complex tenses; or (ii) by introducing an object-language/meta-language distinction and trying to resolve the contradiction in the object-language using the meta-language (Lowe (1987)); or (iii) by introducing higher-order dimensions of time and resolving the contradiction in one time-dimension using another time-dimension (Schlesinger (1982)). The form of McTaggart's argument is the same in each case: there is a contradiction in the tensed position at level 1. Either we adopt tenseless terms to resolve the contradiction at level 1, or we resolve it using tensed terms at level 2. However, the contradiction re-emerges in using the tensed terms at level 2, so either we invoke yet higher levels *ad infinitum*, which is unsatisfactory, or we resolve it using tenseless terms; and if we do this at level n we may as well do it at level 1. Thus, these tensed responses fail as solutions to McTaggart's argument.

(b) Type 2 response: invoke the notion of succession

Smith (1986) argues that McTaggart's argument works only if it assumed that objects have tenses 'nonsuccessively'. The contradiction, according to Smith, is resolved by saying: *first* the object is F, *then* N, and *then* P. But, as Oaklander (1987) points out, this would be unacceptable to McTaggart, for to say that the object is F first is to say that F is had *earlier than* N is had. (That is, if we understand this proposal as something different to the iterated tenses proposal above.) On McTaggart's view, this is circular since it is the flow of time which generates the temporal relations such as *earlier than*; thus invoking such relations to explain how time can flow, i.e., how objects can have the tenses P, N, and F, successively, is circular. Furthermore, for McTaggart, if the *earlier than* relation is taken to be fundamental, then this is to admit that the tenseless position is correct after all.

However, as noted in the introduction (§II(b)), it is a mistake to think of the *earlier than* relation as a purely B-series relation, and so invoking it is not necessarily to admit that the tenseless position is correct. But invoking the notion of succession or *earlier than* will not help anyway since, although tenses are had successively, objects *change* these tenses, and it is the attempt to say *when* they do so in A-series terms which generates the contradiction. Suppose, for instance, we get someone to admit that there is a time that will become present. We then ask *when* it is that that time will become present. The answer is: in the future (or, if you like, later than the present). But this concedes that there is a time in the future that is present (and so on *mutatis mutandis* for all other locations in time). But a time cannot be both present and future. Thus we have a contradiction. And introducing more tenses just generates more contradiction. Thus, we are no better off. (Note that a contradiction does not emerge in the B-series since, if asked *when* these objects occur, a *date* can be given which is a fixed and unchanging property of the object.)

Some have thought, e.g., Levison (1987), that this problem is caused by ascribing temporal *properties* to *events*, that it is a mistake to think that the tensed position involves the sempiternal existence of events which continually change their temporal properties or location in the A-series, as McTaggart originally described it, and that, if we eliminate talk of such changes in events in favour of talk of changes in things (following Prior (1968a)), then there can *be* no events to recede in time and, hence, to have incompatible properties. McTaggart's argument is thereby avoided.

But this is a red herring: the same contradiction survives when we replace talk of events with talk of facts throughout the argument (as I showed how to do in the introduction (§II(b))). The question then becomes not one of how events can have incompatible properties but how the very same propositions can have different truth-values (as in Le Poidevin's (1991: 24–33) and Mellor's (1998: 78–81) formulations of the argument). In short, the root of the problem is thinking of anything—events, facts, or whatever—as *existing* in 'the past' or 'the future'—i.e., as already being located there with those ontologically significant tenses. Eliminating an event ontology is, therefore, irrelevant to avoiding contradiction; rather, it needs to be shown how to eliminate talk of the past and future as locations where objects of any kind reside with these ontologically significant tenses.

I say McTaggart's argument is valid, but only affects tensed positions which assert that more than one tense is ever had by an object.[2] I do

---

[2] It is not true to say, therefore, that McTaggart's argument relies on a false metaphysical assumption, as Prior (1968a), Levison (1987), and others have it, namely that it presupposes an ontology of sempiternally existing objects that instantiate various temporal properties. Prior is correct to deny that the tensed theory must conform to the conception that McTaggart

not, however, need to argue this case in any more detail. For all I am interested in showing is that *presentism* escapes the contradiction, whether or not the other tensed theories do. After all, the argument of Chapter 1 is enough to write off those theories anyway.

III How ersatzer presentism avoids McTaggart's argument

Presentism can avoid McTaggart's conclusion, not by asserting that objects have such tenses at different times, but by denying that they ever have more than one of them. For it is the having of all three—or indeed of any two—incompatible tenses which generates the contradiction. Therefore, presentism should take McTaggart's argument to prove not that tense is unreal but that only one of the three tenses can have instances. The only plausible option for tensed theorists at this stage, then, is to deny the existence of past and future objects, and thus to embrace presentism.[3]

According to ersatzer presentism, the proposition that

(3.1) Tubbs is suckling pigs

is made true by the concrete present fact that Tubbs is suckling pigs. This proposition, according to ersatzer presentism, changes in truth-value over time: it is true *simpliciter* only at some times, namely when

---

originally described. But this cannot be said to be a *flaw* in McTaggart's argument: it is perfectly sound for the tensed position he considers; the fault lies not in the argument itself, but rather in the limitations McTaggart set concerning the variety of possible tensed positions available. For McTaggart dismisses as nonsense the idea that temporal becoming amounts to a change in *existence* (what Broad (1938: 120) called 'absolute becoming'), and for this reason only considers the view that temporal becoming amounts to a change in temporal *properties*, i.e., the view that events exist sempiternally and what changes is their tensed properties. Indeed, the reaction of Prior (and others) here is very telling, for in objecting that this conception is not what the tensed theory amounts to (as he and others understand it), he tacitly concedes the point that the conception under consideration in McTaggart's argument *is* contradictory. But it is not as if nobody does hold such a tensed position. It is not as if Prior has the 'correct' tensed position in mind, and that McTaggart merely misconceives it and addresses a straw man. So it is still quite a substantial claim, for it is such a position that McTaggart shows to be contradictory: he never was after the presentist with this argument.

[3] Le Poidevin (1991: 33–5) recognizes this option.

Tubbs's suckling pigs is present, and false at others, namely when Tubbs is not suckling pigs. The flow of time can then be characterized as the change in truth-value of tensed propositions over time.

According to tensed theories, propositions about the present are made true by present facts; the differences between the various tensed positions arise in how they account for propositions about the past and the future. For some tensed theorists accept the existence of the past and the future as well as the present, and invoke past facts (meaning facts that are located in the past), present facts, and future facts to make propositions about the past, present, and future true, respectively. For example, the proposition that

(3.2) Tubbs was suckling pigs

is made true, for those tensed theorists who at least believe in the existence of the past and the present, by Tubbs's suckling pigs in the past, and the proposition that

(3.3) Tubbs will be suckling pigs

is made true, for those tensed theorists who also believe in the existence of the future, by Tubbs's suckling pigs in the future.

This is the position that McTaggart's argument shows to be contradictory. For, according to these theories, it is Tubbs's suckling pigs being present in the past, i.e., the location in the past of the present fact that Tubbs is suckling pigs, that makes (3.2) true, and the location in the future of the present fact that Tubbs is suckling pigs, that makes (3.3) true. This is contradictory: facts cannot be past and present, or present and future. In other words, suppose it is true that

(3.4) Tubbs is not suckling pigs.

This, if true, is made true by present facts. But there are plenty of facts scattered around that would make it *false*, such as the one we supposed makes (3.2) true, for that fact is the fact that Tubbs *is* suckling pigs. On this conception, then, (3.4) is both true and not true. The solution, therefore, is either to deny the existence of tensed facts which are located anywhere other than the present, or go tenseless and reject any ontologically substantial notions of pastness, presentness and futurity.

Ersatz presentism rejects the existence of past- and future-located tensed facts. According to it, all concrete facts are present facts and all other facts are abstract, and hence tenseless. (3.2) and (3.3), if true, are not made true by present facts located in the past and future. They are, if true, made true by there being one time (i.e., set of u-propositions, etc.) that is made true by present facts and that time being appropriately related to the past and future times that contain the set of present-tensed propositions of which the proposition that Tubbs is suckling pigs is a member. It is never the case, then, that facts instantiate more than one tense: they are either present or tenseless. It can never, then, be that contradictory present-tensed propositions are made true by present facts. Furthermore, if asked *when* Tubbs was suckling pigs, we can give the date. If asked *when* (3.2) is true, we can answer 'now', and state the truthmakers for it. And if asked in general *when* a time is present, we can answer 'when its propositions are true *simpliciter*'. There is nothing more to be said; and what is said is not contradictory.

Problem 2 A DEONTIC, SEMANTIC, AND PARADOXICAL NEED FOR OTHER TIMES

I The deontic need

Tomberlin (2003) puts forward a novel deontic example to argue against presentism. Suppose that Jones is alone, secluded, and comatose from eating highly toxic mushrooms. Now consider the following argument:

(3.5) for any individual x, if x is a moral agent and x is available and able to come to Jones's assistance, x ought prima facie to provide Jones with aid;

(3.6) no presently existing moral agent is available and able to come to Jones's assistance;

(3.7) for any individual x, if x is a moral agent who is available and able to come to Jones's assistance, x ought not prima facie to provide Jones with aid.

The challenge for presentism is to find a way of making (3.5) and (3.6) true and (3.7) false, where 'the [objectual] quantifiers range over presently existing individuals only' (451).

This is a nice problem. But it is not a problem for presentism as such, since it is not as if holding any other theory of time will help in any way; it is not as if invoking concrete past or future people can assist in any way. What we require are *presently* existing individuals; but these are nowhere to be seen on either theory's understanding of that notion. It is rather a problem for anyone (whether they hold a tensed or tenseless position) who believes in *actual* stuff only. But, of course, presentists do not have to be actualists any more than tenseless theorists have to be: presentists can believe in more than presently located individuals, whilst remaining presentists, so long as those individuals do not actually exist in time. So Tomberlin's problem, nice as it is, is entirely about our commitment to *possibilia* and independent of the philosophy of time.

II The semantic need

Tomberlin is not alone in mistakenly thinking that presentists can only believe in presently existing individuals. Lepore and Ludwig (2003), for example, develop a truth-conditional semantics for tensed sentences, dealing with various temporal linguistic constructions, adopting a rather Davidsonian approach: any adequate semantic theory will offer, among its virtues, a transparent account of inference; and if we have a theory which can accommodate a whole host of temporal constructions in a systematic way (and does it better than the rest), then this lends support to that being the correct view, thereby committing us to whatever it tells us there is. This is the way Lepore and Ludwig argue for the existence of times. For, given that their theory refers to and quantifies over times, times exist. The implication they draw for the metaphysics of time is that presentism, which, they say, is the view that 'only the present time is real', must be false (84).

But Lepore and Ludwig make the same mistake as Tomberlin: presentism need not be restricted in this way, for presentism is a theory about what actually exists in time; it says nothing about the existence of anything else. Presentism, like any other theory of time, can have more in its ontology than just objects located in the present (so long as they are not located in time). Of course, presentists *might* go on to deny the existence of abstract objects, but they need not. And they should not, if they are to deal adequately with considerations like those of Lepore and Ludwig, as well as the truthmaking considerations which I raised in Chapter 2. In other words, my version of presentism is immune to Lepore and Ludwig's argument. A semantic theory, if we accept it as true, might tell us that there are times; but it does not tell us what times *are*. I say that they need not be concrete, and thus presentism can survive in its ersatzer formulation.

III The paradoxical need

Le Poidevin (2002: 70) construes Zeno's Arrow argument as creating a difficulty for presentism as follows:

- (A) The dynamic account of motion: an object's motion at a time is an irreducible property, independent of the object's state at other times.
- (B) The static account of motion: an object moves at a time by virtue of its position at that time and at other times.
- (1) If motion is possible, then either (A) or (B) is the correct account of it.
- (2) If presentism is true, (A) is false.
- (3) If presentism is true, (B) is false.

From (1), (2), and (3):

- (4) If presentism is true, motion is impossible.

The argument for (2) is

[According to the dynamic account] an object's being in motion is a primitive event, not further analysable in terms of objects, properties and times.[4] Now

---

[4] This is the best of a bad lot of versions of the dynamic account. Le Poidevin (65–6) dismisses two other accounts.

for these primitive events to exist, on the presentist reading, they must be capable of existing in the present. But events, being changes, are not instantaneous items: they take up time. So, at best, what exists in the present are *parts* of events. The idea of events having parts that are not themselves events, however, conflicts with the primitive status of events. To the question, what are these parts? the obvious answer seems to be: instantaneous states of an object. Presentism is therefore incompatible with primitivism about events. (Le Poidevin (2002: 68))

The argument for (3) relies on a particular conception of presentism. For Le Poidevin acknowledges that presentism seems compatible with the static account of motion:

The presentist can allow that x was in a different position from the one it now occupies, but has to insist that this is made true by present fact. So one set of present facts makes true 'x was at s_1', another set makes true 'x is at s_2', and yet another set 'x will be at s_3'. Thus present fact can, in principle, make it true that x is moving, even when we understand motion in terms of the static analysis. (Le Poidevin (2002: 68))

The difficulty for presentism is that

anything less than a fully deterministic universe will leave some propositions concerning the past without a determinate truth-value (this feature is peculiar to presentism, of course). (Le Poidevin (2002: 68))

And so the concrete present is simply not rich enough to ground the required facts that x was at s_1, x is at s_2, etc. I agree, and welcome this as another reason to reject reductive presentism. But the argument hardly refutes ersatzer presentism, which can quite easily accommodate facts about where x is at a particular time. Similarly, in so far as I understand the dynamic view, where 'talk of "motion at a time" must always be interpreted as motion in an arbitrarily small interval' (66), ersatzer presentism has available to it facts which can ground such a notion. Anything the tenseless theory can do, the ersatzer presentist can do equally. Thus motion does not require the existence of more than one concrete time. Presentism avoids paradox, if the tenseless theory does.

Problem 3 FUTURE CONTINGENTS, NON-CONTRADICTION, AND THE LAW OF EXCLUDED MIDDLE MUDDLE

> I can I can't?!
> *The League of Gentlemen*

One of the advantages that tensed theories which deny at least the existence of the future are commonly thought to have over the tenseless theory is that they are the only positions which allow for 'real freedom' (Prior (1996b: 48)); and it is Prior's belief in freedom which is one of his motivations for his belief in tense, because he thinks that the tenseless position, in claiming that the future is in some sense already laid out before us—i.e., that propositions about it are already determinately either true or false—does not allow for freedom (Prior (1953) following to some extent Aristotle, *De Interpretatione* IX, and Łukasiewicz (1951)). Łukasiewicz (in)famously writes:

> I can assume without contradiction that my presence in Warsaw at a certain moment of next year, e.g., at noon on 21 December, is at the present time determined neither positively nor negatively. Hence it is possible, but not necessary, that I shall be present in Warsaw at the given time. On this assumption the proposition 'I shall be in Warsaw at noon on 21 December of next year', can at the present time be neither true nor false. For if it were true now, my future presence in Warsaw would have to be necessary, which is contradictory to the assumption. If it were false now, on the other hand, my future presence in Warsaw would be impossible, which is also contradictory to the assumption. Therefore the proposition considered is at the moment *neither true nor false* and must possess a third value, different from '0' or falsity and '1' or truth. This value we can designate by '½'. It represents 'the possible' and joins 'the true' and 'the false' as a third value.
> The three-valued system of propositional logic owes its origin to this line of thought.   (Łukasiewicz (1930: 53))

However, if the claim is that the tenseless theory (or bivalence) commits us to fatalism (which is Łukasiewicz's concern), then so do tensed theories. For just as it is not possible to change what *is* to what *is not*, by parity of reasoning it is not possible to change what *will be* to what *will not*, for it is a necessary truth that what will be will be. Thus, on this particular point, the tense theorist is in the same boat here as the tenseless theorist.

But, in any case, neither theory is subject to fatalism. For, although according to the tenseless theory, if a proposition is true at all, then it is true for all time, this is not to say that things could not have been otherwise; that is, it is a modal fallacy to infer *if it happens, then it necessarily happens* (in symbols, $(p \supset \Box p)$), from *necessarily, if it happens, then it happens* (in symbols, $\Box(p \supset p)$). The force of the fatalist argument, if it has any, comes from confusing the undeniable but benign '$\Box(p \supset p)$', with the clearly false and malicious '$(p \supset \Box p)$'. Likewise, in tensed terms, it is necessary that what will be will be, but this is not to say that we could not have brought something else about; that is, it is not to say that what will be will happen of necessity (see, for instance, Gale (1967: §III, Introduction)).

However, fatalism (which concerns *logical* necessity) is a different matter from determinism (which concerns *physical* necessity); but determinism is also held by these philosophers to be incompatible with freedom. Similarly, these philosophers think that denying that future contingents have a determinate truth-value helps them to avoid determinism. However, it is clear that the question of whether the universe is deterministic or indeterministic is independent of whether the principle of bivalence applies to propositions about the future. Consider the tenseless theory. It might be that the laws of nature and the present state of the universe are not sufficient to determine whether an atom decays tomorrow (the same set-up could lead to a different outcome). But nevertheless when considering the time in question it is either true that the atom decays or true that the atom does not decay. Thus, future contingents *can* have a determinate truth-value, even in an indeterministic universe. These considerations are sufficient to show that the notion of determinism is distinct from the notion of determinateness, and consequently that for bivalence to have any bearing on freedom, a link has to be made between determinism and determinateness,[5] and then it has to be shown that determinism is incompatible with freedom. I deny that any of these

---

[5] One way of tying what *will be* true to what is *made true* in some causal sense by the present state of the universe has already been shown in Ch. 2: §IV to be untenable.

stages can be achieved: bivalence is neither here nor there on the issue of freedom.

Nevertheless, Aristotle, in *De interpretatione* IX, for instance, held that only those propositions about the future which are either necessarily true, or necessarily false, or 'predetermined' in some way have a determinate truth-value. This led Łukasiewicz in 1920 to construct a three-valued logic in an attempt to formalize Aristotle's position by giving the truth-value $1/2 =$ indeterminate to future contingents and defining '∼', '&' and '∨', where $1 =$ true and $0 =$ false, as in Figs. 3.1, 3.2, and 3.3.

We can see that the purely determinate entries match the tables of the classical two-valued system; thus, what needs justification are the other entries. Let us take negation to illustrate. We may treat indeterminateness as something to be resolved one way or the other: it will eventually be either true or false. Thus the truth-value of the negation of an indeterminate proposition must itself be indeterminate,

	∼
1	0
½	½
0	1

FIG. 3.1

&	1	½	0
1	1	½	0
½	½	½	0
0	0	0	0

FIG. 3.2

∨	1	½	0
1	1	1	1
½	1	½	½
0	1	½	0

FIG. 3.3

since if the initial proposition could be resolved either way, so must its negation. This reasoning similarly justifies the '½' entries in the other tables.

Now, this system works smoothly for most cases of future contingent statements. Suppose, for example, I say

(3.8) Either I will drown my sorrows or I will buy a Ducati 916 motorcycle.

We would intuitively think that if both of the disjuncts are indeterminate, then the whole disjunction must be indeterminate. This is precisely the answer given by Łukasiewicz's truth-tables. However, the trouble begins when we consider cases where one disjunct is the negation of the other. For suppose I say

(3.9) Either I will buy a Ducati or I will not buy a Ducati.

Because there is no middle ground to be had—either I will or I will not buy a Ducati—we must agree that (3.9) is determinately true. The problem is that both disjuncts are future contingent propositions and therefore indeterminate; but then, according to Łukasiewicz's tables, the whole disjunction must be indeterminate. Łukasiewicz's system gives us the wrong answer.

But not only is the law of excluded middle ($p \vee \sim p$) no longer a logical truth in this system, the law of non-contradiction ($\sim(p \,\&\sim p)$) isn't either, for it too takes the value ½ when $p = ½$. Furthermore, this system cannot be the correct formalization of Aristotle either, since, as noted above, necessary truths such as ($p \vee \sim p$) for Aristotle have the determinate value = true.

So was Aristotle just horribly confused in thinking it is possible to have a non-bivalent logic whilst retaining as logical truths the laws of excluded middle and non-contradiction? Kneale and Kneale (1962: 47 ff.) think so, and Quine calls Aristotle's desire 'fantasy'.[6] I disagree: adopting a non-bivalent logic does not have to result in our abandoning the laws of excluded middle and non-contradiction. And just as well, because my version of ersatzer presentism has a branching future, and so most statements about the future must be neither determinately true nor determinately false. But this is not because, as Broad (1923: 73) and Tooley (1997) think, there is *no* future as of a given time, but rather because there is no *unique* future as of a given time (see Chapter 2: §V(d) for more on my view of the future).[7] I require, then, a non-bivalent logic. But if this meant we must abandon the laws of excluded middle and non-contradiction, I'd take it as a serious objection.

In light of our discussion so far, there are two options for a solution to this problem: either we adopt Łukasiewicz's system and drop some other assumption, or we construct some new system.

Tooley (1997) opts for the first. He adopts Łukasiewicz's system, but the assumption he drops is that the connectives in three-valued logic are truth-functional. This is because, for instance, some disjunctions ($p \vee q$) with indeterminate disjuncts are indeterminate, whereas others ($p \vee \sim p$) are determinately true. So the truth-value of the whole sentence in three-valued logic is not a function of its component

---

[6] Of course, establishing the correct interpretation of the real Aristotle is neither here nor there, for we can discuss whether it is possible to have a non-bivalent logic whilst retaining the laws of excluded middle and non-contradiction, whether or not these were Aristotle's concerns.

[7] Putnam writes: '... to use a 3-valued logic means to adopt a different way of using logical words. More exactly, it corresponds to the *ordinary* way in the case of molecular sentences in which the truth-value of all the components is known... but a man reveals that he is using 3-valued logic and not the ordinary 2-valued logic... by the way he handles sentences which contain components whose truth-value is not known' (Putnam (1957: 169)). But I take it that the assignment of 'indeterminate' to statements is for *metaphysical* reasons, not epistemological. Further, my proposed system has the advantage over Putnam's in that we needn't 'adopt a different way of using logical words'. And it is worth pointing out that I think Tooley (1997: 148–50) is wrong to think that statements cannot be indeterminate *simpliciter*. Because I take future-tensed statements to be made true by sets of, let's call them '*F*-related times', and since there is no unique set of *F*-related times to make it determinately true or false *simpliciter*, it must be that the future-tensed statement is indeterminate *simpliciter*.

parts. This is a quite natural reaction: some sentences, we may think, just are different from others because they are true simply in virtue of their form (what Tooley calls 'logical truths' (139)), whereas others require truthmakers external to the proposition to make them true (what Tooley calls 'factual truths' (139)).

But although this solution might initially appeal, it is not a satisfactory one. For we are left wondering *why* it is that such sentences have a privileged status in three-valued logic. What is so special about these sentences that Tooley feels warranted in holding them to be determinately true in order to draw the conclusion that the connectives in three-valued logic must therefore be non-truth-functional? Certainly, they are logical truths in two-valued logic; they are true under all assignments of truth-values to the component parts and this is what justifies us in privileging them. But given the truth-tables for the connectives in three-valued logic, the sentences '$p \vee \sim p$' and '$\sim(p \,\&\, \sim p)$' are not true under all possible interpretations; they are not 'true in virtue of their form', so in what sense are they logical truths? In other words, why does Tooley think they *are* necessary truths given he thinks the world is governed by three-valued logic? I cannot see any.

Thus, we should take the second option: construct a different system from Łukasiewicz's. The following systems allow us to keep the connectives truth-functional, allow us to keep the laws of excluded middle and non-contradiction as logical truths, they don't introduce a distinction between logical and factual truths, and they allow us to keep the notion of logical truth as true under all interpretations, both for two- and three-valued logic. All this and non-bivalence! This, then, is something along the lines that we've been after.

The solution rests on the following observation: it is the definition of '$\sim$' that causes the trouble. Thus we should stop trying to patch up the obvious deficiencies in Łukasiewicz's system (as Tooley does) and deal with the root directly. For not only does Łukasiewicz's definition of '$\sim$' create the difficulty, I see no reason to think that it is correct, and thus altering it is not fudging it. I claim that the truth-table in Fig. 3.4 is more suitable. The justification for the $\sim (1/2) = 1$ entry is as follows: given that p is indeterminate, then it isn't the case that p; so to say that it is not the case that p is clearly to

	~
1	0
½	1
0	1

FIG. 3.4

say something true. Thus, there is no justification for holding that the negation of a proposition can only be true if that proposition is false, as in Łukasiewicz's system.

Such a definition of '~' is employed in Bochvar's (1938) 'external' system, which also defines '&' and '∨' as in Figs. 3.5 and 3.6. Bochvar used this for the purpose of solving certain paradoxes of

&	1	½	0
1	1	0	0
½	0	0	0
0	0	0	0

FIG. 3.5

∨	1	½	0
1	1	1	1
½	1	0	0
0	1	0	0

FIG. 3.6

classical logic and set theory, and Halldén (1949) uses these tables to develop systems for dealing with vagueness and the logic of nonsense; so it is a system that is well understood. Moreover, it is a three-valued system where the classical laws remain valid. However, there are serious disadvantages to the Bochvar truth-tables *for our purposes*. For, if we adopt these truth-tables, *why* is it that under composition we lose indeterminate truth-values? There are good reasons for *Bochvar's* purposes why this occurs, but his concerns are not ours. *For the purposes of constructing a plausible system for future contingents*, as we saw in (3.8) above, we want certain compound sentences with indeterminate components to remain indeterminate. This is not the system for us.

However, the solution now is clear. As noted, it was the definition of '∼' in Łukasiewicz's system that caused the trouble. But, as we have seen with (3.8), the rest of Łukasiewicz's system works well. So, if we construct a system based on these two desirable features, then the laws of non-contradiction and excluded middle remain logical truths—and, moreover, fall out as natural consequences of intuitive independent reasoning, unlike with Tooley's reasoning—and the truth-values of molecular propositions remain intuitive. Thus, those who wish to keep hold of a non-bivalent logic for future contingents can do so plausibly without having to abandon those logical laws, by working with the following truth-tables given in Figs. 3.7, 3.8, and 3.9. I also take it that the most uncontroversial reading of 'P ⊃ Q' is '∼(P & ∼Q)', in which case, see Fig. 3.10. Some comment, however, is in order. Let **F** (read 'It will be the case that') be a future-tense operator on present-tense propositions. Take the proposition

(3.10) Dr Foster will go to Gloucester

and the proposition

(3.11) Dr Foster will not go to Gloucester.

	~
1	0
½	1
0	1

FIG. 3.7

&	1	½	0
1	1	½	0
½	½	½	0
0	0	0	0

FIG. 3.8

∨	1	½	0
1	1	1	1
½	1	½	½
0	1	½	0

FIG. 3.9

⊃	1	½	0
1	1	0	0
½	1	1	1
0	1	1	1

FIG. 3.10

It may be thought if one assigns ½ to (3.10), then (3.11) must be assigned the value 1—*even if Dr Foster does end up going to Gloucester!* So what has gone wrong? Nothing, I say; and this is obvious so long as we understand these propositions correctly. Obviously, proposition (3.10) is to be analysed as follows:

(3.10*) **F**(Dr Foster goes to Gloucester)

Care must be taken, however, when analysing (3.11) if we require it to be the negation of (3.10). The incorrect analysis is where the future-tensed operator has wide scope over the present-tensed proposition:

(3.11×) **F**∼(Dr Foster goes to Gloucester).

The reason why this must be the incorrect analysis of the negation of (3.10) is clear: the present-tensed proposition that *Dr Foster goes to Gloucester* has a determinate truth-value—it is either true or false depending on whether there is a present fact that Dr Foster goes to Gloucester to make it true. The negation of this proposition—*Dr Foster does not go to Gloucester*—is likewise either determinately true or false. But because these propositions fall within the future-tensed operator, both (3.10*) and (3.11 ×) *as a whole* have the value 'indeterminate'. Now, this does not destroy the law of excluded middle because the future-tensed proposition (3.11 ×), i.e., (3.11 ×) taken as a whole, is not the negation of the future-tensed proposition (3.10*), i.e., (3.10*) taken as a whole—it matters not a jot that the embedded present-tensed proposition in (3.11 ×) is the negation of the embedded present-tensed proposition in (3.10*). We may as well represent (3.10*) as p and (3.11 ×) as q to highlight the fact that the pair (3.10*) and (3.11 ×) is no counterexample to $(p \vee \sim p)$. The correct analysis of the negation of (3.10) is

(3.11*) ∼**F**(Dr Foster goes to Gloucester)

which is of the form $\sim p$, as required. It seems to me that (3.11*) clearly says something true, given that it isn't the case that p. But, of course, to say (3.11*) is true is *not* to say that Dr Foster *won't* go to Gloucester. That would be to confuse (3.11*) with (3.11 ×), which would be a howler: to say that it is not the case that p is not to say that q! Thus even if it turns out that Dr Foster does go to Gloucester, we should still be happy to assign truth to (3.11*). (It might still be misleading to assert the truth of (3.11*) because of scope ambiguity and the rest (see, e.g., Grice (1989: Part I)), but this in no way invalidates my reasoning).

This helps us deal with a slightly different problem. Consider

(3.12) $\mathbf{F}(p \vee \sim p)$

Since $(p \vee \sim p)$ falls within the future-tense operator, does this mean we should assign (3.12) an indeterminate truth-value? Thankfully not, since (3.12) is clearly true. The reason why not is that the future-tense operator only renders statements indeterminate when it operates on contingent propositions; thus, since logical truths are a species of necessary truth, (3.12) is true. And my reasons for saying $(p \vee \sim p)$ is a logical truth are the very reasons given above. What this means is that we cannot accept the equivalence

(3.13) $\mathbf{F}(p \vee q) \equiv \mathbf{F}p \vee \mathbf{F}q$

which we should be happy to reject, since if we take $q = \sim p$ we can see (3.13) mistakenly equates (3.11 ×) with (3.11*).

There are, however, important cases of future-tensed propositions which we cannot afford to be indeterminate, but which do not operate on logical truths. Take, for instance, the truth-value links that we are so keen to preserve, such as

(3.14) $p \equiv \mathbf{F}^n\mathbf{P}^m p,$ where $n = m$.

We require (3.14) to be a necessary truth, but due to the future-tensed proposition on the right-hand side, it looks like it takes the value $= 1/2$. Thankfully, however, we need look no further than the truth-conditions for future-tensed propositions given in Chapter 2. For it follows from what is said there that propositions like $\mathbf{F}\mathbf{P}p$ are true *simpliciter* when the proposition that $\mathbf{P}p$ is true at all times later than the present, i.e., on all possible future branches accessible from that time, which, of course, it is if the proposition p is true. And '$\mathbf{F}\mathbf{P}p$' is false *simpliciter* when '$\mathbf{P}p$' is true at no time later than the present, i.e., on no possible future branches accessible from that time, which it won't be, if the proposition p is false. (3.14), therefore, remains necessarily true, as required.

A related case was brought to my attention by Patrick Hawley (private correspondence). Suppose that I will buy a motorcycle, can only buy one motorcycle, and must choose between a Ducati and an MV Agusta. Then

> Either I will buy a Ducati or I will buy an MV Agusta

should be true; but it appears that I must say that it is indeterminate. However, in cases of this form, we should not formulate them simply as

$$P \vee Q$$

since this does not capture the conditions imposed on the situation. The way one should formulate such cases is rather

$$(P \equiv \sim Q) \supset (P \vee Q)$$

which, under my truth-tables, is a tautology, as we required it to be.

Hawley objects to this solution because it also renders

> Either I will buy a Ducati or I will buy a Ducati

i.e.,

$$(P \equiv \sim Q) \supset (P \vee P)$$

true, which, he says, it intuitively isn't—or at least, intuitively has a different truth-value than the previous case. But I disagree. I see no compelling reason to think that these cases should have different truth-values—I am as equally convinced of the intuitive truth of both of them. This can clearly be seen in the equivalence

$$(P \supset Q) \equiv \sim(P \,\&\, \sim Q)$$

For then

$$\sim((P \equiv \sim Q) \,\&\, \sim(P \vee P))$$

when both sides are indeterminate seems to me to be unproblematically true, since if the conjunction is indeterminate, then it isn't the case; so to say that it isn't the case is to say something true. So it is true; there is no contrast in truth-value between the two cases. What is important is that they have different truth-*conditions*, which, indeed, they do (contrast the case of P = 0 and Q = 1). But why I should grant that they have different truth-*values* needs argument. Indeed, I say that if everyone is aware of the equivalence of 'P ⊃ Q' with '∼(P & ∼Q)', then intuition, so far as it is worth anything in this rather complex example, is firmly on my side. In complex cases like this, asking people about their intuitions is as reliable as asking people whether 'the present king of France is bald' is true, or whether 'if it is raining then it isn't raining' is true, said when it isn't raining. Phrased in this way, such questions are more likely to be puzzling rather than something that people have strong intuitions about. However, when it is spelled out exactly what is being asked (e.g., by rephrasing conditionals in terms of negations and conjunctions, and definite descriptions in terms of quantifier phrases, and so on), then that is the real test for whether a given pronouncement on the truth-value should be respected or not. In short, I recognize that the two cases are different; but the contrast is one of truth-conditions, not truth-value.

This system has recognizably classical features: from simple truth-table tests we can see '&' and '∨' are both commutative and associative; 'P ⊃ P' is true (unlike Bochvar's full systems!); 'P ⊃ Q' is equivalent to '∼Q ⊃ ∼P'; the distributive laws [(P ∨ (Q & R)) ≡ ((P ∨ Q) & (P ∨ R)) and (P & (Q ∨ R)) ≡ ((P & Q) ∨ (P & R))] hold; and a form of de Morgan's laws hold [(∼(P & Q) ≡ (∼P ∨ ∼Q)) and ∼(P ∨ Q) ≡ (∼P & ∼Q)], although because of the definition of negation, we lose the equivalence between '&' and '∨' of the form 'P & Q ≡ ∼(∼P ∨ ∼Q)' and '∼(∼P & ∼Q) ≡ (P ∨ Q)', as well as the equivalence '(∼P ∨ Q) ≡ (P ⊃ Q)' because of the case where P = 1 and Q = ½. It must also be said that, as with many many-valued systems (including Łukasiewicz's before Słupecki's (1936) work) this system is not functionally complete. But the sorts of truth-functions that cannot be generated by the connectives of this system have no application anyway, and so can be ignored.

We can also see clearly from this system why the redundancy theory of truth (e.g., Ramsey (1927)), as well as Prior's redundancy theory of the present mentioned in Chapter 2, needs qualification. For the semantic thesis that 'It is true that P' is equivalent to 'P' cannot be right, since if 'P' is indeterminate (as it is if it is a future contingent statement), 'It is true that P' is false (rather than being itself indeterminate), showing that the semantic equivalence does not hold. Similarly, if we interpret the present-tense operator as 'It is now true that', then biconditionals, such as $\mathbf{NF}p \equiv \mathbf{F}p$, equally do not hold. The problem with the redundancy theory of truth is that it conflates the metalinguistic notion of bivalence with a theorem of the object language, namely the law of excluded middle. And so once it is shown, as I have done, that the two notions peel apart in important ways—one having to do with a view of truth and falsity, the other having more to do with a view about negation—we see that it is not the notion of truth but the redundancy theory itself which should take early retirement.

Thus, so long as Dr Foster doesn't fall into a muddle with the law of excluded middle, it is possible to have what my 'Aristotle' desires, namely a non-bivalent logic where classical laws remain intact. Thus it should really be *this* system and not Łukasiewicz's, as Prior (1953: 317) has it, which is known as the 'classical system of three-valued logic'.

Problem 4 TRANSTEMPORAL RELATIONS (I)

> Presentism complicates the treatment of transtemporal relations
> Adams (1986: 321)

It is widely held, and I think correctly so, that a necessary condition for the existence of relations is that both of the *relata* exist. However, according to presentism, only things that are present exist. The general problem then arises: how should presentism deal with relations where at least one of the *relata* lies in the past, and is therefore non-existent? I shall show how presentism should deal systematically with such relations in general.

First, presentists should say that if there are any genuine relations at all between spatio-temporal objects, then they are all either (a) spatio-temporal or (b) causal relations. (Indeed, I think this is true independently of what the presentist needs to say.) There do, however, seem to be relations that hold between objects existing at different times, such as *taller than*, which are neither spatio-temporal nor causal. I say that these cases fall into the class of *determinables*, which I deny are genuine relations. Other (so-called) relations that may trouble presentism because of the possible lack of a *relatum*, such as *father of*, should be viewed as really causal: '*a* is the father of *b*', for instance, essentially amounts to '*a* caused *b* to exist'. Thus, the presentist's general strategy here should be to first reduce all supposed transtemporal relations (that are not spatio-temporal) either to determinables or causal relations. If it is reduced to a causal relation, the next step is to deny that *causes* is a genuine relation. Because of the importance of causation, I shall not discuss it here, but shall devote the next chapter to it. First, though, because I have not yet stated this explicitly, we must have an account of temporal relations themselves.

I *Earlier than* and defining tenses

Temporal relations themselves are transtemporal, so I should briefly say how presentism can deal with them. This approach has an attractive feature for those tensed theorists who wish to dispose of the relations *earlier than*, *later than*, and *simultaneous with*, in favour of *past*, *future*, and *present*. For simultaneity can be defined as follows. If p is the u-proposition that e occurs, then $\mathbf{N}p$ amounts simply to p. And similarly for $\mathbf{N}q$, if q is the u-proposition that e^* occurs. So events e and e^* can be represented as being simultaneous by a true instance of:

(3.15) p & q.

Here, the events e and e^* are not bound together with a simultaneity relation, but rather the u-propositions that they occur are bound together using a conjunction. Of course, care must be taken when expressing what it is to say that things *were* or *will be* simultaneous. For neither

(3.16) $\mathbf{P}p$ & $\mathbf{P}q$

nor

(3.17) $\mathbf{F}p$ & $\mathbf{F}q$

imply that e and e^* are simultaneous: e may occur before e^*, yet both may occur in the past. We would have to add that they are simultaneous, which would render the definition circular. This, however, can be dealt with by binding e and e^* together using a conjunction of the propositions p and q, and then operating on the whole conjunction rather than on each conjunct, i.e.,

(3.18) $\mathbf{P}(p\&q)$

and

(3.19) $\mathbf{F}(p\&q)$,

respectively.

Now, of course, some events are more past than others, and how are we to say this without saying that some past events are *earlier than* others? This is easy once we have metric tense operators in place (see Chapter 2: n. 2). For suppose that e and e^* were simultaneous events, that f and f^* were simultaneous events, that e occurred earlier than f, that both are past, and that p, q, r, and s are the u-propositions that e, e^*, f, f^* occur, respectively. We can capture this by writing:

(3.20) $\mathbf{P}^m(p\&q)$ & $\mathbf{P}^n(r\&s)$ & $m > n$, where $m, n \in \mathbb{R}$

and then give the truth-conditions for past-tensed propositions that I have given in the previous chapter (§V(c)). (Here the superscripts indicate how far in the past or future we should go in evaluating the truth-value of the propositions, in which case we would just add or subtract the superscript to or from the present date, accordingly.) That is to say, the past is all of those actually *E*-related times with dates less than the date of the time that is presently realized. And *mutatis mutandis* for the future. This is a perfectly natural way of expressing our understanding of the past- and future-tenses. Here we have no need for B-series relations, nor primitive notions of pastness and futurity, just conjunction, the notion of truth *simpliciter* for u-propositions, and the *greater than* relation defined over the real numbers.

II Determinables

How can we account for statements such as 'I am taller than my great-grandfather' when the statement '*a* is taller than *b*' seems to require the existence of *a*, *b*, and the relation *taller than* to make it true? I say that all that is really required to make it true is the fact that *a* is, say, 6 feet tall and *b* is (or rather was), say, 5 feet tall and that the 'relation' between them is simply a logical consequence of these facts. (Remember that to say that *b* was 5 feet tall is to say: **P**(5 feet tall(*b*)), which is true iff (5 feet tall(*b*)) is true at an earlier *E*-related time.)

Now, we could take this to mean that such relations *supervene* on the fact that *a* is such a height and *b* was such a height and can, therefore, be disposed of (ontologically speaking) altogether. Alternatively, and my preference, we can take this to mean that the relation between *a* and *b* has simply been shifted to talk of relations between the relative magnitudes of lengths. And since numbers are used to represent (proportionally) the magnitudes of these quantities, the relation between *a* and *b* is ultimately reduced to the relations between numbers (i.e., 6 > 5). (Whether such relations between lengths, or numbers, or whatever, can themselves be reduced by claiming that it supervenes on the natures of the numbers, etc., themselves is an interesting but independent matter.) Either of these options is available to presentism, since both do the job. For presentism is required here only to account for seeming relations, such as *taller than*, between existing objects, such as myself, and non-existing objects, such as my great-grandfather. Since this can be done by appealing to objects that *do* exist (facts about me and facts about my great-grandfather, construed in the way I treat past-tensed statements, and relations between eternally existing objects such as numbers), such relations as *taller than* are not problematic for presentism.

III Qualitative relations

Not all supposed relations can be accounted for in this way, however; for they won't all be subject to a quantitative treatment. For instance, suppose we are reminiscing about growing up in a more innocent age. This may well be true, but comparing two times in terms of innocence does not lend itself well to a quantitative assessment. Yet whatever concrete facts constitute an innocent age will be facts that are represented by the abstract story about what happens at that time. Since these abstract objects *are* the facts, for ersatzer presentism, the truth of statements involving qualitative relations will supervene on the contents of these times. The same goes for the typical example involving the admiration of Socrates. For 'I admire Socrates' can be dealt with so long as Socrates can be represented somehow. But that is a problem about how we can talk about *Socrates*, and not a problem, as some philosophers seem to suggest, with accounting for the spurious relation of *admiration* itself. For the sentence is ambiguous between admiring the *qualities and achievements* of Socrates, and admiring *Socrates*. The former is not a particular problem for presentism, since time is irrelevant to whether we can admire certain qualities and achievements, whereas the latter is the problem of how to pin-point who we are talking about, i.e., a problem concerning reference (something I shall deal with in the Problem 5). The focus on the relation of *admiration* itself is a red herring.

So all of these purported relations can be accounted for—at least if the reference relation, which is often a transtemporal relation, can. Because the reference relation is an important relation, we should deal with it as a problem in its own right.

Problem 5 TRANSTEMPORAL RELATIONS (II): REFERENCE

I Prior, proper names, and presentism

According to presentism, the only concrete objects that exist are those that are presently realized: 'Socrates' and many other names for past objects no longer have a referent. But this raises a problem for presentism: are statements involving the name 'Socrates' rendered meaningless, and, if so, is this not a good reason for rejecting presentism, given that they are not?

Names (and definite descriptions) seem to be paradigm cases of referring expressions, and if they are, presentism is in trouble, for we do want to say that statements involving 'Socrates' and 'Plato', such as that Socrates taught Plato, assert something rather than nothing.

Prior's solution is a compromise. He writes: 'there are no *facts* about x to be stated except where x exists' (1968e: 259), and so in this sense concedes (or rather positively endorses the view) that no fact has been stated in saying 'Socrates is wise'. But this is not as counterintuitive as it appears, for Prior draws the conclusion that this problem shows merely that proper names (at least for past objects) should be treated not as referring expressions, but as quantifier phrases, in the style of Russell's theory of ordinary proper names (e.g. Russell ((1911); (1918–19))), which utilizes his theory of descriptions (e.g., Russell ((1905); (1919: 167–80))). That is,

(3.21) Socrates was the teacher of Plato

is construed (where **P** is the propositional operator *It was the case that*, G is the property *snub-nosed wise philosopher who drinks hemlock*, and H the property *author of The Republic*) as something like:

(3.22) $\mathbf{P}(\exists x)(\exists y)(Gx$ & $(\forall z)(Gz \supset z = x)$ & Hy & $(\forall w)$ $(Hw \supset w = y)$ & teaches (x, y) & $x \neq y)$.

Prior's denying that there are any facts about x when x does not exist, then, is a rather misleading way of putting it. It is better to say that although no *singular* statements can be made about past individuals, *general* statements can (Prior (1968a: 19)).

To dispel any doubts about this solution, it is worth filling out the Russellian treatment here, in order to make clear how it works. In Chapter 2: §V(c), I gave the truth-conditions for past-tensed quantified propositions using the objectual interpretation of the quantifiers. The alternative would be to say that '$(\forall x)Fx$' is true iff all its substitution instances, 'Fa', 'Fb', 'Fc', etc., are true; and '$(\exists x)Fx$' is true iff some substitution instance, 'Fa', 'Fb', 'Fc', etc., is true. But this relies on everything in the domain of quantification having a name, which, of course, they might not. And if they don't, then '$(\forall x)Fx$' might still be false even if all named things are F, since some unnamed thing might not be F; and '$(\exists x)Fx$' might still be true even if no named thing is F, since some unnamed thing might still be F. The objectual interpretation of the quantifiers has the obvious advantage here because it does not treat the quantifiers as generalizing about named things, but as generalizing about objects whether or not they have names. And this is just as well, because having to rely on names in the truth-conditions for the quantifiers would render this approach circular.

So how do I see the story working? We start with a concrete object (named or otherwise) which, if F, is sufficient to make '$(\exists x)Fx$' true. That proposition is then true-at-a-time t. Time moves on, and we can suppose that that particular object no longer exists. Nevertheless, we can say later that something was F, i.e., hold '$\mathbf{P}(\exists x)Fx$' true, despite that particular not existing, since we are able to talk about its having been F via the fact that '$(\exists x)Fx$' is true-at-a-time t which is E-related to the time which is presently realized. Thus, we do not need the object to exist presently in order to say meaningful things about it. However, we do need *something* to exist to talk about it, even if we do not need the object itself: we can't get away with postulating nothing; something must exist in order to represent it. It is not good enough just to assert '$\mathbf{P}(\exists x)Fx$' as true without any explanation as to *how* it can be true, for this violates the conditions that any good metaphysical theory should meet, namely to transparently explain the mechanisms by which truths can be held to be true (see the introduction: §III). I say that once we unpack the tenses and the quantifiers in the way I have done, and with the ontological commitments to times to represent what happened, we have a perfectly transparent account of how we can talk about past objects without them having to exist.

Of course, this neat solution is a non-starter if the descriptive theory of names is unsatisfactory, but I shall not tackle this issue here.[8] I want to investigate whether presentists *are* committed to being Russellians, by which I mean someone who treats both proper names and descriptions as quantifier phrases. For Russell's theory is not uncontroversial, and it is worthwhile to discuss whether the success of presentism may depend on the success of Russell's theory. I shall show how presentists can adopt a non-Russellian alternative. But, first, a problem.

---

[8] I assume here, with Kripke (1972), that for all my intents and purposes, Frege's (1892) is a kind of description theory. I do not think, then, that any separate discussion is required for this particular theory of names. An obvious difference is that empty names for Frege result in sentences involving them expressing propositions with no truth-value, whereas for Russell the propositions are false. I leave it to the reader to work out how adopting this difference would change some details of the presentist position, and how unimportant such differences are for my argument.

II Rigidity for Russellians

Consider the well-known rigidity argument in the context of modality put forward by Kripke (1972) against treating names as definite descriptions. Names are rigid designators—they name the same object in every world in which that object exists—whereas definite descriptions, it is claimed, are non-rigid designators—they do not always designate the same object in every world. Thus, since names behave differently in modal contexts from definite descriptions, so the argument goes, names cannot be treated as definite descriptions; they have different semantic properties. Interestingly, the same phenomenon can be carried over to the temporal case. Let us call the tallest man in the world 'Lemuel'. Now consider:

(3.23) Lemuel was 2 feet tall.

According to my version of presentism, this is to be understood as:

(3.23′) It was the case that: Lemuel is 2 feet tall.

I take it that both (3.23) and (3.23′) are true, given that before he reached his dizzying heights, Lemuel was a child. But Lemuel is identical to the tallest man in the world, so:

(3.24) The tallest man in the world was 2 feet tall

is true too. But, according to presentism, this is to be understood as:

(3.24′) It was the case that: the tallest man in the world is 2 feet tall.

And here lies the problem. For whereas (3.24) is true, (3.24′) isn't—surely one has to be taller than 2 feet tall to be included in the *Guinness Book of Records*? So 'The tallest man in the world is 2 feet tall' never was true.

The obvious strategy to tackle such rigidity arguments is to equate the name with a temporally *rigidified* description. For just as '*Actually* the saddest person ever to have held a Martini' designates the same person in all possible worlds where they exist, 'The man who is *at present* the tallest in the world', where 'at present' refers to the time at which the description is uttered, designates the same person across all times. Thus, equating names with temporally rigidified descriptions fends off this particular objection to presentists treating names in the Russellian way.⁹

Supposing, though, that for whatever reason we did not want to be Russellian presentists, what are the alternatives?

III Who wants to be a Millianaire?

Le Poidevin (1991: 40) argues that the causal theory of names in particular is not available to the presentist. He writes:

> Why... can [the presentist] not invoke the *causal theory of names* (Kripke (1972)), in which singular reference to an individual x is achieved *via* a series of causal connections between x (or some naming of x) and my present use of 'x'? The answer is that this theory is simply not open to the [presentist], for he denies the reality of the past states of affairs and/or individuals with which the present event—a token utterance of 'x'—is supposed to be connected. The causal relation thus lacks a *relatum*.   (Le Poidevin (1991: 40))

This paragraph contains two problems for presentism. The first is that, according to the causal theory of reference, the reference relation between the present use of a name and the bearer of the name is to be reduced to (or at least requires) a causal relation of the appropriate kind between the present use of the name and the bearer (or at least with the event of the initial naming). But since it is a necessary condition for the existence of relations that the *relata* exist, the causal relation, and thus the reference relation, cannot. But if this is taken to be the difficulty, the presentist strategy should simply be to deny that causation is a genuine relation between events, as I shall do in the next chapter.

The second problem, however, is the real difficulty. For, whether or not the causal relation is a genuine relation, the fact is that there is still nothing on the other end of the causal connection—so what exactly is being referred to?

---

⁹ Essentially, this is a difference in *de re* and *de dicto* readings of the tense operator. The correct reading in this context is *de re*: 'of the man who is presently the tallest in the world, he was 2 ft tall'. The *de dicto* reading would be true if we were talking of a particularly tall Lilliputian, or of a time of severe malnutrition.

At this point, we must try to specify those components which make up 'the' causal theory of reference, since there is no widespread consensus what it is. Because of its association with the thesis that names need have no *connotations*, some take it to include what we may call the 'Millian' theory of names: the meaning of a name is its *denotation*, the thing it refers to, and nothing else (see Mill (1843: bk 1, chs. 1, 2)). But if we then take the entire meaning of 'Socrates' to be the flesh and blood object Socrates, then without an existent Socrates, the name is literally meaningless. Presentists, then, cannot be Millians—that's part and parcel of their thesis, if they think meaningful discourse can be had about non-present objects. But, as Frege (1892) saw, there's trouble at t' Mill anyway; so good riddance, I say.

But rejecting the Millian aspect of the causal theory does not preclude the presentist from using the better aspects associated with the causal theory, such as the *historical-causal* component.

IV Passing the nominal parcel

The major advantage of the causal theory of reference over the descriptive theory is in its treatment of ignorance and error. We often do not have a uniquely identifying description in mind when we use a name, and sometimes we may even have a false description in mind. If we do associate a false description with a name, then the Russellian definite description will, if satisfied at all, be satisfied by the wrong thing. Similarly, if we lack uniquely identifying knowledge, then it isn't determinate who we are talking about.[10] The causal theory lifts this epistemic burden. For my ability to talk about Socrates is not the result of having a definite description in mind, but rather the result of the name being passed from one person to another along a causal chain (consisting of appropriately connected facts). This allows us to

---

[10] I think the descriptive theory can say a lot in response to this, including building the causal aspect into the story. This indeed results in a hybrid theory which takes the best bits from the causal theory and leaves the bad bits behind, such as the minimal semantic content that names would have if they were stripped of all connotation. It is not for me to discuss this debate here, but see McCulloch (1989) for a nice discussion.

talk about Socrates, without having to have an implausible amount of knowledge about him.

So how do I see this working for the presentist? We start with the event of the initial naming ceremony whereby Socrates was named. We can write this as follows:

(3.25) $\mathbf{P}(\exists x)(\exists y)(\exists z)(x = \text{Socrates} \ \& \ \textit{refers to}(y, x, z))$,

where x ranges over people, y over producers of the name, z over names, and where the *refers to* relation is left to philosophers of language to make precise, but which corresponds to a commonplace notion.[11] In English it says: someone referred to Socrates using some name. It seems to me that (3.25) no more needs Socrates to exist to be meaningful than (3.22) does. All we need, then, to talk about Socrates, is for our present use of the name 'Socrates' to be causally related (in an appropriate way, again to be filled out by philosophers of language) to such facts. To expand: when Socrates existed, he himself was a flesh-and-blood constituent of certain facts which made propositions, such as $(\exists x)(\exists y)(\exists z)(x = \text{Socrates} \ \& \ \textit{refers to}(y, x, z))$, true *simpliciter*. So, even though Socrates no longer exists, what enables us to talk about Socrates is the fact that $\mathbf{P}(\exists x)(\exists y)(\exists z)(x = \text{Socrates} \ \& \ \textit{refers to}(y, x, z))$ and the fact that this fact is causally connected in an appropriate way to our use of the name 'Socrates'.

Now, this is not reference in the sense that requires, as a necessary condition to succeed, an existent particular. But presentists do not need reference in this sense in order to help themselves to the nice aspects of the causal theory. Indeed, the thought that presentists require particulars to be referents in order to talk about Socrates has lead to some mishandling of the situation. As discussed in Chapter 2: §III, Craig (2003: 395) states that 'the proper name "Socrates" expresses an individual essence of Socrates rather than denotes nonconnotatively the actual object Socrates and so does not require Socrates to exist in order for the name to refer'. Let us set aside reservations about the ontology here, since even if we adopt the ontology, it is not clear that this is the correct thing to say. For if it is the essence which is referred

---

[11] We could, of course, specify the ys or the zs either in the same way the xs have been or by using definite descriptions to specify them uniquely. But we need not complicate matters until it is shown that we must.

to and not the actual object Socrates, then the flesh and blood creature *never is* referred to by the name 'Socrates'. Yet the original problem was how to refer to Socrates—nobody cares whether 'Socrates' can be said to refer to something else. To put the point another way, ersatzer presentists should not commit themselves to the view that Socrates becomes an abstract object when he dies. That doesn't capture what we'd like to say about the situation at all. It is much more like it to say that the abstract objects are used to *represent* Socrates rather than act as referents for the name: we should no more mistake what *represents* Socrates with Socrates himself than we should mistake a drawing of an egg with an egg. It is rather like how Lewis's counterparts work. When I say 'I could have been a contender', what I don't do is refer to my counterpart who is a contender, but rather use my counterpart to represent what I—the person to whom I am referring—could have done. So the notion of representation is different from that of reference, and even though we don't have a fully worked-out theory of representation (as explained in Chapter 2: n. 6), we can still talk about how we should think of reference. It may turn out that ersatzer presentists require essences to be constituents of the abstract propositions to give a full account of how representation is possible, which is why I set aside reservations about the ontology; but whatever presentists require for representation, they shouldn't say that these are the entities to which we refer. Rather, what captures what we want to say is (3.25). For this allows us to say that there *was* a time when reference was made, not to an abstract essence, but to the flesh and blood *Socrates*, the genuine article. This is a much more plausible and, more importantly, more useful thing to be able to say, because it is this very fact which allows presentism to adopt the nice aspects of the causal theory (without it having to be genuine reference, i.e., where an existing object is required to be the referent). For it obviates the need for the fully complete and accurate descriptions of Socrates required by the Russellian in order to be able to talk about him and nobody else. The issue of ignorance and error is the only substantial worry when going with the Russellian view. But since this can be bypassed with (3.25) and the causal story, presentists need not be worried that their theory depends on the success of the descriptive theory of names. The issue of genuine reference is neither here nor there.

With that said, let's fill out the presentist's version of the causal theory. Note that (3.25) as it stands allows for any old instance of naming; so at least one constraint on the process has to be that the naming must be done by authorities on Socrates, such as those immediately acquainted with him. But so long as we rub up against such producers of the name (or at least rub up against consumers of the name who rubbed up against such producers, or rub up against consumers who have rubbed up against consumers who ... and so on) in an appropriate way, then we'll be able to talk about Socrates.[12]

Note also that (3.25) leaves it open just what Socrates *was* named. After all, the way we write 'Socrates' is different from the way the Greeks wrote it, and the way they say 'Socrates' may have differed. But we need not specify what strings of symbols the producers inscribed, or which sounds they uttered. All that matters is that our use of the name 'Socrates' is causally related to the naming of Socrates, so that in using 'Socrates' we are able to talk about him, regardless of the names the original producers used to talk about him.

(3.25) also assumes that there is an unproblematic relation between Socrates and the event of his naming. This would indeed be the case if there was a time at which Socrates and the fact he was named both existed. However, it might be that the thing named is named after it has ceased to be. Yet so long as there was an appropriate causal connection between the producer(s) and the bearer, and so long as there was an appropriate causal connection between the later naming and the fact that the bearer and the producer(s) were related, then the causal theory can take off. We can write these conditions as follows:

(3.26) **P**[causally connected in an appropriate way $((\exists y)(\exists z)$ (produces (y, z)), **P**$(\exists x)(\exists y)$ (causally connected in an appropriate way $(x, y)))$]

where, again, x ranges over people, y over producers of the name, z over names. This story assumes that the causal theory requires there to be a causal connection between the use of a name and the *bearer*, and not merely a causal connection between the use of a name and the *production* of a name. The latter version of the theory would

---

[12] See Evans (1982) for the producer/consumer terminology.

allow for reference to be made by consumers to mathematical objects, for instance, through being causally connected to expert producers of mathematical terms, even though the experts themselves had no causal interaction with the bearers. This version of the theory, by employing (3.25), is unproblematic for presentists, if they want it. The former, stronger formulation of the theory, however, is particularly useful. For externalists about meaning press the point that causal interaction with the object named is vital to the semantic content of certain propositions—it is that which makes my thought about one thing rather than another (see Putnam (1981), for instance). So what is it that makes my thoughts about Socrates and not his Doppelganger in Twin Athens? Since what determines what my thought is about is fixed by facts about the causal chain linking facts about the bearer with facts about my use of certain names in certain sentences expressing certain thoughts or propositions, then so long as presentism can represent such facts, then those thoughts will determinately be about that particular thing (Socrates) and nothing else (his twin). Presentists can help themselves to all of this, if they want it.

So either way, whether we insist on a causal link with the bearer itself or not, presentism can adopt these useful features of the causal theory, for I have already shown in the last chapter how presentism accommodates facts about the past. All I have to show is how it deals with the causal connections between the facts. This is what I shall now do.

4

Transtemporal relations (III): causation

Being able to accommodate causation is an important project in its own right, but it is especially pressing here given the close links between it and time. Causation is one thing (independently of the tensed–tenseless debate) that distinguishes time from space in time's being the dimension in which change takes place, and it is causation which accounts for our experience of change. Many people coming to the tensed–tenseless debate for the first time have to coax themselves into thinking that causation fits into the tenseless view. Initially, the tenseless view looks so causally inert that only a dynamic account of time seems to capture it: how can some fact bring about another fact when all of the facts already exist? But any clear-headed person soon sees that the tenseless theory has no trouble reconciling the existence of these facts with the more popular accounts of causation. The counterfactual claim that if fact F had not obtained then fact G wouldn't have either, for instance, is consistent with this view. It remains to be seen, however, whether the tenseless view can use causation (or something else) to give the direction of time, which is something they need to do, given that, according to them, time itself does not flow. I tackle this issue in §II below.

In any case, despite the first impression that the notion of causation fits more favourably into a dynamic account of time, on further reflection it seems that presentism has more of a difficulty: it seems that it cannot accommodate causation at all. Let c and e be events. Whenever we have a true instance of 'c causes e', it seems to follow at least that both c and e exist. Furthermore, one widely accepted connotation of causation is that c is earlier than e. But, if c is earlier than e, then it follows, according to presentism, that when c exists, e does not yet exist, and when e exists, c has ceased to exist; thus, if causation is a relation, then presentism cannot account for it.

Presentism should, then, deny that causation *is* a genuine transtemporal relation between events, and that '*causes* (c, e)' is the correct form of causal statements (*pace* Davidson (1967b)). This is not as radical as it initially sounds, since, after all, many accounts of causation, as we shall see, do not take the form of causal statements to require transtemporal relations.

Since it is the transtemporalness that causes the problem for presentism and not the event ontology, I shall not discuss here any reasons for thinking that events are not the causal *relata* (for this, see, e.g., Mellor (1995)). Whether or not we think that ultimately causation must link events or facts or whatever, what matters here is that presentists can represent that an event occurs (or occurred), etc., and show how it is possible to state past-tensed truths concerning it. If this can be done, then presentists can use whichever *relata* they feel appropriate for causal contexts.

The first issue to tackle, then, is how presentism can even formulate a theory of causation. Naturally, I cannot discuss all of the various theories of causation, so I shall concentrate on three well-worked out accounts. I shall then discuss the general issue of whether causation can give the direction to time, and end by discussing the possibility of backwards causation and why it matters.

I Formulating theories of causation within presentism

(a) *The regularity theory*

> We may define a cause to be *an object followed by another, and where all the objects, similar to the first, are followed by objects similar to the second.*
> David Hume, *An Enquiry Concerning Human Understanding*: §7.

Let us first consider the regularity account of causation, which treats causation as nothing more than 'constant conjunction'. Here we can represent causal relations between events *c* and *e* using propositions joined by a connective. Thus, where C is the proposition that *c* occurs, and E is the proposition that *e* occurs, we rephrase '*c* causes *e*' in terms of a constant conjunction between C and E using the connective '&'. This account has a very minimal ontology in that it commits us to believing (ontologically speaking) in nothing more than regular conjunctions of events. Thus causation need not be treated as a transtemporal relation. At least, it need not be treated as a genuine relation in its own right, since the regularity account is an attempt to reduce the causal relation between events to certain spatio-temporal relations between events. And as we have seen, spatio-temporal relations are unproblematic for presentism.

Whether or not the regularity account is entirely satisfactory as an account of causation is a question for another time. The project here is to see whether a presentist could adopt this view, if desired.

One problem is that a causal 'C&E' (whatever that amounts to) is never true-at-a-time (understood in the ersatzer presentist way), for one connotation of causation is that the cause occurs earlier than the effect. One way to capture this temporal asymmetry is to write '**P**(C)&E'. This certainly can be true-at-a-time and is true *simpliciter* iff C is true at a past time and E is true at the present time. But, of course, '**P**(C)&E' could be true in the past, present, or future; so in order to capture this we just need to add a tense operator such that '**P**(C)&E' falls within its scope, as in '**P**(**P**(C)&E)' and '**F**(**P**(C)&E)'. More complex tenses can be achieved by iteration of various operators.

A further condition for a causal conjunction is usually that the *relata* are contiguous in space and time. Just how this is to be understood, and whether it is true can be left for another time. It will do for our purposes to say that the condition will amount to something like this: spatio-temporal locations of the events $l(c)$, $l(e)$ must be sufficiently close in time and space for us to take it as a causal link. Whatever 'sufficiently close' is taken to be, we can certainly represent the spatio-temporal location of the various events, since at each time, the spatial location (in a given frame of reference) of an event can be given. Thus this further condition could be incorporated into the ersatzer presentist account of causation if needed.[1]

So far, so good. But according to the regularity theory, whether a particular conjunction of events is causal or not depends on whether those types of event are regularly conjoined. That is to say, whether an event c with properties F causes an event e with properties G depends on what happens to all other F-type and G-type events. As Hume recognizes (*Enquiry*: §7.2), the causal relation turns out to depend on matters *extrinsic* to the particular circumstances concerning the events c and e.

Whether this is palatable is again a question for another time, but this does raise the issue of how a presentist can accommodate this theory. At first sight, it looks easy: we generalize to $(\forall x)(Fx \supset Gx)$, where the quantifier ranges over all events past, present, and future. The problem here is that when we fill this out explicitly, it entails

(4.1) $\mathbf{P}(\forall x)(Fx \supset Gx) \& (\forall x)(Fx \supset Gx) \& \mathbf{F}(\forall x)(Fx \supset Gx)$

This is fine for presentism if it adopts a linear view of time; but since I have developed a branching view, this statement cannot be true because the last conjunct has an indeterminate truth-value. In other words, we'd have to say that at a given time it is indeterminate whether a particular F-event is the cause of a particular G-event. Whether it

---

[1] Similarly, suppose we adopt the view that causation involves the transference of energy or momentum from a given object to another at the point of contact. Here, the spatio-temporal notion of motion and contact can be accommodated in the same way. However, specifying the amount of energy at a time or the momentum of a particle at a particular location is complicated by quantum mechanics. Take Heisenberg's Uncertainty Principle for energy and time: there is a fundamental limit to our knowledge of a particle's energy E over a finite time interval. So, where ΔE is the uncertainty in the energy and Δt is the time interval during which the energy is known to be within the range ΔE, the uncertainty relationship is described by $\Delta E \Delta t \geq \hbar/2$, where $\hbar = h/2\pi$ and h is Planck's constant. A more precise specification of the energy (small ΔE) requires a longer period of time (large Δt), and vice versa; indeed, in order to establish a particle's energy exactly, it must be confirmed that its probability wave is infinitely long, which would take an infinitely long period of time. But if the Uncertainty Principle is interpreted as an epistemological feature concerning the limitations of our knowledge, then whatever the facts are which determine the energy at a time will be reflected in the propositions which are true at various times, even though we can't know them. On the other hand, if the principle reflects a genuine indeterminacy and not mere uncertainty over the energy at a time, this, too, will be reflected in the propositions true at a time. Either way, ersatzer presentism is no worse off than the tenseless theory in this respect.

was the cause would only emerge (if it did at all) once time's flow had made determinate all F-type events and determined whether they had been followed by G-type events. This is stranger than the linear version of the regularity-view, where the facts are determinate. This is, perhaps, another reason for rejecting the regularity-view. But if one buys the extrinsic nature of causation anyway, it is not clear that the branching version is all that strange. (It has at least one advocate in McCall (1994), although I dismissed his particular theory of time in Chapter 1: §II(b).) But, certainly, there are no more epistemological problems with the branching view than there are with the linear view. Thus, whether or not this is a satisfactory account of causation, presentists can certainly give a story along these lines.[2]

(b) The counterfactual theory

> Or, in other words *where, if the first object had not been, the second never had existed.*
> David Hume, *An Enquiry Concerning Human Understanding*: §7.

An alternative to the regularity account is the counterfactual account of causation (e.g., Lewis (1973a)). Where C is the proposition that a particular event c occurs, and E is the proposition that a particular event e occurs, we can rephrase 'c causes e' in terms of counterfactual dependence between C and E by using the connective '$\square\rightarrow$'. The causal dependence between c and e on this account is analysed in terms of the truth of two counterfactuals:

(4.2) 'C$\square\rightarrow$E' ('if c were the case, then e would be the case'), and

(4.3) '$\sim$C$\square\rightarrow\sim$E' ('if c weren't the case, then e wouldn't be the case').

If c and e do not actually occur, then (4.3) is automatically true: so e depends causally on c iff (4.2) holds. But if c and e do actually occur, then (4.2) is automatically true: so e depends causally on c iff (4.3) holds. Therefore, since causal dependence implies causation, it *cannot* be that

---

[2] The regularity view does not seem quite strong enough, however, to support the causal theory of names, which seems to require a singular account of causation.

causation is a genuine relation between *c* and *e*. For '*c* causes *e*' is analysed as 'if *c* were *not* the case, then *e* would *not* be the case', i.e., in terms of the actual *non*-occurrence of *c* and *e*. It follows that, since relations cannot exist without existent *relata*, causation, on this account, cannot be a relation. At least, again, it cannot be an *intrinsic* relation between *c* and *e*, since whether *c* causes *e* depends on what happens elsewhere (such as other possible worlds). Thus, if it isn't a genuine relation, it can hardly be a transtemporal relation; and at most it is a trans*world* relation. So all that needs to be noted is that presentists have a way of representing counterfactual dependence between past, present, or future facts or events. This is easily achieved by adding the appropriate tense operators to the present-tensed C and E joined with '$\Box\to$', and then evaluating the counterfactual in whichever way we deem appropriate.

(c) Causes as raising the chances of effects

> Because, because, because, because, becaaause ...
> *The Wizard of Oz*

Alternatively, we might prefer to analyse causation in terms of the connective 'because' (as in Mellor (1995)) as representing causation as a connection between facts. The relevant features of this account here are that a true instance of 'E because C' implies that 'C' and 'E' are (at least at some time) true and that 'C before E' is true. Presentism can easily formulate '*c* causes *e*', then, as either:

(4.4) E because **P**(C),
(4.5) **P**(E because **P**(C)),

or

(4.6) **F**(E because **P**(C)).

In order for any of these to be true, however, Mellor (1995) imposes the condition that causes must raise the chances of their effects. It is straightforward for presentism to represent this theory, as follows. If we follow Mellor and write '$ch_C(E)$' to represent the chance of the fact E holding with fact C and '$ch_{\sim C}(E)$' to represent the chance of the fact E holding without the fact C, then 'E because C' is true when $ch_C(E) > ch_{\sim C}(E)$. Note that the chances of E holding with or without C are properties of facts before E and are independent of whether E actually obtains (but whether Mellor can explain why, on his account, they must be earlier is questioned in §III below). To give a concrete example, the chances of dying while skydiving relate to such facts as the way the plane has been exited and whether somebody forgot the parachutes. Such chances of dying will change during the drop (so long as there *is* a parachute), and may rise or fall over time. But such chances still exist whether or not someone dies. (Note that, even though the chances of dying while skydiving are lower than not dying while skydiving, the skydiving can be cited as the cause of death since the chances of dying were increased by the skydiving, i.e., were much higher than if the person had not gone skydiving at all.) Now, if such chances exist and attach to various facts, then these facts will at each time make true various propositions concerning them, such as the proposition that $ch_C(E) = p$. Included in the ersatz times, then, will be such propositions representing such chances (on which propositions such as $ch_C(E) > ch_{\sim C}(E)$ supervene), and these will serve as truthmakers for any causal statements. Ersatzer presentists, then, can have a rather nice account of singular causation without invoking transtemporal relations.

II The direction of time and causation: the counterfactual connotation of causation

There's only one direction
'One Vision', Queen

On the regularity theory, how do we distinguish the cause from the effect? After all, conjunctions are just conjunctions: they have no direction. Regularity theorists may just stipulate that the cause is the earlier of the two events. But if they do, then they would just be asserting the temporal asymmetry connotation of causation without explaining it. This is particularly unattractive if, like many theories of time, you want to explain time's direction in terms of the direction of causation: it is circular to give the direction of time in terms of the direction of causation if you simply define causes to be earlier than effects.

Lewis (1979a) has a well-worked out theory for how the counterfactual theory can account for the direction of causation, and thus of time. So let's discuss this. As we saw briefly above (§I(b)), Lewis (1973a) analyses causation in terms of causal dependence, and then analyses causal dependence in terms of counterfactual dependence. He then gives the truth conditions for counterfactual statements using the framework of possible worlds and a notion of comparative similarity: 'C$\square\rightarrow$E' is true if in the closest world (or worlds) in which C is true, E is also true. Before we continue, then, we need to discuss the notion of comparative similarity.

(a) Similarity

Lewis expounds the notion of similarity by appealing to our intuitions about when counterfactuals should come out true. Call the actual world $W_@$. Lewis says that we intuitively take the closest world to $W_@$ to be W_1, where the past is identical to that of $W_@$ up until a very short time before the antecedent event c at time t. The antecedent event then occurs and W_1 then continues to evolve according to the laws of that world. To take a concrete example, consider:

(4.7) If Nixon had pressed the button, there would have been a nuclear holocaust

Assume that in $W_@$ Nixon does not press the button at t, but in W_1 he does. For the sake of argument, Lewis assumes that *determinism* is true: the present state of the world plus the laws of nature are enough to determine all past and future states of the world. Given this assumption, after time t, W_1 differs from $W_@$ in matters of particular fact. For example, in W_1 the pressing of the button follows the laws of nature to result in a nuclear holocaust, whereas in $W_@$ there is no such holocaust. Lewis says that when $W_@$ and W_1 diverge, i.e. just before t, a little *miracle* takes place in W_1. By 'miracle' he does not mean a breach in the laws of nature of W_1, since they are deterministic, but rather a violation of the laws of nature of $W_@$ in W_1. So the miracle at W_1 is relative to $W_@$. Since it is W_1 that is the closest to $W_@$, it is this world that determines the truth-value of the counterfactual (4.7).

And since in W_1 the consequent as well as the antecedent is true, (4.7) is true.

Lewis then argues that it takes much more of a miracle for two worlds to *converge* than it does for them to *diverge*. Divergence requires only a small, localized miracle, whereas convergence would need widespread violations of the laws of nature—a big miracle. Having identified these intuitions, Lewis then ranks the features of similarity between worlds in order of importance as follows:

(i) we should avoid big widespread miracles;
(ii) we should maximize spatio-temporal region of perfect match of particular fact;
(iii) we should avoid small miracles,
(iv) we should not bother too much to secure approximate similarity of particular fact.

This ranking, then, determines which world, or set of worlds, is most similar to $W_@$. And with this in place we are in a better position to understand Lewis's account of the direction of causation.

(b) Direction

According to Lewis, the earlier–later orientation of causation is explained by the *asymmetry of counterfactual dependence*, i.e., the future depends counterfactually on the past, but not the other way round. It is clear, however, that this just shifts the burden of explanation, since we now need to know why it is that counterfactual dependence is asymmetric in the way that it is. After all, counterfactuals seem to be symmetric. For instance, we could hold true:

(4.8) If the match hadn't been struck, then there wouldn't have been a fire.

As well as

(4.9) If there were a fire, then there would have been a striking of a match.

Yet, only the match was the cause of the fire; the fire was not the cause of the striking. Intuitively, we'd see (4.9) as stating that the fire is *evidence* for a match being struck, but not as its *cause*.

Lewis notes that there *are* certain situations in which we *may* be inclined to accept a 'back-tracking' counterfactual, and explains this in terms of vagueness: counterfactuals are vague, and different ways of resolving the vagueness are appropriate in different circumstances (1979a: 34). Usually we resolve the vagueness according to the 'standard resolution', which takes counterfactual dependence to be asymmetric, and we judge comparative similarity in the way described above. Under this standard resolution, back-tracking counterfactuals are false. However, some special contexts allow other resolutions, ones where back-tracking may be permitted. When the need for this special resolution comes to an end, however, we switch back to the standard resolution. But what justifies us in adopting the 'standard' treatment of counterfactuals?

Lewis argues that the direction of counterfactual dependence is fixed by a feature of the physical world, namely the *asymmetry of overdetermination* (1979a: 49). Any particular fact in the world is predetermined throughout the past and postdetermined throughout the future. For a fact to be determined there must exist a minimal set of conditions that is jointly sufficient for the existence of the fact, given the laws of nature. (Members of the set may include causes of the fact and traces of it.) Lewis calls this set of conditions a *determinant*. So for a fact to be *pre*determined, it must have a determinant prior to the fact obtaining, and for it to be *post*determined, it must have a determinant after the fact has obtained.

To generalize, at any time, a particular fact has at least one determinant. If some fact has more than one determinant, we can say that it is *overdetermined*. The asymmetry of overdetermination is then found in the fact that there is considerably more overdetermination with respect to the past than there is with respect to the future. To support this claim, Lewis notes that we have only a few examples of overdetermination of later affairs by earlier ones—hearts being simultaneously pierced by two bullets and the like. Therefore, we can expect much more overdetermination of past events than of future ones (1979a: 49–51).

It is this asymmetry of overdetermination that explains the asymmetry discussed above between divergence and convergence due to miracles. What a miracle does is break the link between a determinant and the fact it determines. Now, to *diverge*, only one link needs to be broken between a determinant and fact, since after that if the world evolves according to the laws of nature it will continue to diverge. To *converge*, however, many links need to be broken. For suppose that Nixon had pressed the button. To converge back to $W_@$ after t, there is a multitude of links that have to be broken, e.g., between the conditions that determine that a holocaust will occur and the holocaust occurring, and between the conditions that determine that Nixon's fingerprints are on the button and his fingerprints actually being there, and so on. And this is explained by the fact that the more overdetermination there is, the more links need breaking. Thus the direction of counterfactual dependence, which anchors the direction of causation, is explained by the asymmetry of overdetermination.

But what about the asymmetry of overdetermination itself? Lewis says this is explained by contingent, *de facto* features of our world (1979a: 50). Since his account ultimately rests on these *de facto* features of the world, I'll discuss the difficulties with this and set aside any other objections that might be made to his theory.

Price (1996: 147–50) argues that the asymmetry of overdetermination that Lewis's account relies on does not exist, at least not at the microphysical level—i.e., the level where we talk in terms of microscopic elements, such as fundamental particles. He picks on Lewis's (1979a: 50) use of an asymmetry noted by Popper: there are processes of radiation in which a spherical wave expands outward from a point source to infinity, and yet the reverse process where the wave contracts towards a point never occurs, even though it would obey the laws of nature equally well. We can illustrate this by thinking of the former as like the waves that go outward when something is dropped into a pool of water—this type of process is called a 'source'—and the latter as like when the plug is pulled in a pool of water and the waves go inward—this type of process is called a 'sink'. Lewis says that a process of either sort exhibits overdetermination in one direction, and in the ones that in fact occur, the overdetermination is towards the past. From this special case, Lewis suggests we generalize.

Price's objection is based on the observation that, at the micro level, there is no asymmetry of radiation. The asymmetry only arises because 'the universe contains big, coherent sources of radiation, but no corresponding big sinks' (1996: 148). So, when we get to the macro level, it appears that there is a genuine asymmetry in the processes of radiation itself. Therefore, Lewis's account cannot be correct since it relies upon a non-existent physical feature of the world.

Now, assuming this physical observation is correct, what are the implications? At first glance it seems that if the asymmetry of overdetermination (of which the asymmetry of radiation is a special case) doesn't exist, then it can't explain the asymmetry of causation. And, if this is so, Lewis's account cannot be correct. However, this diagnosis is too quick. For we mustn't overlook the fact that it has been conceded by all sides that at the macro level there *is* an asymmetry of overdetermination. We can thus acknowledge Price's point but say that, at the macroscopic level, there is an asymmetry, even though when we get down to the microscopic level it disappears. In accounting for the direction of time, we are accounting for how the world appears to *us*. And we are macroscopic creatures. Thus, it matters little that what grounds the earlier–later direction of causation does not hold all the way down to the micro level. Note that here we need not say that there is no causation at the micro level, for there might well be counterfactual dependence there. For what is required for causation is the counterfactual dependence *itself* and not that counterfactual dependence has a *direction*. Thus, it is not so much that 'there is no right answer to the question as to which of a pair of events is the cause and which is the effect' (Price (1996: 151)), but rather that since counterfactual dependence is symmetric, so is causation: C is a cause of E, since E depends counterfactually on C, and since C counterfactually depends on E, E is also a cause of C. This is not a contradiction unless one assumes that causation is asymmetric, which we cannot do here. However, it does leave us with a causal loop, which some have thought impossible. But, as we shall see below (§IV), there is no good reason for thinking this on the tenseless view.

An initial reaction to the idea that causation at the micro level is symmetric will probably be that it is very strange; so any view that countenances it may appear implausible. But further reflection shows that it isn't. Consider the intuitions that we have about causation that make the existence of causal loops look implausible, that ground Lewis's contention that causation has something to do with non-back-tracking counterfactuals, and that provide the basis for thinking that causation has only one direction. These intuitions are all driven by *macro* phenomena. At the macro level, Lewis's counterfactual account delivers all the results that match our intuitions. At the micro level, the account still works; it is just that it delivers some results that we didn't expect. But no wonder: our intuitive conception of future-orientated causation is guided by everyday occurrences at the macro level, and so long as at the macro level it is as a matter of fact that there is an asymmetry (regardless of how we explain this given the symmetry at the micro level), then this is enough to ground our intuitions. Thus we can dismiss considerations based on its appearing intuitively implausible since here we are gauging plausibility according to our intuitions that apply at the macro level. So Lewis's contention that causation has to do with counterfactuals that are true under the standard resolution of vagueness, i.e., ones that are not back-tracking, holds because he is appealing to our intuitive notion of causation, where the resolution is 'standard' since it accounts for our standard experience, which is macroscopic. We need not conclude, then, that the direction of causation has to be imposed on the world by our minds (cf. Price (1996: 162–94)). It does have a factual basis at the macro level. This is not to say that backwards causation is impossible, but just that our world is such that it so happens that there is an asymmetry of overdetermination. This account seems to be quite good then in terms of what it is trying to achieve. The standard reservations about *defining* time's direction in terms of physical processes, however, would still remain: would we want to say that causation or time went backwards as soon as these physical processes reversed? And we are also still left wondering what the explanation is for why backwards causation does not actually occur.

III The direction of time and causation: the means—end connotation of causation

Mellor (1995: 60) holds that there are a number of connotations of causation which should be captured by any adequate account of causation, such as that causes and effects are *evidence* for each other, that causes *explain* their effects, and that causes *precede* their effects. By far the most important, however, is the *means–end* connotation: causes are *means* to bringing about their effects. Mellor (1995: ch. 7) then goes on to explain what a means is in non-causal, decision-theoretic terms, thereby giving an analysis of causation. The upshot is that any cause C of any effect E is a means to E iff in the circumstances it raises the chance of E, i.e., iff $ch_C(E) > ch_{\sim C}(E)$ (as explained in §I(c) above).

Nice as this analysis is, however, analysing causation in decision-theoretic terms fails to guarantee that the means always precedes the end, i.e., that causes always precede their effects. This creates a difficulty for giving the direction of time in terms of the direction of causation, as Mellor wants to do. To illustrate this difficulty, I shall use the fun and famous decision-theoretic problem known as 'Newcomb's problem'. It shows that the means to a given end can occur later than the end's occurring. (It also satisfies the evidential and explanatory connotations.) In light of this, Mellor must find a way to rule out these cases. He argues that backwards causation creates a causal loop, and since causal loops are impossible, so are these cases. I shall go on to reject this argument (§IV). First, however, we need to acquaint ourselves with Newcomb's problem and what it is usually taken to illustrate.

(a) Newcomb's problem and backwards causation

I shall start by defending so-called 'non-causal decision theory' against 'causal decision theory' by arguing that if the decision matrices are construed correctly, we shall (1) only need to adopt one principle of decision-making, what is known as the *principle of maximizing expected utility*, and no conflict between this and what is known as the *principle of dominance* arises; and (2) avoid making the wrong decisions in the so-called 'down-to-earth Newcomb situations'. This solution will show that the assumption that causation in this case runs from earlier to later is unwarranted.

The standard exposition of Newcomb's problem, **Problem 1**, is as follows.

Problem 1: There are two boxes: b_1 contains £1,000 and b_2 contains either £0 or £1,000,000 (£M)—we don't know which. A predictor, Π, gives us the following choice:

A_1: take b_2 only,

or

A_2: take both boxes.

We are told: if Π predicted at t_0 that we shall choose b_2 at t_1, then

Π_1 : Π has placed £M in b_2,

and if Π predicted at t_0 that we shall choose both boxes at t_1, then

Π_2 : Π has left b_2 empty,

where t_0 is before t_1. This is represented in the *utility* matrix given in fig. 4.1.[3] A_1 and A_2 are 'acts'; Π_1 and Π_2 'states', and the results of doing certain acts in certain states are 'outcomes'.

Further, whenever choosers have taken both boxes, b_2 has been empty; and, whenever choosers have taken only b_2, it has contained £M. This is represented in the *probability* matrix given in Fig. 4.2. Now consider this variation:

Problem 2: As **Problem 1**, except Π at t_0 places £1,000 in b_1; we then perform either A_1 or A_2 at t_1, and *then* Π at t_2 places either

	Π_1	Π_2
A_1	£M	£0
A_2	£M + £1,000	£1,000

FIG. 4.1. Utility matrix

	Π_1	Π_2
A_1	1	0
A_2	0	1

FIG. 4.2. Probability matrix

---

[3] For simplicity, I assume that money can represent utility, and is approximately linear.

£M or £0 in b_2. Matrices 1 and 2 equally represent **Problem 2**; the *only* difference between **Problems 1** and **2** is that Π plays before us in **Problem 1**, but we play before Π in **Problem 2**.

Problem 1 is used mainly (e.g., Nozick (1969)) to show how two intuitive principles of decision-making can conflict. The first is the *principle of dominance*:

PDOM: Perform the dominant act (if there is one).

An act dominates another if it is at least as good under all outcomes and better under some.

PDOM recommends A_2 because when we choose, b_2 already either does or does not contain £M. If $Π_1$ obtains then we are better off doing A_2 than doing A_1. If $Π_2$ obtains then we are better off doing A_2 than doing A_1. Hence, whichever state obtains we are better off doing A_2.

However, this conflicts with the *principle of maximizing expected utility*:

PMEU: If $ExpU(A_m) > ExpU(A_n)$, then perform A_m rather than A_n, where $ExpU(A)$ is the expected utility of act A.

The expected utility of an act A is calculated by multiplying the respective cells of the utility and probability matrices, and summing the outcomes of the given act A, as in Fig. 4.3. Since, $ExpU(A_1) = $ £M $> ExpU(A_2) = $ £1,000, PMEU recommends A_1.

There is, then, conflict between PMEU, which recommends A1, and PDOM, which recommends A_2. My solution is based on this consideration: since **Problem 1** is exactly like **Problem 2** in respect of the probability and utility matrices, we should be able to generate a similar conflict in **Problem 2**. If such a conflict cannot be generated in **Problem 2**, then the root of the conflict must lie in the difference between the two problems. Since the *only* difference between the two

	$Π_1$	$Π_2$
A_1	£M	£0
A_2	£0	£1,000

FIG. 4.3. Expected utility matrix

problems lies in the order of play, this is where the conflict can be resolved.

It can be shown that conflicting recommendations do *not* emerge in **Problem 2**. In **Problem 2**, PDOM is universally acknowledged as bad advice, for performing the dominant act, A_2, is likely to bring about state Π_2, and consequently we miss the opportunity to become millionaires. Performing A_1, however, is likely to bring about Π_1, in which case we would be millionaires. In other words, choosing the one box is a *means* to the end of becoming a millionaire. Therefore, we should perform A_1, i.e., follow PMEU.

Generalizing: PDOM should only be followed when which state obtains is independent of which act is performed. Independence is represented in the probability matrix in Fig. 4.4. Comparing with Fig. 4.2, we can see that there is dependence in both **Problems 1** and **2**. Indeed, that dependence in **Problem 2** is *causal* is a natural assumption to make in the set-up described. In **Problem 2**, then, we should follow PMEU, for there is no good argument for PDOM here, i.e., there is no conflict.

Furthermore, in the case where there *is* independence, PDOM (when it can be applied) agrees with the advice given by PMEU, as illustrated in Fig. 4.5.

Since $1 \geq p \geq 0$, $\text{ExpU}(A_2) = £Mp + £1,000 > \text{ExpU}(A_1) = £Mp$. PDOM now agrees with PMEU: perform A_2.

	Π_1	Π_2
A_1	p	1-p
A_2	p	1-p

FIG. 4.4. Independence

	Π_1	Π_2
A_1	$£Mp$	$£0$
A_2	$(£M + £1,000)p$	$£1,000(1-p)$

FIG. 4.5. PDOM agrees with PMEU

Therefore, in **Problem 1** there is a more important underlying issue than a conflict between PMEU and PDOM. For when there is dependence PDOM is bad advice and PMEU should be followed; when there is independence, PDOM is good advice, but this is because it agrees with PMEU. It seems, then, that in either case we should follow PMEU, *and yet it remains controversial whether we should follow PMEU in* **Problem 1**.

The crucial issue concerns *dependence*. In **Problem 1**, the probabilistic dependence between acts and states is the same as in **Problem 2**. However, in this case it is controversial whether PDOM is invalid, since believing that which state obtains *causally* depends on which act is performed is not a natural assumption to make. Simply claiming that PDOM is bad advice where states are probabilistically dependent on acts assumes that *probabilistic* dependence is equivalent to *causal* dependence. These, however, are not always equivalent (see §b(ii) below). The present point is that the *only* difference between **Problems 1** and **2** is the order of play, and if there is causal dependence in **Problem 2**, then there is causal dependence in **Problem 1**, i.e., my later act brings about the earlier state. This resolves the conflict between arguments for A_1 and arguments for A_2: we should follow PMEU and perform A_1.

Before defending this claim further it is necessary to make explicit how 'probability' is to be interpreted, and how causation is to be understood, for Newcomb's Problem arises from not saying how the probability matrix is to be construed, which, in turn, has ramifications for causation. (This is why PMEU was not fully specified earlier as either the principle of maximizing *subjective* expected utility, which involves multiplying probabilities construed as credences or *objective* expected utility, which involves multiplying probabilities construed as objective probabilities. But, of course, we shall now see that this matters.)

Objective interpretations of probability, such as *frequency* and *chance*, have their relative merits. I do not need to get into this debate: either interpretation will suffice for my needs.[4] For whatever the truthmaker

---

[4] Presentism, however, will have a certain amount of trouble with aspects of the frequency interpretation in much the same way that they do with the regularity account of

of probability statements—be it the frequency of similar cases in the total population, or an irreducible single-case property, chance—there is an intimate connection between these interpretations and causation, which may be restated either way. Thus we may say that causes must raise the chances of their effects, even if we cash out chance in terms of frequency. The point is that, whether frequencies are the probabilities we need or merely evidence for them (chances), if we construe Fig 4.2 in these terms, **Problems 1** and **2** support the causal thesis, i.e., that in both problems my acts bring about certain states, because the acts raise the chances of the effects.

The *credence* interpretation of probability is a measure of my degree of belief that p is true and is in this sense subjective. Nevertheless, it is generally agreed that, where the relevant frequencies or chances are known, they should influence our credences (see Lewis's (1980) Principal Principle).

(b) Decision-theory in light of Newcomb's problem

Newcomb's problem is meant to illustrate by those who set it up that PMEU is not sufficient in some cases (called 'Newcomb situations', e.g., Eells (1982: 92)) to recommend the correct act. For it is claimed by some that PMEU is insensitive to causal dependence, and therefore decision theories based on it (non-causal decision theories, **NCDT**) are inadequate and need supplementing. On the assumption that the states are causally independent of the acts in Newcomb's problem, A_2 is the correct choice, whereas PMEU by recommending A_1, supposedly shows its insensitivity to causality, which is why it gives the wrong recommendation.

Causal decision theory, **CDT**, (e.g., Gibbard and Harper (1978); Skyrms (1980); Lewis (1981)) invokes all the concepts of **NCDT**, but adds causal concepts. Some supporters of **NCDT**, (e.g., Eells (1982)) argue that sufficient constraints are, or can be, built into their theory to make it recommend the 'correct' choice in Newcomb's problem, namely A_2. In both cases, the assumption that A_2 *is* the choice that the

---

causation in §I(a). For it is indeterminate what happens in the future and so indeterminate what any actual frequency is. But there are good reasons for preferring the chance view, anyway (see e.g., Mellor (2005b)).

correct decision theory must recommend is based on the assumption that causation must run from earlier to later.

In saying that we should perform A_1, I am not necessarily disagreeing with **CDT** or these versions of **NCDT**: I agree that our decisions need to be sensitive to causality. Disagreement comes with the assumption that in Newcomb's problem causation runs from earlier to later. In other words, I *could* adopt a causal decision theory without ruling out backwards causation. This would enable the theory to recommend A_1 in Newcomb's problem, while still ruling out the wrong decision in down-to-earth Newcomb situations where there is no backwards causation (see §b(ii) below). Alternatively, I could argue that PMEU *is* sensitive to causality, and that there *is* causal dependence between acts and states in Newcomb's problem and therefore **NCDT** is adequate. I take the latter view, but shall first discuss why I reject the **CDT**s that have been proposed.

(i) The Skyrms–Lewis approach The Skyrms–Lewis approach (Skyrms (1980: 133); Lewis (1981: 313)) is to specify which states are outside the influence of our actions and then restricting PMEU by limiting its applications to states that may be influenced by our actions. By assuming that earlier states are not influenced by later actions, this allows it to give the right answers in **Problem 2** (and down-to-earth Newcomb situations), while giving the 'correct' recommendation of A_2 in **Problem 1**.

However, the question of which states are 'outside the influence of' acts is the very question at issue, and the Skyrms–Lewis approach begs it by assuming that there is no backwards causation in **Problem 1**. For if there is backwards causal influence in Newcomb's problem, we have an argument for A_1 anyway, and the Skyrms–Lewis restriction on PMEU becomes redundant.

(ii) The Gibbard and Harper approach Gibbard and Harper (1978: 180) think Newcomb's problem illustrates a conflict between two kinds of expected utility maximization: **V**-maximization and **U**-maximization.

> **V**(A) is the expected utility of A calculated from conditional credences, and is given by the formula: $\mathbf{V}(A) = \sum_j \mathrm{Cr}(O_j/A) u O_j$, where u is the utility of the outcomes $O_1, \ldots O_m$, of act A.

U(A) is the expected utility of A calculated from credences in counterfactuals, and is given by the formula: $U(A) = \sum_j Cr(A \square \rightarrow O_j)\, uO_j$.

Gibbard and Harper take a conditional credence like $Cr(O_j/A)$ to be an *epistemic* probability measuring A as *evidence* for O_j, rather than as a way of bringing O_j about. To illustrate, consider the down-to-earth Newcomb situation of an executive E being tested for promotion P on day 1, the result to be announced on day 3 (1978: 165). On day 2, E learns that the criterion tested for on day 1 is ruthlessness, a quality he can exercise on day 2 by sacking someone, S. The conditional credence $Cr(P/S)$ is higher than $Cr(P/\sim S)$, but all this shows is that S is *evidence* that E will be promoted, not that it is a *way* of getting the promotion; *this* is determined by the result of the earlier test. However, V-maximization recommends the sacking.

On the other hand, Gibbard and Harper take belief in counterfactuals to represent our belief in *causal* dependence between antecedent and consequent. For this reason, they would not attach higher credence to $(S \square \rightarrow P)$ than to $(\sim S \square \rightarrow P)$. And this is why they think decisions should use U-maximization rather than V-maximization: U-maximization recommends leniency because it is sensitive to the belief that the sacking won't help bring about E's promotion.

But why accept this? Our $Cr(S \square \rightarrow P)$ may well be higher than our $Cr(\sim S \square \rightarrow P)$, and, if it is, V-maximization and U-maximization give the same answer. As Eells notes:

> Conditional probabilities 'backtrack', but nonbacktracking counterfactuals don't. It is the nonbacktracking interpretation of counterfactual conditionals that makes [U-maximization] sensitive to causal information...to which it appears [V-maximization] is insensitive. (Eells (1982: 98))

Gibbard and Harper don't have an independent reason to rule out back-tracking counterfactuals and banning them on the basis that causes must occur before their effects begs the question.

Gibbard and Harper's theory is, therefore, unsatisfactory. However, they have highlighted where **NCDT** is faulty, namely in using *conditional probabilities* in calculating expected utility, rather than unconditional probabilities. For, if we use unconditional probabilities and require these to be not just epistemic or subjective but real frequencies or chances, we can make PMEU sensitive to causality. For now we can read Fig. 4.2 as saying what the *chances* (or frequencies) of the states are, as opposed to the mere epistemic probabilities, if we do A_1 or A_2. Anyone who denies backwards causation will then deny the truth of Fig. 4.2, since they will deny that the chances of Π_1 and Π_2 depend on my choice of action. Thus, for example, nobody will believe Fig. 4.6 with epistemic probabilities replaced by chances. Conversely, to accept Fig. 4.2 is to accept backwards causation. This leads to the following criticism. I claim that a world without backwards causation will be a world without any Newcomb games to cause trouble. It is, therefore, disingenuous of those who do not believe in backwards causation to set up Newcomb's problem to show the need for **CDT**. The whole conflict is brought about, then, by setting up a case of backwards causation and then assuming that there is none! That this is the case is shown when dropping such an assumption, for it resolves the conflict in **Problem 1** and never arises in **Problem 2**.

So, causal decision theory either begs the question by assuming that causes always precede their effects, or would give the A_1 recommendation if it allowed for backwards causation, which is, I argue, the correct choice. Non-causal decision theory is preferable because if backwards causation *is* possible, non-causal decision theory, if construed correctly, will give the correct answers, since it does not rule out backwards causation a priori, as **CDT** does. And if there is *no* backwards causation, then non-causal decision theory has nothing to fear, for, if formulated correctly, problematic cases would not even arise. **CDT** is, therefore, unnecessary.

The only credible explanation of the problematic Newcomb problem, then, is that it involves backwards causation, where causation is defined by chance-raising as outlined above. The reason this situation seems problematic is simply that we assume, as Nozick *et al.* do, that there *is* no backwards causation. But then the right conclusion to be

	Promoted	Not Promoted
Sack W	1	0
Leniency towards W	0	1

FIG. 4.6. Implausible case when interpreted with chances

drawn is not that we need **CDT**, but simply that these problematic cases will not occur. As, indeed, they do not—a fact of which our combination of PMEU and the lack of backwards causation provides not only the simplest but the only explanation.

But why backwards causation does not occur, though, evidently *cannot* be explained by analysing causation decision-theoretically. Choosing the one box is a means to winning a million; it explains why we are a millionaire, if we are, and having a million is evidence that we chose only one box as much as choosing the one box is evidence that we are millionaires. Mellor must find some independent way, then, to rule out such cases.

IV Mellor's argument against causal loops

That causes raise the chances of their effects is not essential to Mellor's (1998: 132–5) argument against the possibility of causal loops. What is central is his view that the chances of an effect E obtaining are independent properties of facts before the effect E obtains. We have already seen this in the skydiving case above (§I(c)). Let us remind ourselves with the different example of a coin toss. The chance of an unbiased coin landing heads at the point at which we toss it is equal to 1/2. Thus chances are properties of facts before the fact we are interested in. Further, these chances exist *independently* of whether or not the coin actually does land heads: if it lands tails, then the chance of it landing heads at the time it was tossed is still equal to 1/2.

Using this, Mellor sets up an example. Suppose the following. We have a population of 20 million people, half of whom smoke, the other half of whom do not. The chances of getting cancer if you smoke = p = 0.6. The chances of getting cancer if you do not smoke = p' = 0.2. So the number of people in this population who will get cancer, N(cancer), will be approximately 8 million, and the number who will not get cancer, N(not cancer), will be approximately 12 million.

Now, we have established that the chances of smoking if you get cancer (q) and the chances of smoking if you do not get cancer (q') are independent of chances of getting cancer. So p, p', q and q' can take any values between 0 and 1. But suppose in that case that we choose q = 0.5 and q′ = 0.25. Then, approximately half of those who have cancer and approximately a quarter of those who do not have cancer will be smokers, i.e., approximately 7 million, leaving approximately 13 million of our 20 million people non-smokers. But this contradicts our original starting figure of there being 10 million smokers and 10 million non-smokers. Thus, the only assumption to reject, according to Mellor, is that causal loops are impossible.

This argument, however, relies on equivocation. For it is misleading just to assert that the chances involved are all independent of one another: in one sense, p, p′, q and q′ *can* take any values, but in another sense, they *cannot*. They can in the sense that they could have been otherwise: p could have been equal to 0.75 and q equal to 0.4. But once it is fixed by certain other facts that, say, there *are* a certain amount of smokers, then there *are* constraints on what values p, p′, q and q′ can take.

We can see this in the case of time travel. Is it possible to go back and kill your grandfather? You can in the sense that you have the gun ready, he's in front of you, and there's nothing else stopping you. But you can't in the sense that, if your grandfather was not killed at that time, then there is nothing you can do to kill him (see Lewis (1976)). All that independence requires is that we could go back in time or not go back in time, and the grandfather could be killed or not be killed. But once we've fixed whether he was killed, then we are constrained in what other features of the situation we can have. But this is not good enough to rule out backwards causation any more than the fact that it not being possible to shoot your grandfather in the future, when you didn't actually shoot him—but you *could* have; you had the gun ready!—is enough to rule out forwards causation. This is precisely the same answer that we should give to Mellor's generalization of this to the probabilistic case. In one sense, p, p′, q and q′ *can* take any values, but in another sense, they *cannot*. Once the equivocation is resolved, Mellor's argument loses its force.

The way to make Mellor's scenario consistent is to set q = q′ = 0.5—after all, that's what we'd expect, given that we already know that half of the 20 million are smokers and the other half not. And consistency, here, is enough to show that causal loops are possible. It follows that Mellor has not given any explanation for why backwards causation does not occur (because he has not shown what he set out to show, namely that it *cannot* occur), and so cannot define time's direction in terms of the direction of causation. Nevertheless, it is still possible to say that the asymmetries that we actually see are explained by the direction that causation just *actually* happens to have, namely from earlier to later, even if causation does not necessarily have this direction. But no explanation for this has been successful, such as that it is impossible for it not to be like this; it just has to be taken to be a brute fact.

Given this discussion, I endorse the possibility of time travel for such tenseless worlds. It is worth mentioning, however, that it is common to think that time travel is available only in such worlds, and is ruled out automatically by presentism simply because there is no past time to travel back to. I think this is mistaken. What time travel amounts to, according to Lewis (1976), is the same person setting off on a journey where there is a discrepancy between the time it takes in terms of the person's 'personal' time and the time it takes in 'external' time, where, in order for it to be the same person travelling, there has to be some appropriate form of connectedness between the person who departs and the person who arrives. Given this, we can tell the following time-travel story. It is presently 1976. Horace walks out of a time machine complete with memories of his recent stepping into a time machine in 2076, a journey which was bought for him for a treat for his thirtieth birthday. It seems to Horace that his journey only took five minutes. Time moves on. In 2046, Horace is born. And so on.[5]

This story was given in terms entirely consistent with the presentist ontology: the existence or non-existence of the past is neither here nor there for establishing whether time travel is possible. This, however, is not to say that time travel *is* possible according to my version of presentism. For time travel requires that the person who arrives is the same as the person who departs. But the very notion of being the same person requires there to be an appropriate connectedness between the two people. But this, in turn, relies on there being a causal connection between them: the memories and everything

[5] Keller and Nelson (2001) have also endorsed this story.

else that constitutes the psychological make-up of Horace in 1976 were caused by events that occur in 2076. The very notion of them being the same person, then, relies on the possibility of backwards causation. That is, whether backwards time travel is possible according to presentism has nothing to do with the non-existence of the past, but rests wholly on the possibility of backwards causation. But backwards causation is incompatible with presentism.

V Presentism and backwards causation

This whole issue arises from tenseless theorists trying to account for the direction of time in terms of causation. But there is an alternative justification for using Lewis's method of keeping the past fixed, and Mellor's assumption that the chances of E obtaining are properties of facts located earlier than E, namely *the very fact that the past is determinately fixed and the future is not*. This is precisely what a branching future and a linear past gives you, and precisely the version of presentism I have been advocating. This would also give us an explanation for why backwards causation doesn't actually occur, namely because it *can't* occur, on this view. This is not, as some might think, because the future doesn't *exist*: as I've shown, forwards causation is perfectly possible for the presentist, even though the past does not exist; so the non-existence of the future is no bar to backwards causation occurring. (Thus the popular view that only the tenseless theory allows for backwards causation is false. For if time were linear for the presentist, then there *would* be a determinate fact about what will happen, showing that the future qua *non-existent* is not the crucial issue in establishing whether backwards causation is possible any more than the non-existence of the past is for forwards causation.) Rather, the correct reason for rejecting the possibility of backwards causation is due to the *indeterminateness* of the future: if it is indeterminate which facts will obtain, then *nothing* can be said to be the cause of the previous fact's obtaining.

This should not be confused with indetermin*ism*. Indeterministic causation is perfectly comprehensible. For what we have with indeterministic causation is *some* determinate contingent fact F obtaining that *actually* brought about another determinate contingent fact G, even though G might not have obtained even though F did. With indeterminateness, however, there is *no* determinate fact F, although there is a determinate fact G. And under these circumstances, it is hard to see how F could be said to have brought about G.

We should not even be tempted to suppose that F may well have caused G, if F does end up obtaining. Neither should the converse of this claim be confused with a bad argument which is commonly employed against the possibility of backwards causation: we should not say that F was not the cause just because F might not have come about, or that we could have done something to stop F coming about, even though we actually didn't. For think of the analogous situation in the context of the tenseless theory: facts F and G obtain, and F is located later than G. We cannot argue that we can rule out F being the cause of G just because after G obtains, but before F obtains, we could have done something to prevent F (although we actually didn't, since F obtains), without our thereby preventing G. For had F been prevented, it may be that G would not have occurred—we just don't know; it seems quite possible to me, and would be the case if backwards causation were in place. And if F didn't obtain, maybe something else brought about G, but F would have done had it not been prevented. Note the symmetry between forwards causation and backwards causation here, and note the fact that in the case of forwards causation we would naturally object to such a 'bilking' argument that it does not show much about whether F caused G. At best, the bilking argument is inconclusive. Yet what does show conclusively that F was not the cause of G (on my version of presentism) is the fact that *when* G became determinate, F was not. It is nothing to do with whether F might or might not eventually obtain.

Thus, as presentists, we say that the process of temporal becoming creates more and more determinate truths as time moves on. So *time* gives time its direction, and this in turn gives causation its. So, ultimately, time's flow does explain our experience of time's flow, since it does this by giving causation its direction, through which we are able to experience the world. As well as its being more ontologically parsimonious, then, presentism also has the explanatory advantage on why backwards causation does not occur.

PART II
Presentism and Relativity

Now that we have successfully negotiated the purely philosophical obstacles in presentism's way, it is time to tackle another issue which is commonly taken to be the other great hurdle for any tensed theory of time: modern physics.

Tensed theorists in general have been accused by many of not being able to reconcile their views with the special theory of relativity.[1] It is about time, then, that they struck back. The mistakes of the past have been due to presentists, and tense theorists in general, making the wrong dialectical moves, for this whole debate rests on the participants from both sides not being able to see the wood for the trees. As we shall see in the next couple of chapters, the initial set-up of the debate is biased towards the tenseless theory, and so it is unsurprising that the presentists end up licking their wounds rather than their tenseless opposition. It is on this, then, that presentism needs to focus its attention.

Although authors such as Gödel (1949b) had already noted the tension between special relativity and tensed theories of time, Putnam's (1967) thesis initiated the current dialogue concerning the status of the present in the context of special relativity. Stein's (1968), on the other hand, is taken by most to be the antithesis to Putnam's arguments, for Putnam says tense is not compatible with special relativity, whereas Stein says it is. Dividing the debate into these two camps is how much of the dispute over tense in special relativity has been carried out since. I shall show, however, that the party lines should be drawn in a different place. For Stein (and his cohort) misunderstands the dialectical situation that Putnam is engaged in with tense theorists: Stein, in fact, falls on the same side of the debate with Putnam. Once this and other dialectical situations that have arisen in this whole debate are spelled out, we shall see that a plausible way of reconciling the traditional tensed theories of time with special relativity becomes viable.

Special relativity, however, is not the whole story. For general relativity is also of some relevance to whether presentism is viable.

---

[1] Among those that think STR refutes presentism are Putnam (1967); Weingard (1972); Mellor (1974); Maxwell (1985); Shimony (1993); Callender (2000); Savitt (2000); and Saunders (2002).

Whether, and to what extent, this is true will be discussed in the last two chapters.

I shall begin, however, by presenting as much physics as is required for understanding the philosophical issues surrounding special relativity and presentism. I hope to keep those with no physics background on board by presupposing very little prior knowledge and by making this as much as possible a self-contained book. Those with more knowledge of physics can skip this material. Any other relevant physics will be discussed as and when the need arises.

5

Physics for philosophers

I Basic notions

The special theory of relativity originated in a 1905 paper by Einstein. It is now familiar not only to physicists and many philosophers but to much of the non-academic public. But since it is not familiar to all, it is first necessary to introduce some of the fundamental notions before we even consider its philosophical significance. Let us start with defining our terms.

Newton's first law of motion (aka the law of inertia) states that neither the direction of motion nor the speed of an object changes unless it is acted on by an unbalanced force. In other words, the natural state of an object is to move in straight lines; so we should not think of objects needing something to *move* them (as in the old Aristotelian physics), but rather should think of objects needing something to *stop* them from continuing on this course (such as frictional forces).

We specify the location of an event using a coordinate system. The most familiar kind are Cartesian coordinate systems, which require a reference point, three axes (x_1, x_2, x_3) (in three-dimensional space) such that each point can be assigned a unique triple of coordinates (the easiest way of guaranteeing this being to have them at right-angles to each other), and some way of defining a unit of length (e.g., metre) so that the axes are equally calibrated. (Alternatively, we could use other coordinate systems, such as spherical polar coordinates.) But to characterize fully the location of an event, we need to specify the position of a particle at a given instant of time t. An event's location, then, is given by four numbers (t, x_1, x_2, x_3). This specification assumes a particular coordinate system and time-scale. It is this combination of coordinate system and time-scale that we call a **frame of reference**.

The line plotting the successive events characterizing the motion of a particle in four dimensions is called the **worldline** of the particle. In practice, we are able to draw diagrams only in three dimensions, one of which must be reserved for plotting time. Thus we can only plot motion occurring in at most two spatial dimensions rather than three. To keep things simple, let us plot the motion of a particle in one dimension of space against the dimension of time. (This will be helpful later for those who are not familiar with Minkowski space–time diagrams.)

A particle which remains stationary over time, then, will have the worldline labelled (a) in Fig. 5.1. The **velocity** of a particle is its speed together with its direction. Since velocity is the change in position of a particle over time, a particle moving in the positive x-direction is represented by worldline (b). **Acceleration**, in turn, is a change in velocity over time, and so is represented by a curved worldline, such as (c).

We can now define the notion of an **inertial frame of reference**, namely, as a frame of reference in which Newton's first law of motion is valid. In other words, we can think of them simply as non-accelerating coordinate systems. Any frame of reference that moves with constant velocity relative to an inertial frame is also an inertial frame.

We could consider the motion in Fig. 5.1 from the point of view of the particle tracing out worldline (b), as in Fig. 5.2. For, according to it, it is stationary and the particle tracing out worldline (a) is moving away. In fact, there is nothing to physically determine which particle is 'really' moving. For instance, we might wake up to find ourselves in a box with opaque walls located in an inertial frame of reference

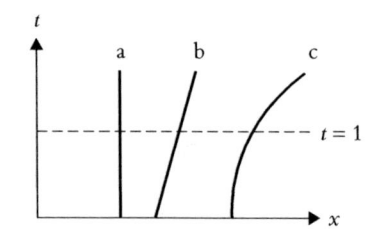

FIG. 5.1. Worldlines of particles in various states of motion where a is at rest

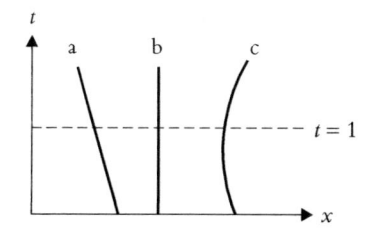

FIG. 5.2. Worldlines of particles in various states of motion where b is at rest

with a small window on one side which allows us to see other boxes passing in a certain direction. In this predicament, we could not tell whether we were stationary with the boxes moving past us with constant velocity, or whether we were moving with constant velocity past the stationary boxes, or whether we were moving with constant velocity but more slowly than the other boxes moving with constant velocity. Certainly none of these situations would feel any different to us. But there is a frame of reference in which each of these is described as being the case: the question over which box is moving is taken to make sense only relative to a frame of reference. Contrast this with the case of being on a motorcycle accelerating away from some impressed girl standing on the pavement. It is obvious that there is an asymmetry in this case: it might look like the girl could be described as accelerating away, but whatever else it is that she feels when she watches me accelerate off into the distance, she doesn't feel any acceleration. In other words, the person on the bike feels an *inertial force* (a force experienced due to acceleration). The bike, then, is *really* accelerating; the girl is not. Thus accelerations are not relative; they are absolute.

But just because there is no way of physically discerning whether there is a frame of reference which is absolutely at rest, which then determines whether other frames are absolutely moving and by how much, this is not to say that there is no such frame. Newton himself thought that there was such an absolute rest frame, in part because of the fact that it is possible to tell whether someone is accelerating, that is, that there is a fact of the matter who is accelerating. For since acceleration is absolute and is a change in velocity, and velocity is a change in position, it seems to follow that there must be a fact of the matter over whether someone is travelling with a certain velocity, and a fact of the matter which locations they have occupied.

But considerations of inertial effects are not enough to establish that there is such an absolute frame, since this can be accounted for in so-called 'neo-Newtonian' or 'Galilean' space–time. For, just as in Newtonian space–time, straight worldlines represent the inertial structure of space–time: straight lines in one inertial frame will remain straight in all other inertial frames, and curved lines (accelerating particles) will remain curved. Indeed, this is precisely what was shown in Fig. 5.2: the physical situation can be described just as well without the assumption that there are absolute velocities or positions. It is an open question, then, whether there is such an absolute frame. But, in any case, an important question to ask at this point is: *if two people observe the same motion from different reference frames, K and K′, what is the relationship between their descriptions?*

According to the pre-relativistic Newtonian world-view (with either the Newtonian or neo-Newtonian space–time), the relationship is given by the Galilean transformations:

Galilean transformations between frames of reference:

$$t' = t$$
$$\mathbf{x}'(t) = \mathbf{x}(t) - \mathbf{u}t$$
$$\mathbf{v}'(t) = \mathbf{v}(t) - \mathbf{u}$$
$$\mathbf{a}'(t) = \mathbf{a}(t)$$

where the first line captures the time transformation, the second line the coordinate transformations, the third line the velocity transformations, the fourth line the acceleration transformations, and where $\mathbf{u}$ is the velocity of the origin of frame of reference K' as measured by frame of reference K.

For ease, let us from now on only consider the coordinate transformations between frames of reference. The relationship between the coordinates assigned to the point P (in Fig. 5.3) in frame K, where $P = (x_1, x_2, x_3)$, and in frame K', where $P = (x'_1, x'_2, x'_3)$ is given by the first two lines of the Galilean transformations. (The x_2- and x'_2-axes have been left off the diagram.) Note here that these transformations assume that the frames K and K' are in **standard**

configuration, i.e., where the origins of frames K and K' coincide at $t = t' = 0$.

Let us plug in some values to the Galilean coordinate transformations to get a feel for them. We assume $t = t'$ and deal with the spatial coordinates. In K, $P = (2, 0, 3)$, and let us suppose that the velocity of K' with respect to K is $\mathbf{u} = (1, 0, 0)$, i.e., it travels in the x_1 direction at the rate of one unit of space per unit of time. Then after, say, 10 units of time, we can see from using the Galilean coordinate transformations that the coordinates of P in terms of reference frame K' will be $P = (2, 0, 3) - 10(1, 0, 0) = (-8, 0, 3)$ (which indeed looks like the correct answer from inspection of Fig. 5.3).

A consequence of these transformation is that the time interval $(t_2 - t_1)$ measured in the frame K will be identical to the same time interval $(t'_2 - t'_1)$ measured in the frame K', since it is assumed that $t_2 = t'_2$ and $t_1 = t'_1$. Most physicists up to 1900 would have expected this, and it confirms Newton's famous statement about the nature of time:

absolute, true, and mathematical time, of itself, and from its own nature, flows equably, without relation to anything external... (Newton, *Principia Mathematica*, Book I, Scholium after Definitions)

Another point to note is that the length of something with end points P and Q is the same in both frames K and K'. Let us suppose that such a line, PQ, is parallel to the x_1 axis, and thus also parallel to the x'_1 axis. Suppose that, in K, P is at point a on the x_1 axis, and Q is at point b on the x_1 axis, when measured at time t, and P is at a' and Q is at b', when

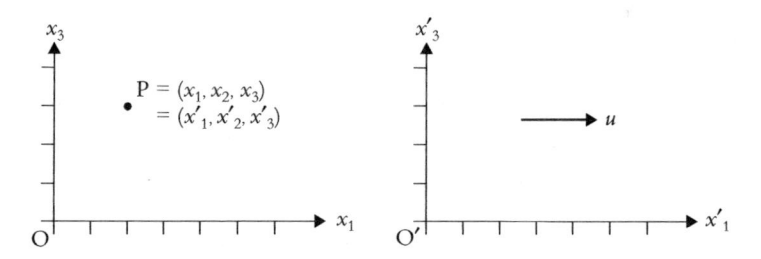

FIG. 5.3. A point P considered from two inertial frames of reference, K and K'

measured at time t'. Since, $t = t'$, then the length of PQ in frame $K = b - a$, and in frame $K' = (b' - a') = (b - ut) - (a - ut) = (b - a)$.

Thus, in either Newtonian or neo-Newtonian space–time, as encapsulated by the Galilean transformations, measurements of length and duration are **invariant** quantities: each frame will agree on the distance and duration between two events.

II Essentials of special relativity

Now that we have these basic notions in mind, we can consider the special theory of relativity (STR). There are two essential elements that comprise STR that I shall refer to as the *core* elements of STR:

i **the Principle of Relativity**: all inertial frameworks are equivalent for the description of all physical phenomena: the same laws hold in all inertial frames;

and

ii **the Law of the Propagation of Light**: light (*in vacuo*) is propagated in straight lines with a constant speed c (approx 300,000,000 ms^{-1}, or, to make it more intuitive, 186,000 miles per second...)

The Principle of Relativity has been in operation since Galileo, but here the 'physical phenomena' is extended to include much more than Galileo ever considered, such as electrodynamics.

The Law of the Propagation of Light originates from a constant that appears in Maxwell's equations (formulated around the 1860s) governing electromagnetic phenomena. This constant gives the speed with which electromagnetic waves propagate. Since light is a form of electromagnetic radiation, it has this constant speed. And since the speed of light is a constant in these laws of nature, it must, by the Principle of Relativity, be a constant in all inertial frames of reference.

One thing novel about Einstein's approach was that he elevated these two assumptions to the status of postulates where previously they had been, at best, conjectures. But, regardless of their status, these two assumptions, although not apparent at first, lead to rather odd consequences. For we ordinarily think in the following way (as formalized in the Galilean transformations above). If we walk past a tree at 3 mph, then relative to us the tree will recede from us at 3 mph. If we ride past a tree at 80 mph, the tree will recede from us at 80 mph. But, according to STR, light always recedes at a constant speed no matter how fast we are travelling. As a consequence of this, we have:

  iii **the Limit Principle**: no matter how fast an observer travels, they can never overtake a ray of light: however near their speed approaches that of light, light still retreats at c.

This has strange consequences, which leads to what is known as the doctrine of the relativity of simultaneity.

The relativity of simultaneity

Imagine that after the domination by Ducati of the World Superbikes Championship, the regulations were changed in order to give the other motorcycle manufacturers a chance. In turn, however, Ducati responded by producing the first Super-Duperbike, capable of travelling close to the speed of light. Let $Foggy_1$ and $Foggy_2$ be the riders on Super-Duperbike$_1$ and Super-Duperbike$_2$, respectively, and let Penelope be in the pit stop at the side of the track. Ducati wish to help in an experiment. The Super-Duperbike$_1$ is kitted out with screens at the front and rear, each an equal distance away from the rider's position, and $Foggy_1$ is given a device for emitting light pulses towards the screens. $Foggy_1$ sends out a light pulse and observes that the pulse reaches both front and back screens simultaneously. Penelope, at the side of the track, on the other hand, observes the light pulse to reach the rear screen of Super-Duperbike$_1$ first as it races past her. This is because, for Penelope, the pulse travels equally fast along the track and therefore, since relative to Penelope, Super-Duperbike$_1$ is in motion, the rear screen will be hit by the pulse before the light-pulse catches up with the front screen. Furthermore, if $Foggy_2$ on Super-Duperbike$_2$ riding parallel to Super-Duperbike$_1$ were to ride faster than Super-Duperbike$_1$ and pass it, relative to Super-Duperbike$_2$, Super-Duperbike$_1$ would be going in the opposite direction, and $Foggy_2$ would observe the front screen to be hit by the pulse before the light pulse catches up with the rear screen.

The question is: do the light signals arrive at the front and rear screens simultaneously or not, and how are we to understand 'simultaneity' here? Einstein questioned whether there is any sense in the statement that two events occur simultaneously before a definition of simultaneity had been given, so he offered the following conditions for a definition of simultaneity:

> VER: The definition should supply us with a method by which we can decide by experiment whether given events occurred simultaneously   (Einstein (1920: §VIII))

Now, according to Einstein, all assignments of time to events involve the concept of simultaneity: 'If, for instance, I say, "That train arrives here at 7 o'clock," I mean something like this: "The pointing of the small hand of my watch to 7 and the arrival of the train are simultaneous events"' (Einstein (1905: §A.1)). Thus, according to Einstein, the assignment of times to events involves judgements of simultaneity. Events occurring simultaneously at the *same* point in space according to one inertial observer are observed by all inertial observers to be simultaneous. The assignment of times to events in the immediate vicinity of a clock is taken to be simple and unambiguous. The question remains, however, of how to determine simultaneity and how to attach times to events in a single inertial reference frame when the events are separated in space. What we might use for this, in principle at least, are many clocks, all synchronized with each other. We can then imagine placing a synchronized clock, at rest, at the location of every event to which we wish to assign a time. In this way, the time of every event can be read off a stationary clock, located at the event, by an observer located at that clock. To synchronize these clocks (in a given inertial frame), Einstein suggested we use the following method involving light signals:

If at the point A of space there is a [stationary] clock, an observer at A can determine the time values of events in the immediate proximity of A by finding the positions of the hands which are simultaneous with these events. If there is at the point B of space another [stationary] clock in all respects resembling the one at A, it is possible for an observer at B to determine the time values of events in the immediate neighbourhood of B. But it is not possible without further assumption to compare, in respect of time, an event at A with an event at B. We have so far defined only an 'A time' and a 'B time'. We have not defined a common 'time' for A and B. The latter time can now be defined in establishing *by definition* that the 'time' required by light to travel from A to B equals the 'time' it requires to travel from B to A. Let a ray of light start at the 'A time' t_A from A towards B, let it at the 'B time' t_B be reflected at B in the direction of A, and arrive again at A at the 'A time' t'_A. (Einstein (1905: §A.1))

So clock B is synchronized with clock A if $(t_B - t_A) = (t'_A - t_B)$, i.e., if the clock at B is set to read such that $t_B = 1/2 \, (t'_A + t_A)$. Note that this procedure rests on the following assumption:

ONE-WAY: the speed of light is the same in both directions.

The point is that by synchronizing clocks according to this procedure, we have defined a measure of time for all points within our frame of reference by means of a set of clocks at rest in our frame of reference. Furthermore, this method is equally valid for synchronizing clocks at rest within *any* particular inertial frame of reference. This leads to the following definition:

DEF: If an observer, under the above conditions and definitions, judges some given events to occur at the same time, then they are simultaneous.

This, however, immediately leads to the doctrine of the **relativity of simultaneity**. For simultaneous events with reference to the coordinate system of Foggy$_1$ are not necessarily simultaneous with reference to the coordinate system of Foggy$_2$, and similarly with the coordinate system of Penelope. In sum, every coordinate system has its own simultaneity relations and unless we are told the coordinate system to which a statement of time refers, the statement, according to Einstein, is meaningless.

The Lorentz transformations
It is clear, then, that the Galilean transformations do not work in STR. Because the speed of light is taken to be an invariant, and this involves distance travelled over time, the distances and times measured by people in different states of motion must vary from frame to frame in order for this speed to be constant for all observers.

Limiting ourselves to considering just coordinate transformations between different observers that are required to account for this, we get the **Lorentz transformations**,[1] which, in one dimension (which is the dimension which corresponds to the direction of v, the velocity of frame K' relative to frame K) are:

$$x' = \gamma(x - vt)$$
$$t' = \gamma \left(t - \left(\frac{vx}{c^2}\right)\right)$$

where $\gamma = \dfrac{1}{\sqrt{1 - \left(\dfrac{v}{c}\right)^2}}$

We can see clearly that at low velocity v (with respect to the speed of light), the γ factor is approximately $= 1$, which is what is meant by Newtonian mechanics approximating special relativity at low speeds, since the Lorentz transformations reduce to the Galilean transformations as v tends to 0.

The notorious consequences of these transformations are:

time dilation: $t' = \gamma t_0$ (where t' is time on a moving clock and t_0 is proper time, i.e., time as measured by a clock in a frame of reference at rest). The closer v approaches c, the slower the moving clock goes (from the perspective of the rest frame).

length contraction: $l' = l_0/\gamma$ (where l' is length of a moving object and l_0 is the proper length, i.e., length as measured in the rest frame of the object). The closer v approaches c, the shorter the moving object becomes (from the perspective of the rest frame).

Thus different inertial observers, O, O^* will not necessarily judge the spatial distance $\Delta x_{(e^*,e)}$ and temporal duration $\Delta t_{(e^*,e)}$ between two events, e, e^*, to be the same. Note the difference here between the consequences for measurements of length and duration as given by the Galilean transformations with those given by the Lorentz transformations: they are invariant quantities under the Galilean transformations

---

[1] Einstein independently came up with these transformations, and they are sometimes referred to as the 'Lorentz–Einstein' transformations in acknowledgement. This noted, I shall use the shorter term for ease.

but not under the Lorentz transformations. Nevertheless, there is a measurement that O and O* can make which will be the same, namely the **space–time interval**, ΔS, between the two events, e and e^*. This, in one spatial dimension, is defined to be:

$$(5.1) \quad (\Delta S_{(e^*,e)})^2 = c^2 (\Delta t_{(e^*,e)})^2 - (\Delta x_{(e^*,e)})^2$$

It is easier to see these implications of the Lorentz transformations by using the geometrical representation of them in Minkowski space–time diagrams. Not only are they helpful for understanding special relativity but they are essential to understanding the philosophical arguments that are couched in terms of them.

III Minkowski space–time diagrams[2]

In Fig. 5.1, we plotted the positions of three particles in various states of motion against time. However, in space–time diagrams, we plot spatial position not against the time variable t, but against the variable ct (time multiplied by the speed of light). This is simply because it allows us to present the Lorentz transformations in a conveniently symmetric form:

Lorentz transformations in symmetric form:

$$x_1' = \gamma \left(x_1 - \left(\frac{v x_0}{c} \right) \right)$$

$$x_0' = \gamma \left(x_0 - \left(\frac{v x_1}{c} \right) \right)$$

where $\gamma = \dfrac{1}{\sqrt{1 - \left(\dfrac{v}{c}\right)^2}}$, $x_0 = ct$, and where v is the velocity of the frame of reference K' as measured by frame of reference K

We thus use ct as the temporal component of the particle's location, even though it has the dimensions of length. We also assume that when the origins of frames K and K' are co-incident (as they pass by

---

[2] In some of what follows, I have used Zimmer (1993).

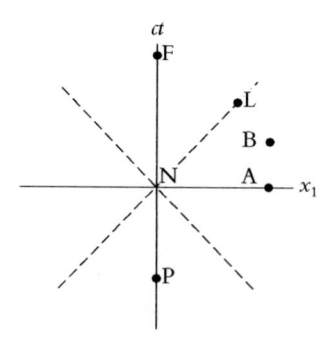

FIG. 5.4. Minkowski space–time diagram

each other), the clocks at the respective origins both read zero. This is an arbitrary assumption, but makes the transformations much easier.

Now consider an event N at the origin (0,0) of a coordinate system. Because we use the axis ct, the worldline of a light pulse in the positive x-direction passing through (0,0) will be $x = ct$, whereas the worldline in the negative x-direction will be $x = -ct$. We represent this in Fig. 5.4. We can see quite clearly from substituting the coordinates of various events into the equation for the space–time interval that any events (such as N and L) *along* the worldline of the light pulse will have a space–time interval of 0. Thus, when $(\Delta S)^2 = 0$, the events are said to be **light-like** separated. Similarly, any events (such as the pair (N,F) or the pair (N,P)) *within* the light-cone[3] mapped out by the worldline of the light pulse will have a space–time interval such that $(\Delta S)^2 > 0$, and are said to be **time-like** separated. And likewise, any events (such as the pair (N,A) or the pair (N,B)) *outside* the 'cone' mapped out by the worldline of the light pulse will have a space–time interval such that $(\Delta S)^2 < 0$, and are said to be **space-like** separated. (Thus the space–time interval, despite being a measurement of distance, does not accord with our everyday notion of distance, since events with different locations can, in case of light-like separation, have

---

[3] They are known as 'light-cones' because when we introduce a second spatial axis the surface defined when $(\Delta S)^2 = 0$ is given as $x_1^2 + x_2^2 = (ct)^2$, which sweeps out around the ct axis an upper cone and a lower cone whose noses meet at (0,0). The remaining third spatial axis can also be defined mathematically in this way, but one will have a hard job trying to draw it.

no space–time distance between them, or in the case of space-like separations, have values involving imaginary numbers.)

All inertial observers will find the same value for $(\Delta S)^2$, i.e., the classification of these intervals into light-like, space-like and time-like is **Lorentz invariant**: all inertial observers using the Lorentz transformations will agree on which pairs of events fall into which classification. Given this, there are some absolute claims concerning time that can be made within special relativity: not everything is relative. For we can say the following:

P, representing any arbitrary event in the lower light-cone, is in N's **absolute past**: all events in the lower light-cone of N will be judged to be in N's past by all inertial observers; there is no frame of reference in which P is not in N's lower light-cone. F, representing any arbitrary event in the upper light-cone of N, is in N's **absolute future**: all events in the upper light-cone of N will be judged to be in N's future by all inertial observers; there is no frame of reference in which F is not in N's upper light-cone. A and B, representing any arbitrary events outside the light-cone, are in N's **absolute elsewhere**: all events outside the light-cone of N will be judged to be in N's elsewhere region by all inertial observers; there is no frame of reference in which A and B are not outside N's light-cone. We can also say that any events occurring at the same spatio-temporal location, the co-called **space–time conjunction** of those events, will be judged by all inertial observers to be simultaneous; and so there is a notion of **absolute simultaneity** in special relativity.

Further, because in STR there is a limit on how fast signals can be transmitted, namely the speed of light, it follows that only those events on or within N's light cone are **causally connectible** with N: any worldline of a particle passing through (0,0) will fall on or within N's light-cone (for to stray outside the light-cone is to have a velocity greater than light). So all events in the lower light-cone of N can physically influence N, and no event falling outside the lower light-cone can physically influence N. (To see this, just consider any such event and draw its light-cone—it won't include N!) Similarly, N can physically influence only those events in the upper light-cone of N, and cannot physically influence any event falling outside the upper light-cone.

It is only when we consider events that are space-like separated from N (such as A and B) that the notion of simultaneity becomes relative. We can see this by considering another inertial observer O' and considering their frame of reference K' with respect to the frame of reference K of the inertial observer O, who we will consider to be at rest (Fig. 5.5). Here, the x-axis is the spatial axis and the ct-axis is the temporal axis in the inertial frame of reference for observer O at rest within that frame K. For convenience, we draw this frame of reference such that the axes are at right-angles to each other. The x-axis is the line along which $ct = 0$, and the ct-axis is the line along which $x = 0$. Similarly, the frame of reference K' of an inertial observer O' moving at speed v with respect to O will have the x'-axis as their spatial axis and the ct'-axis as their temporal axis. The x'-axis is the line along which $ct' = 0$, and the ct'-axis is the line along which $x' = 0$. Determining what the axes of observer O' look like is straight-forward: plug $ct' = 0$ and $x' = 0$ into the Lorentz transformations. This gives the x'-axis as a line of slope v/c through (0,0), and the ct'-axis as a line of slope c/v through (0,0). So if the observer O' is moving at half the speed of light with respect to observer O, $v/c = 0.5$, as shown on the diagram. As v slows down (i.e., tends to 0), the axes move closer to the axes of the rest frame (as is expected, since this frame is at rest). As v/c tends to 1 (i.e., as the velocity v of observer O' moves closer to the speed of light), the axes move closer to the worldline of the light pulse running through (0,0), again as we would expect.

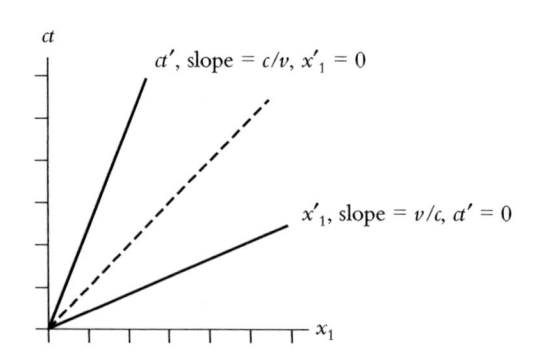

FIG. 5.5. Representing the axes of a frame K' in terms of the axes of frame K taken to be at rest

Once the axes are in place, we can show how the scale works along them. This is easy to show when we consider the various intercepting lines. To find out where the line $x' = 1$ intercepts the x-axis, we just set $x' = 1$ and $t = 0$ in the Lorentz transformations. It intercepts at $x = 1/\gamma$. Similarly, $x' = 2$ intercepts the x-axis at $x = 2/\gamma$, and so on. Next we find where the line $ct' = 1$ intercepts the ct-axis, by setting $ct' = 1$ and $x = 0$ in the Lorentz transformations. It intercepts the ct-axis at $ct = 1/\gamma$. Similarly, $ct' = 2$ intercepts the ct-axis at $ct = 2/\gamma$, and so on. Adding this to Fig. 5.5, we can represent the coordinate system of K' in terms of the coordinate system K (Fig. 5.6). We are now in a position to appreciate the relativity of simultaneity. The horizontal lines at $ct = 0$, $ct = 1$, $ct = 2$, etc., represent the progression of time according to the observer O at rest in coordinate system K, where events spread out across space along the same horizontal lines are taken to be simultaneous. Thus, events N and A in Fig. 5.4 are simultaneous in coordinate system K. However, the inclined lines at $ct' = 0$, $ct' = 1$, $ct' = 2$, etc. represent the progression of time according to the observer O' at rest in coordinate system K', where events spread out across space along the same inclined lines are taken to be simultaneous. Thus, there will be an inertial frame where the events N and B in Fig. 5.4 are simultaneous. So although event B is simultaneous with N in some coordinate system K'', it is later than N in K. Suppose, for instance, that B is at $ct' = 0$, $x' = 2$. From the

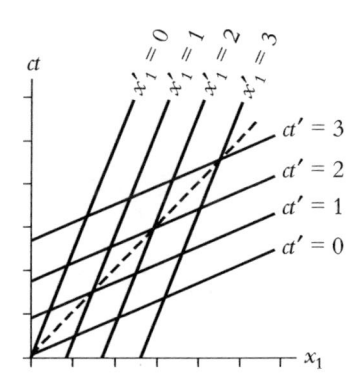

FIG. 5.6. Representing the coordinates of a frame K' in terms of the coordinates of frame K taken to be at rest

Lorentz transformations, we can see that B is at $ct = \gamma(v/c)x'_1$, which is later than $ct = 0$, whereas both N and B are at $ct' = 0$. But notice that B is also at a greater spatial distance in K than it is in K', for $\Delta x' = 2$, whereas $\Delta x = 2\gamma$. This is a consequence of the space–time interval being invariant: a difference in temporal intervals is compensated for by a difference in spatial intervals.

We can also see geometrically from Fig. 5.7 how to understand the notion of time dilation. Suppose two events occur at the same place but at a different time in the reference frame K' which is stationary with respect to observer O', but moving with respect to an observer O in reference frame K. Suppose the time interval ($\Delta ct'$) is 3 units for O' (as represented by thick black line), then for O in K, the interval ($\Delta ct'$) will be 3γ units, where $3\gamma > 3$.

Similarly, the notion of length contraction can be understood from looking at Fig. 5.8. Take the thick black line to represent a rigid rod. In the diagram on the left, it is at rest in frame K'. At any one time then, such as $ct' = 1$, the rod has a length $\Delta x' = 2$ units. However, when it is measured at any one time from the point of view of frame K, such as $ct = 1$, the rod has length $\Delta x = 2/\gamma$, where $2 > 2/\gamma$. Thus we see that a rod moving with respect to a frame of reference will be measured as being shorter in that frame of reference than it is in the frame of reference in which it is considered as being at rest.

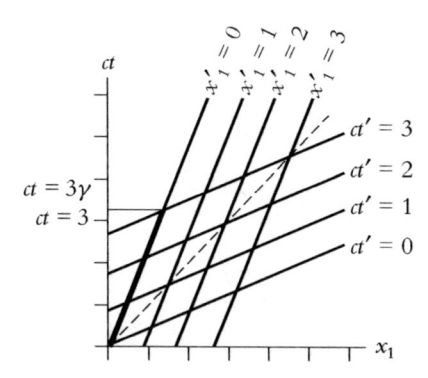

FIG. 5.7. Time dilation represented geometrically

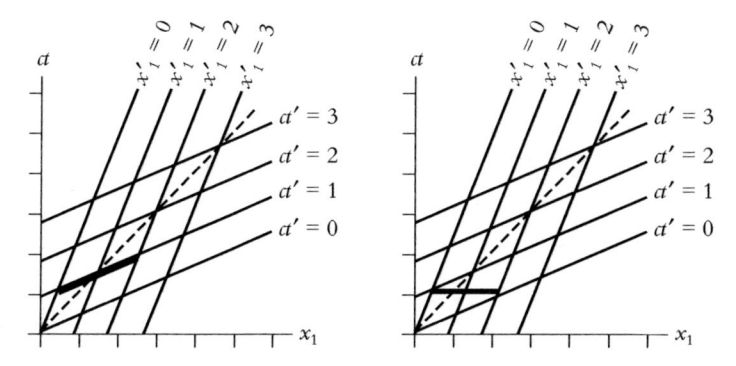

FIG. 5.8. Length contraction represented geometrically

IV Minkowski's philosophical conclusions

From the fact that measurements of length and duration differ from inertial frame to inertial frame, Minkowski draws the conclusion that length and duration in not being invariant quantities cannot be objective features of reality: invariance means objectivity. Minkowski (1908) famously comments:

> The views of space and time which I wish to lay before you have sprung from the soil of experimental physics, and therein lies their strength. They are radical. Henceforth, space by itself, and time by itself, are doomed to fade away into mere shadows, and only a kind of union of the two will preserve an independent reality. (Minkowski (1908: 297))

But just from the fact that different measurements of time and space can be made does not show that there is no absolute frame, and thus does not show that 'space by itself, and time by itself' need to be rejected as entities in their own right. Nor does it show that they are not independent entities; it rather shows that *measurements* of time and space are not independent. For if there is an absolute frame and the different inertial observers are simply measuring that from their particular perspectives, we would expect the measurements of the spatial and temporal aspects of given events to be dependent. The differences and dependences between spatial and temporal measurements are perfectly compatible with there being an objective fact of the matter concerning the distances and durations between events.

Neither need we draw the conclusion that space and time need to be considered alike, even if they do form the aspects of an underlying objective entity known as 'space–time'. For the only reason for thinking this is that the temporal component of space–time—the ct-axis—has dimensions of length,[4] just like the other spatial dimensions of space–time. But, as I explained above, using a ct-axis, rather than a t-axis is adopted purely because it allows the Lorentz transformations to be expressed in a conveniently symmetric form. Nevertheless, the non-symmetric form has also been stated and would have done just as well. In other words, considerations of this kind of convenience can hardly carry the weight of the metaphysical claim that time is just like space.

Further, as Mellor argues, following Reichenbach (1928: §16), just because something is represented spatially, we cannot draw the conclusion that it is a spatial dimension or that it is in anyway analogous to a spatial dimension. For consider the 'colour space' in Fig. 5.9 (taken from Mellor (2005a)). This is a two-dimensional spatial representation of a three-dimensional colour space which illustrates the possible ways in which things can match in colour. But it would be misconceived to draw the conclusion that brightness, hue, and saturation were each spatial dimensions, just because they were represented spatially. And to go on to conclude that each of these dimensions must be alike just because they comprise the different dimensions of colour space would be equally fallacious, since they're not. We should, then, be equally wary of drawing conclusions from Minkowski space–time diagrams.

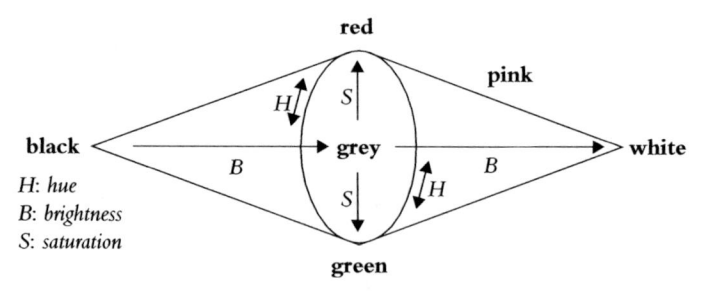

FIG. 5.9. A colour space

H: *hue*
B: *brightness*
S: *saturation*

---

[4] c is the speed of light and so has units of metres per second; t is time and so has units of seconds; thus, (m/s)s = m.

Yet the most compelling reason for not drawing the conclusion that time is like space just from considerations of special relativity is that special relativity itself treats them differently. For, as we have seen, the space–time interval distinguishes the temporal from the spatial. For the space–time interval $\Delta S_{(e^*,e)}$ between events e^* and e is defined to be:

(5.2) $(\Delta S_{(e^*,e)})^2 = c^2(\Delta t_{(e^*,e)})^2 - [(\Delta x_{1(e^*,e)})^2 + (\Delta x_{2(e^*,e)})^2 + (\Delta x_{3(e^*,e)})^2]$

which explicitly states that the temporal component of space–time has a different sign than the spatial components. So although, according to Minkowski, it is the invariant quantities which are objectively real (and so we should not consider temporal and spatial quantities to represent something objective), since the right-hand side of (5.2) taken as a whole is an invariant quantity that distinguishes clearly between the temporal and spatial components,[5] this distinction itself should be taken to represent something objective. Special relativity thus treats time differently from space.

Note also that although physics concerns itself with searching for invariant quantities because of the link between invariance and objectivity, this is only one side of the equation. For although invariance implies objectivity, it doesn't follow that this is the only route to objectivity: there may be extra facts about time with which physics does not concern itself.

One reason why it is a welcome result for presentism that time has been shown to differ significantly from space (both in terms of its treatment in special relativity as well as for the reasons given in the last chapter concerning causation) is that it sidesteps the worry that presentism about time should be matched by some kind of 'presentism' about space. If we did have to hold the analogous position concerning space, I would take it as a serious objection to presentism about time. But, as I have shown, we need not.

---

[5] Note that this has the form of Pythagoras' theorem $|PQ|^2 = (x_Q - x_P)^2 + (y_Q - y_P)^2 + (z_Q - z_P)^2$, which is the way to measure the distance between P and Q in Euclidean geometry (i.e., the familiar geometry where the interior angles of a triangle sum to 180° and the circumference of a circle is equal to $2\pi r$). Gauss was able to show that the whole structure of Euclid's geometry can be derived from his formula, and so can be seen as an expression of Euclidean geometry. It follows that Minkowski space–time is Euclidean in nature.

6

The present dialectic in special relativity

We are now ready to engage with the philosophical implications that some have drawn from special relativity (STR) for the viability of tensed theory of time, as described in the introduction to this part of the book.

I Putnam's thesis

Putnam (1967) argues that the relativity of simultaneity raises a major problem for any theory of time that ascribes a privileged ontological status to the present. Since we are only concerned with presentism, I shall set up the problem in presentist terms, but it can be reformulated *mutatis mutandis* for the other tensed theories. Putnam's argument (ARG) is essentially as follows:

> (ARG): Presentism states that only what is present exists; hence only things simultaneous with the present exist. STR, however, states that there is no absolute (i.e., frame-independent) simultaneity relation between spatially separated events, and hence no privileged set of events that constitute the present—there is no *absolute* present. The best that can be said according to STR is that what is present (i.e., simultaneous with an event we suppose to be present) is *relative* to a frame of reference. But then, if both STR and presentism are true, it follows that what *exists* is relative to a frame of reference. But

PRESENT DIALECTIC IN SPECIAL RELATIVITY   161

what exists is an absolute matter, not relative. Therefore, we must reject either presentism or STR. And, since STR is one of our most successful scientific theories, we should reject presentism rather than abandon STR.

There are three options open to presentism at this point. Either *all* spatially separated events are simultaneous with N, or *some* but not all are, or *none* is. Consider again the Minkowski space–time diagram from the last chapter (Fig. 5.4). If all events spatially separated from N are considered to be simultaneous with N, and therefore present, then A and B are simultaneous with N, and therefore present. But a light-cone centred on B, for instance, would not include F within it. Thus F would have to be considered simultaneous with B and therefore present. But F cannot be both present and future. In order to avoid contradiction, then, we'd have to relativize presentness to a space–time location, which is not the presentist's conception of the present.

Similarly, suppose we said that only some but not all spatially separated events are simultaneous with N, such as those on particular spatial axes at the same time, like N and A. This is the notion of simultaneity we employed in the last chapter and, as we saw, there are frames of reference in which N and B fall along the same spatial axis. Thus, if we are to avoid B being said to be both future and present, we have to relativize presentness to a frame of reference, again conceding that presentism is false.

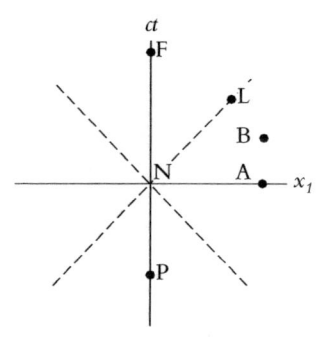

FIG. 5.4. Minkowski space–time diagram

The final alternative—that no events in the elsewhere region are present when N is present—is suggested by Stein.

II Stein's antithesis

Stein says the notion of 'becoming' may be epitomized as follows:

> For an event—a man considering, for example—at a space–time point a, those events, and only those, *have already become* (real or determinate), which occur at points in the topological closure of the past of a. (Stein (1968: 14))

Let us call *Pasties* those that hold that 'only statements about events in the lower half of my light-cone have a truth-value; only events that are in "my past" according to *all* observers are determined' (Stein (1968: 14)).

Putnam's strongest objection to Pasties relies on the fact that an object (Oscar) can be in space-like relation to *me-now*, but occur in the lower light-cone of *me-later*. This can be seen in Fig. 6.1. When N is present, A is outside its light-cone; but if we take Oscar's worldline to be the line linking N and F, then at F, A does fall within the lower light-cone of F. The problem this creates for Pasties is that:

> when that future becomes present, it will become true that Oscar *existed*, although it will never have [been true] to say in the present tense 'Oscar

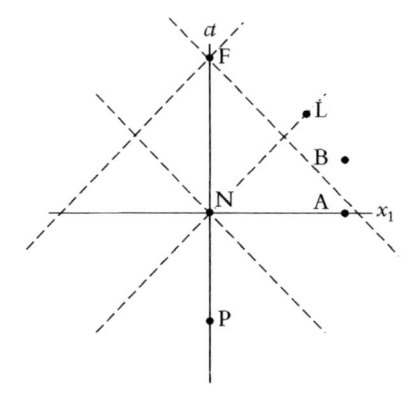

FIG. 6.1. A is at one time outside the light-cone of N but inside the light-cone of F

exists now'. Things could come to *have been*, without its ever having been true that they *are*! (Putnam (1967: 204))

Stein's objection is that this does sound disturbing if we bring along our pre-relativistic conceptions in evaluating this consequence, but that in special relativity we cannot use the relativistically invariant notions (such as simultaneity) of pre-relativistic space–times. That is, the argument merely highlights the difference between relativistic and pre-relativistic space–times. Thus Stein diagnoses the fallacy in Putnam's argument as one of employing illegitimate notions about time in the context of Einstein–Minkowski space–time. Stein writes:

in Einstein–Minkowski space–time *an event's present is constituted by itself alone.* In this theory, therefore, the present tense can *never* be applied correctly to 'foreign' objects. (Stein (1968: 15))

Stein writes further:

having stated the 'man in the street's view' that 'real' means 'presently existing' and having correctly shown that this is incompatible with special relativity (if one assumes 'real' to have an objective meaning—i.e., to be relativistically invariant), Putnam bases the rest of his discussion upon 'our desire to preserve... one-half' of that view: namely, the principle that all presently existing things are real. (Stein (1968: 18))

The bracketed clause raises a question of how to interpret Stein's positive thesis, given that he holds that special relativity is *not* incompatible with tense. He does not want to reject special relativity, so should we interpret him as saying that reality *is* a relative notion: what is real for me is not necessarily what is real for you? Or should we interpret him as saying that we should conclude that reality is not relative, but that only the *here-now* is real? Or has he something less metaphysically loaded in mind?

a) The minimalist interpretation

Stein continues:

If... instead of maintaining the implication 'present implies real,' we were to insist upon the converse—i.e., that *only* things that exist now are real—, we should be led by an argument like Putnam's to conclude that *for any event, it and it alone is real;* and then, instead of the interesting result that special relativity implies [we should be tenseless theorists], we should have the interesting result that special relativity implies a particularly extreme (but pluralistic!) form of solipsism. (Stein (1968: 18))

The tone of this paragraph suggests that Stein is not proposing 'solipsism' proper—that only the *here-now* exists—since he also says it is solipsism of a 'pluralistic' kind. It sounds, then, that what he may be offering is a form of *minimalism* concerning the notion of becoming and existence.

The minimalist interpretation of becoming and existence is based on an argument from *meaninglessness*: it is based on the claim that the only notion of 'present' that makes sense in the context of Einstein–Minkowski space–time is that of the *here-now* (recall: '*an event's present is constituted by itself alone*' and 'the present tense can *never* be applied correctly to "foreign" objects' (Stein (1968: 15)). The idea then, according to this interpretation, is to say that, of any event, it is present relative to itself and to nothing else: it and it alone is present.

Some are attracted to this kind of minimalism about tense.[1] These authors appeal to the seemingly trivial truth that it is ridiculous to think that we can talk of other objects existing at times and places other than the times and places at which they are. Just as we talk of a chair that exists here, it makes no sense to ask whether that chair also exists over there. (Consider Dorato (2002: 270): '... it is non-controversial to grant that for an event to *occur at a time* just means for it to *exist at that time*'.)

This 'trivial truth', however, is far from obviously true once we distinguish *existing* at a place/time, from being *located* at a place/time. Just as I can say that Socrates exists as of this time (if I believe in the real existence of the past), I can say that Australia exists as of this place (given I don't think that England is the only real place). But this is, of course, not to say that Socrates is located now, or that Australia is located here. Thus, I maintain, it *does* make sense to talk about, and is perfectly natural to talk about, objects existing at times and places

---

[1] e.g., see Dorato (2002) and Savitt (2002). Savitt in particular tries to use these minimalist considerations to show that the debate between the tensed and tenseless theorists can be 'dissolved'. I have shown in Ch. 2: §VII(a) the debate between tensed and tenseless theories of time is more substantial than that.

other than those at which they are located: it is true of every place that this particular chair, for example, exists, even though this chair is only located at one of them.

Thus the minimalist interpretation, if based on this philosophical argument from meaningless, is far from compelling. However, Stein argues more from the meaninglessness of ascribing existence to objects that are not located here-now *within Einstein–Minkowski space–time*:

> 'at a given time' is not a relativistically invariant notion, and the question of definiteness of truth value, *to make sense at all* for Einstein–Minkowski space–time, has to be interpreted as meaning 'definiteness at a given space–time point (or event)'—to be vivid: 'definiteness for me now'. (Stein (1968:14))

But here it must be said that this is the very question at issue: *does* it make sense to ascribe the present tense to 'foreign objects'? To simply state that it doesn't merely begs the question against traditional tense theorists who hold that it does. I discuss this in detail below. Nevertheless, the minimalist interpretation is suggested by what Stein says later:

> In the context of special relativity ... we cannot think of temporal evolution as the development of the world *in time*, but have to consider instead ... the more complicated structure constituted by, so to speak, the 'chronological perspective' of each space–time point. The leading principle that connects this mathematical structure with the notions of 'process' and 'evolution' (and justifies the use of our notion of 'becoming' in relativistic space–time) is this: At a space–time point *a* there can be cognisance of—or information or influence propagated from—only such events as occur at points in the past of *a*. (Stein (1968: 16))

The point I wish to make here is that Stein's conception of becoming does not allow us to express any kind of substantial thesis concerning tense. Stein offers a definition of temporal becoming in Einstein–Minkowski space–time that is so deflated as to be indistinguishable from the tenseless theory: how is his view of the reality of the past and irreality of the future any different from the tenseless theorist's explanation for why we *think* there is an *ontological* asymmetry between past and future; and how is his use of 'present' any different from the tenseless theorist's indexical use of 'present'? True, Stein's indexicals refer not just to temporal locations but *spatio*-temporal locations, and in this sense extends the tenseless theory of *time*, but it essentially amounts to treating 'present' as an indexical and nothing more. Thus, although this is a notion of 'becoming' that a tenseless theorist would be happy to assent to, this is not a solution to the problem that any traditional tense theorist would adopt. In other words, adopting this solution would be to concede that tense proper *is* incompatible with STR, and Putnam and Stein would find themselves on the same side of the debate, and in essential agreement rather than arch-enemies.

(b) The relativist interpretation

Putnam's other objection to Pasties is his requirement that there be *no Privileged Observers*. The idea here is essentially that if for an observer O_1 an event e is real, then e is real for all other real observers $O_2 \ldots O_n$: no observer is privileged. Putnam writes of Pasties (which, recall, are those that hold that 'only statements about events in the lower half of my light-cone have a truth-value; only events that are in "my past" according to *all* observers are determined' (Stein (1968: 14))) that

[The Pastie] flagrantly violates the idea that there are no Privileged Observers. Why should a statement's having or not having a truth value depend upon the relation of the events referred to in the statement to just one special human being, *me?* (Putnam (1967: 203))

But Stein objects that this argument loses much of its force when we ask: why should a statement's having or not having a truth-value depend upon the relation of the events referred to in the statement to just one special time, *now*? For this is exactly what many who hold that there is an ontological distinction between past and future contend: certain statements are only true at a given time—those about the future, for example, only become true once the fact that it is about becomes determinately the case. But if we are not even going to allow that the truth-value of statements might depend on the time at which they are tokened, then there is no reason to argue from special relativity, since the tensed view will not even get off the ground in the first place. Yet if we do accept this way of talking—i.e., allow the tensed theory at least to get off the ground before we apply an argument specifically generated by concerns of STR—then it is unclear what basis Putnam has for requiring that there be no Privileged Observers.

Although initially persuasive, Stein's argument here, however, will not do. For Stein's argument requires that once we drop one assumption about the properties of the *is real for* relation, then we are at liberty to drop the others. That is no way to argue! Stein's argument would work only if Putnam assumed tense theorists are committed to *is real for* being an *equivalence relation*, for then Stein would be correct to point out that certain tense theorists deny that it is—*no-futurists*, like Tooley (1997), for example, who believe in the real existence of the past and present but not the future, and who hold that the world grows as more and more facts come into existence, hold that although Aristotle is real for Descartes in 1600, Descartes is not real for Aristotle in 365 BCE. But Stein is wrong to think that this has any bearing on the relevant issue at stake. What is at stake is not whether *is real for* is an *equivalence relation*, but whether *is real for* is *transitive*. And Stein's pointing out that many tense theorists do not hold that *is real for* is *symmetric* in no way engages with that! So Stein fails to show with this argument that tense theorists should be happy to drop the assumption of transitivity; but being happy to drop transitivity is exactly what is required for the relativist interpretation to be acceptable to them.

Furthermore, it is obvious why the case of no-futurism is not a relevant counterexample, for Putnam quite clearly states in his requirement that there are no Privileged Observers that

If it is the case that all and only the things that stand in a certain relation R to me-now are real, *and you-now are also real*, then it is also the case that all and only the things that stand in the relation R to you-now are real.   (Putnam (1967: 198), my italics)

So for Stein to use an argument that assumes that the premiss '*you-now are also real*' is false (which it may be for no-futurists) in no way engages with the argument Putnam has set up! So Putnam's no Privileged Observers requirement amounts to: *of everyone that exists, no one is privileged in determining what exists*. To argue, as Stein does, that some things might not exist (e.g., Descartes) when others do (e.g., Aristotle) is irrelevant to this rather modest requirement that most (including no-futurists) would want to accept. Thus the burden is still on Stein to show why we should reject this plausible assumption. Of course, Stein claims that it is meaningless to extend the notion of presentness and thus reality to 'foreign objects'. But, as I have already pointed out, the philosophical argument for this is far from compelling, and whether or not special relativity licenses the ascription of reality to foreign objects is the very question at issue, and one that I deal with below. Consequently, Stein is lacking a non-question-begging conclusive reason for dropping this assumption.

Indeed, there are overwhelming reasons why tense theorists should not drop transitivity, even in the face of STR. For it leaves such a tense theorist either committing suicide or at least suffering severe structural damage to their common-sense world-view. The way of suicide emerges as soon as tense theorists relativize becoming to space–time points, for then, as with the minimalist, they are incapable of expressing a substantially different theory from the tenseless theory. Thus, tense theorists would do well not to take Stein's advice, for even though relativizing becoming seems an obvious way to reconcile tense with STR, this is only because it is the tenseless theory in a thin disguise; ultimately, it is to concede that tense proper is incompatible with STR, and thus not a solution that traditional tense theorists can entertain.

Either that or we really do relativize *existence*: what exists for me is not necessarily what exists for you. What is wrong with that? Well, first, although we may think that existence can be relativized to some things, such as times, it sounds more like a bad joke to think that existence depends on how fast you're going! But, nevertheless, it might well be argued that anyone who accepts STR will accept that simultaneity is frame-relative; so anyone entering into the spirit of special relativity will be happy to accept that existence itself is frame-relative. Well, not quite! Tenseless theorists need not accept it. So because there is a theory available that does not lead to the conclusion that we must relativize existence itself, and because there are no other compelling reasons to relativize existence, tense theorists should not happily swallow this conclusion and take it to be a surprising discovery about existence, but should view it as an unwelcome consequence of adopting this solution.

But why, exactly? Let us take a step back. When we are fishing around for the most satisfactory theory of the world, we all accept that the ideal situation is to find a conservative position that keeps as much of our common-sense view of the world intact as possible. Of course, if no such position is forthcoming, the rules of the game change; but this is not the situation we have here: there *is* a position available where we can keep existence absolute. So isn't the best situation for the tense theorists to find themselves in one where they can, with the tenseless theorist, keep existence absolute? For to give up on absolute existence is to concede that tensed theories (as commonly understood) are incompatible with STR after all, given the other things we already believe about the world. So the real interest lies in discussing whether a full-blooded tense theory survives in STR, i.e., a tense theory that isn't a tenseless theory in disguise or one that has to abandon core presuppositions of our world-view, such as absolute existence. Both Putnam and Stein argue that this cannot be had, and so *both* fall on the opposite side of the debate to traditional tense theorists—it's just that Putnam is conservative with respect to his notions of what STR and tense amount to, whereas Stein is conservative with respect to STR but offers a revisionary (i.e., watered-down!) version of tense that *is* compatible with STR. But Stein's project is rather irrelevant: nobody ever did deny that his bogus tenses were compatible with STR! That never was the project. The interesting issue is whether tense proper, *even with all the other background assumptions that we make*, survives in STR. It is this project to which Putnam is responding. And it is Stein's misunderstanding of the dialectic in which Putnam is engaged that leads him (and others) to think they are enemies when they are not.

An alternative response to ARG for tense theorists would be to remain conservative with respect to the notion of tense (in the sense of not relativizing existence whilst keeping universe-wide planes of simultaneity), but be revisionary with respect to STR. This is Tooley's (1997: ch. 11) strategy, and is discussed briefly below (§VI). But I need not go into this here, since my solution remains conservative both with respect to STR and tense, and thus is the ideal solution for traditional tense theorists, especially as it works within the parameters of the problem as laid down by tenseless theorists, and thus, as with all proper engagement, is a much more effective and convincing response to them.

The question now is what form such a solution should take. We have seen that it requires at least an absolute notion of existence. There are two options for presentism. The first, ironically, is one possible interpretation of what Stein suggests: the idea that only the *here-now* exists. Sklar (1981) is one who has seriously considered this option. The second is my own solution. But first, I shall discuss the *here-now*.

(c) The solipsistic interpretation

How could anyone seriously believe that only the *here-now* exists? Isn't it counter to firmly held beliefs? At first sight, Stein's response is somewhat persuasive:

> The concept of the 'spatially unbounded present' is not, in fact, as 'natural', or (primitively) 'intuitive', as our entrenched habits of thought and speech lead us to suppose. It is at least a plausible anthropological hypothesis that the primitive notion—the notion that first arises 'naturally' in the course of human development and socialisation—is that of contemporaneity *with respect to communication or influence*. At any rate, it is clearly a fact about the historical etymology of our language that the original meaning of the word 'present' was not *now*, but *here-now* (i.e., 'nearby now'). ... That remains a current usage: When a soldier at roll call responds 'Present!' upon hearing his name, he is not merely announcing that he still exists; he means that he is on the spot. (Stein (1991: 159))

This argument certainly shows that we have a legitimate use for the notion of the *here-now*. But this argument does not show that the notion of the *here-now* is primary; less still does it show that we have no conception of the present extending beyond our spatial location. Stein's argument, as it stands, shows only that it is useful to have a variety of indexicals, and that we use whatever indexical is most appropriate in the circumstances. It would be no good to shout 'Present!' if the roll-call were in England and the soldier in Australia. All the argument shows is that the concept of 'nearby now' is also useful, not that it is the primary temporal notion. However, there is a more profound issue that we can use Stein's comments to illustrate: it does give us a plausible story about how we *understand* the notion of simultaneity; and if it is tied to the notion of communication, then Einstein's definition of simultaneity (Chapter 5: §II) in terms of the receiving of signals looks quite attractive. The interesting challenge laid down by Stein's comments, as I see them, then, is that any alternative to Einstein's definition must also supply us with an account of how we *understand* the definition of simultaneity offered. I take up this challenge below (§IV).

Thus the concept of the *here-now* is far from nonsensical, but much more needs to be said if we are to adopt the view that only the *here-now* exists. The motivation seems to come from the following line of thought. Special relativity with its definition of simultaneity is already shot through with verificationist assumptions. So once we adopt this way of thinking about the world, Sklar (1981) asks, what consequences follow for our metaphysics? He says it leaves open an option that 'we will hesitate to take' (136), but one that fits with the verificationist foundations of special relativity and one that fits with what, according to Sklar, motivates presentism in the first place. For Sklar says that what motivates presentism is to be found in the 'epistemic remoteness' of past and future (138). And furthermore:

This ties in the familiar intuition about the irreality of past and future with such familiar verificationist themes as the claim that all propositions about past and future are, unlike those about the present (or, at least, about present immediate experience) 'inferential' in nature. And it ties it in with the further move, so familiar with radical verificationist programs, either to reduce statements about past and future to statements about present evidence or, alternatively, to adopt some kind of 'criterion' theory of meaning of statements about past and future, taking their meaning to be fixed by their relation, in terms of warranted assertability, to statements about present experience which are exhaustive of the body of evidential statements for them. (Sklar (1981: 138))

It is clear that if epistemic remoteness is our criterion for irreality, then not only should we treat the past and future as unreal but also those events that are space-like separated from us. But there was no need to venture into special relativity to achieve this result: in pre-relativistic space–times, spatially distant events are just as epistemically remote. The difference is that Sklar takes STR to show that we are *forced* to treat spatial separation on a par with temporal separation. It follows that if we withhold reality from certain temporally separated events, then we should withhold reality from certain spatially separated events.

Thankfully, however, this is not true: STR does not force us to treat time and space similarly, as we saw in Chapter 5: §IV. Further, presentism need not be motivated by verificationist concerns. In Chapter 2, ersatzer presentism was put forward as a way of having paradise on the cheap, and not as a way of having as much paradise as we could see. Thus, there is no reason for presentists to adopt this radical and implausible view, however compatible it is with STR. Nevertheless, I think Sklar is correct to say that STR, if seen as incorporating Einstein's definition of simultaneity DEF, is shot through with verificationist assumptions. This is my major reason for saying we need not be compelled to adopt it.

III Questioning the grounds for adopting Einstein's definition of simultaneity

As shown in Chapter 5: §II, the doctrine of the relativity of simultaneity is derived from Einstein's premisses VER, ONE-WAY, and DEF.

Consider VER. Einstein argues that so long as we cannot give a definition of simultaneity that supplies us with the method by means of which we can decide whether or not two events occurred simultaneously, any statement involving the concept of simultaneity is meaningless. But, as Smith (1998a) points out, VER then looks like it is based on a verificationist theory of meaning; and verificationism is, if not dead, then at least decrepit.

But it is VER that motivates Einstein's definition of simultaneity, DEF: if an observer perceives two flashes of light at the same time, then they are simultaneous. DEF is an *operational* definition: it is a reductive analysis of simultaneity in terms of observations of light signals under certain specified conditions, and so it satisfies VER. But operationalism is untenable, and any independent support it has derives from accepting VER, which has been rejected.

Of course, dismissing verificationism is not a sufficient ground for dismissing DEF altogether, for there may be other grounds for adopting DEF, such that we may think that it is a good suggestion for a definition, or that we have no alternative but to accept the definition given its inextricable relationship to how current physics is conceived. However, these won't wash either: presentists shouldn't take it to be a good definition (for the reasons already given), nor should they accept that physics shows it to be the only tenable definition (for the reasons I shall give below). It is down to me, then, to supply an alternative definition

IV Understanding and defining absolute simultaneity

We have seen that giving a definition of absolute simultaneity in terms of light signals and clock readings, as Einstein does, results in the relativity of simultaneity, and so subjects tense theorists to ARG. My suggestion is that presentists should formulate a definition of simultaneity in their own terms. This can be done using the same method I used in Chapter 3: Problem 4: §I.

We can let p be the true present-tensed proposition that event e occurs, and let q be the true present-tensed proposition that event e^* occurs. The fact that e and e^* occur together can be represented thus:

(3.15) $p \& q$.

We can then say that they were or will be simultaneous by adding tense operators to the entire conjunction (as explained in Chapter 3: Problem 4: §I). It is then possible to define *absolutely simultaneous with* thus:

(6.1) e is absolutely simultaneous with $e^* =_{def.} \mathbf{P}(p \& q) \vee (p \& q) \vee \mathbf{F}(p \& q)$.

Note how this turns some of the thinking on this matter on its head. For I say that it isn't that the conjunctions are true *because* the events are simultaneous, but rather that they are simultaneous because the conjunctions are true. And, why not? There is no compelling reason to think it must go the other way round. For the truthmaker for the conjunction can quite easily be given without relying on the notion of simultaneity: '$(p \& q)$' is true iff 'p' is true and 'q' is true, each of which just require present facts to make them true. Since, for presentism, there is an ontologically significant and basic sense in which events are present, we should expect that a definition of simultaneity could and would be given in terms of presentness rather than the other way round.

A different reason for not adopting this definition, to which Stein subscribes, is that the issue should be taken to be 'whether a notion of "real becoming" can be coherently formulated in terms of the structure of Einstein–Minkowski space–time' (Stein (1991: 148)). Putnam agrees, but goes further: '[simultaneity is] to be definable in a "tenseless" way in terms of the fundamental notions of physics' (Putnam (1967: 198–9)). But requiring that the definition be given in tenseless terms is an unargued for assumption that I see no compelling reason to adopt, especially from the point of view of the tense theories; and the same goes for formulations in terms of 'fundamental notions of physics'. Rather, the important issue is whether tense as traditionally conceived is *compatible* with STR, whether or not it can be formulated in terms of it. What matters is that a convincing definition of simultaneity can be given.

Some might read VER as rather a demand for a *naturalistic* basis for simultaneity. Stein, for example, writes:

to insist (without supporting argument) upon a notion of 'present (spatially distant) actualities', in assessing special relativity, is simply to beg the question since it is fundamental to that theory that it rejects any such notion.   (Stein (1991: 152))

But Stein seems to forget that he is just as guilty of begging the question against tense theorists here! He writes further on simultaneity:

we know that *within* [Einstein's] theory, there is only one 'reasonable' concept of simultaneity (and in terms of that concept, the velocity of light is indeed as Einstein supposed); therefore an alternative will only present itself if someone succeeds in constructing, not simply a different empirical criterion of simultaneity, but an essentially different (and yet viable) theory of the electrodynamics of systems in motion. No serious alternative is in fact known. (Stein (1991: 154))

But my suggested alternative definition of simultaneity does not alter the mechanics: everything in special relativity remains as it is. Thus, the alternative definition need not be constructed in terms of an 'empirical criterion' which determines an alternative mechanics. The burden, however, is on me to show how we can *understand* this notion of absolute simultaneity, especially given that we can never know which events are absolutely simultaneous with which; and it is also up to me to show how we are to understand the relationship between the old definition of simultaneity and this alternative suggestion.

First, then: *understanding absolute simultaneity*. It is not good enough to say boldly that we just *do* have some sort of understanding of the notion of absolute simultaneity; that, after all, was what Einstein was dissatisfied with. The question is, then, what does it take to understand it?[2] There are two components: how to understand *simultaneity*; and how to understand *absoluteness*. My solution accepts the challenge that our understanding of simultaneity must be tied to our definition of simultaneity, as it was with Einstein's definition. I suggest this: first, we do understand what it is for ourselves to be *absolutely present* and for present-tense propositions to be absolutely true, for it is not possible for us to be anything but correct about whether we are present, if we are presentists: if we exist, we are present. Second, simultaneity is defined in terms of the conjunction of present-tensed propositions. Thus:

1. We can understand what it is for something to be simultaneous because we understand the notion of conjunction, the definition of which is entirely exhausted by the truth-table for '&'.
2. We understand the content of the present-tense propositions involved in such conjunctions by grasping what they represent.

---

[2] Note Einstein's (1924) remarks: '... our concepts and laws of space and time can only claim validity in so far as they stand in a clear relation to our experiences; and that experience could very well lead to the alteration of these concepts and laws'. Note that my alternative definition does 'stand in a clear relation to our experiences', given our grasp of the present tense, but doesn't alter our concept of simultaneity.

For example, I grasp the present-tense proposition that I am sitting because I know what I am and what it is to be sitting.
3. I grasp the notion of the present-tense because it is that of which I have immediate acquaintance.

Thus, I can understand the notion of absolute simultaneity, since there is nothing more to understanding this than understanding the notion of the conjunction of absolutely true present-tensed propositions.

So if we reject verificationism, there is no need to adopt Einstein's definition of simultaneity, and thus no need to accept the relativity of simultaneity. Furthermore, I have shown how a definition of absolute simultaneity can be given and how it can be understood. None of this is in conflict with *core* STR. The question remains, though, of how we *are* to interpret core STR, and how it links with the various notions of simultaneity.

V The interpretation of the Lorentz transformations[3]

It is interesting to note the difference between Einstein's interpretation of the Lorentz transformations and that of Lorentz. At the end of the nineteenth century there was research into how to interpret the results of the Michelson–Morley experiment to detect the earth's motion through the æther, which was thought at that time to be the medium through which light travelled and which defined an absolute frame of reference. George Fitzgerald was the first to suggest that the measuring apparatus used in these experiments did not detect the æther because it systematically contracted in the direction of the earth's motion. Independently, Lorentz thought the same, and from 1892 to 1904 worked out the transformations to describe what length a moving object would be judged to have by observers moving at various velocities, in order that the æther would remain undetected.

---

[3] Miller (1998) was an invaluable source for some of this section.

Einstein, on the other hand, didn't take on all of this baggage. He started afresh and arrived at the transformations by following through the two principles which make up core STR. In this way he was able to show that length contraction, etc. was a consequence of his definition of simultaneity and certain measurement procedures; the bodies themselves do not go through any kind of mechanical change but are just measured to have various lengths in different frames of reference. Thus, the issue of reconciling the null result of the Michelson–Morley experiment with the existence of the æther became redundant; and since there was no other physical need for an absolute frame, the notion was abandoned.

Lorentz later acknowledged the elegance of Einstein's solution:

I should certainly have given a more prominent place to Einstein's theory of relativity by which the theory of electromagnetic phenomena in moving systems gains a simplicity that I had not been able to attain. The chief cause of my failure was my clinging to the idea that the variable t only can be considered as the true time and that my local time t' must be regarded as no more than an auxiliary mathematical quantity. In Einstein's theory, on the contrary, t' plays the same part as t ... (Lorentz (1916))

For Lorentz, then, the Lorentz transformations related the time of inertial frames in motion ('local time') to the time in the absolute rest frame ('true time'), whereas, for Einstein, all of these coordinates were on a par, physically speaking.

As Poincaré (1902) clearly saw, there were great difficulties reconciling Newton's third law of motion (the principle of action and reaction) with the properties that the æther was supposed to have. What kind of mechanical properties does it have if it is to have such an effect on bodies moving through it? He did, however, offer this suggestion to save Lorentz's theory (although in his (1904), he thought that there were further problems with this suggestion):

According to Lorentz, we do not know what the movements of the æther are; and because we do not know this, we may suppose them to be movements compensating those of matter, and re-affirming that action and reaction are equal and opposite. (Poincaré (1902))

Lorentz rejected this, however, because his whole theory relied on the æther being motionless. Nevertheless, Poincaré's real problem with Lorentz's hypothesis of contradiction was that it was *ad hoc*. It is perfectly all right, according to Poincaré, to save the theory by making certain saving assumptions, so long as the assumption helped the theory to explain a wide range of phenomena. If it only serves to explain away one unwelcome result, then it is bad methodology. In evaluating the work of those who tried to explain the null results of the Michelson–Morley experiment, Poincaré praised the success of Lorentz's theory, but was critical of the *ad hoc* contraction hypothesis:

> An explanation [of the null result] was necessary, and was forthcoming; they always are; hypotheses are what we lack the least. (Poincaré (1902))

I should like to avoid this cutting comment! In arguing for an absolute frame of reference, then, I do not want to argue that we should go back to the æther theory. But we do not need to. The æther is one way of defining an absolute frame. But it is not the only one: the process of temporal becoming recognized by presentists also defines an absolute frame. Einstein was right that absolute frames are not required to do the physics of STR; but not all reasons for believing in things have to come from physics. This was acknowledged by the physicist Max von Laue, who worked in this area at the time:

> in my opinion, such problems as whether the æther or absolute time exists can be omitted without damage from physical considerations... I am not asserting that these problems are uninteresting, on the contrary they seem to me of great philosophical meaning. But precisely for this reason they should remain reserved for treatment with the methods of philosophy. (M. von Laue (1912))

So how should we interpret the Lorentz transformations, if we are presentists? We can, with Einstein, reject the existence of the æther as redundant, and maintain that light does not need a medium in order to be propagated. Nevertheless, we can still hold on to an absolute frame. The Lorentz transformations are, then, to be regarded more as recipes for relating the measurements made by some inertial observer to the measurements made by another inertial observer, given a particular well-defined measurement procedure. This is essentially Einstein's way. It follows that the observable content of the theory remains intact and that there is nothing in terms of the physics of the situation which will tell for or against a privileged frame. The only difference comes in saying that one of these frames, defined by the universe-wide process of temporal becoming, is privileged.

Note that this does not violate the *Principle of Relativity*. Although some think this implies that there is no privileged reference frame, there is no such implication. For there is an ambiguity in saying that all inertial frames are 'equivalent' for the *description* of all physical phenomena. For given the Lorentz transformations this is true: two inertial frames, one of which is the ontologically privileged frame K, one of which is not, can equally be used to describe all physical phenomena—so no frame is privileged in this sense—but this is not to say that one reference frame cannot be ontologically privileged. This weaker reading of the Principle has no strict implications for whether there can be an ontologically privileged frame. That is, *core* STR can be accepted both by defenders and critics of privileged frames: the issue of space–time structure is one of the negotiable elements of the theory.

On what basis, then, should one interpretation of the transformations be chosen over another? Are there any principles to which we can appeal, such as simplicity, or economy of postulation, etc. that can arbitrate between such theories? In von Laue's terms, what treatment should we give within the 'methods of philosophy'?

VI The 'conspiracy of silence' objection

The conspiracy of silence objection arises from recognizing that, although the core elements of STR do not imply that there is *no* privileged frame of reference, they do imply that if there *is* a privileged frame of reference, then it cannot possibly be detected by physics. For if it could be detected, then there would be physical laws that would not be invariant under transformations from one inertial frame to another: one frame would be physically privileged; consequently, the *Principle of Relativity*, and hence core STR, would be violated. Thus, if there were a privileged frame, nature would have to conspire systematically to keep such a frame from us; there would be a 'huge conspiracy of silence' (Mackie (1983: 20)). Zahar (1983) puts it as follows:

Nature conspires systematically to conceal from us the asymmetry which marks off one privileged frame from all other inertial systems.... [But] it is unlikely that Nature contains both deep asymmetries and compensatory factors which exactly nullify these asymmetries.... Einstein demanded that there be few accidents in Nature as far as possible—that observational symmetries should manifest more fundamental, more deep-seated, symmetries. (Zahar (1983: 39))

According to Mackie, this argument appeals to *the principle of sufficient reason*, a principle often wielded by those who want to reject that which cannot be observed, such as privileged frames. Mackie dismisses the principle quickly by arguing that it is self-refuting: there is no sufficient reason to accept it. However, as both Dorling (1983) and Zahar (1983) point out, that a principle cannot apply to itself does not invalidate it: it is not put forward as a logical truth, but as a powerful heuristic tool for theory construction. I agree: there must be good grounds for us to adopt certain features of a theory, and that it is less satisfactory for a theory to postulate certain features merely on the grounds that there is nothing to rule them out. We must, then, cite good reasons for postulating absolute planes of simultaneity (especially given that we cannot know which the preferred plane is), other than the reason that there is nothing to rule them out.

There are a number of moves presentists can make. The first is to argue, as Tooley (1997: ch. 11) does, that Einstein's STR also entails a conspiracy of silence, for nature seems to conspire against us when we try to measure the one-way speed of light. Yet it is the assumption of the constancy of the one-way speed of light that justifies ONE-WAY in Einstein's definition of simultaneity. But, so the argument goes, this assumption has no experimental basis and was just adopted by Einstein as a *convention*.[4]

---

[4] See Winnie (1970) for more details and how STR can be formulated if we drop this assumption. Tooley's strategy in light of this is to replace the standard Lorentz transformation, which is only valid in traditional STR, with the ε-Lorentz transformation (see also Reichenbach (1958: 127)). 'ε-Lorentz transformations' are more general than the standard Lorentz transformations. They contain the variable 'ε' that takes values between 0 and 1, corresponding to different assumptions concerning the relevant one-way speed of light. Specifically, if $c+$ is the one-way speed of light in the positive direction along the relevant axis, and c is the round-trip speed of light, then the value of ε is equal to the ratio $c/2c+$. So if the relevant one-way speed of light is equal to the average round-trip speed,

If this manœuvre were successful, presentists could draw strength from the dialectical situation. In order for Einstein's definition of simultaneity to work, ONE-WAY is essential. But ONE-WAY rests on the assumption of the constancy of the one-way speed of light, something that nature conspires to keep us from testing, whereas, in order for the presentist's definition to work, there has to be a privileged frame of reference, something, again, that nature conspires to keep us from detecting. Put this way, it seems that there is very little to choose between these two 'conspiracies'. So at this stage we are left in a stalemate situation which can only be resolved by appeal to principles of good theory construction. The question, then, comes down to this: STR is strange—nobody denies that—but what is stranger: the fact that there *are* no absolutely simultaneous events, or the fact that we cannot *know* which events are absolutely simultaneous? Arguably, the epistemological issue is not that strange: it is no surprise, after all, that we cannot detect such a privileged frame if the measurement procedures for establishing simultaneity are as Einstein sets them up to be. But both interpretations are empirically equivalent and perfectly compatible with core STR. Thus, although it may be argued that our inability to know is explained by there being no fact of the matter, it would equally be perfectly respectable for presentists to adopt the less strange view that we merely cannot know which events are absolutely simultaneous, given their other metaphysical commitments.

However, this 'epistemological' rather than 'ontological' interpretation of the relativity of simultaneity can be put forward without presentists having to rest their case on there being a conspiracy of silence in Einstein's definition. After all, there are many who think that the alternative formulation that drops the constancy of the one-way speed of light is not viable, and thus is not an assumption adopted by convention, but is the only real option. But even if this is true and there is not a conspiracy of silence objection to Einstein's definition, all presentists need to do is be frank and admit that the conspiracy of

---

ε will be equal to $1/2$, and substituting this into the general ε-Lorentz transformations will result in the standard Lorentz transformations. This then paves the way for his preferred definition of absolute simultaneity. Tooley is, then, conservative with respect to the notion of a tensed theory, but revisionary concerning STR, whereas my solution is conservative with respect to both.

silence objection against them only demonstrates one cost of invoking privileged frames. But still, this is only a cost if we only take into consideration the *physics* of the situation. For the presentist can argue that there are good *metaphysical* reasons for invoking privileged frames, which should be weighted equally with considerations from physics. For privileged frames were not invoked to engage in the physical laws, and so it is not surprising that it cannot be detected by physics. Presentists, then, should be happy to take this argument on the chin, for it is necessary to bear this cost in the interest of, according to the presentist, a better total theory.

A related, but different, problem from the conspiracy of silence objection for presentists is the argument from *simplicity and surplus content*: since the universe does not need to be so structured for the relevant laws to hold, invoking such a frame is a superfluous addition to the physical theory. Any physicist and philosopher, therefore, who is guided solely by the considerations of science, has good reason to be suspicious of privileged frames of reference. I shall now discuss this.

VII Simplicity and surplus content

There is an argument which says that it is *simpler* to assume that the only temporal relations that exist are those of the relative kind postulated by the Einsteinian version of STR, rather than assume that there are, in addition, absolute temporal relations.

However, there is no one measure of simplicity. Smith (1998a: 142) uses this point to argue that there is a sense in which to invoke a privileged reference frame is simpler than Einstein's STR. For Einstein's STR postulates a time series for each of the infinitely many inertial frames, yet the advocate of absolute simultaneity postulates only one real time series.

This, however, is a bad argument. As Mackie (1983: 10) notes, reference frames come on the cheap. They are, after all, merely coordinate systems. And, in any case, tense theorists require just as many reference frames; the only difference is that they take one to be privileged. It is misleading, then, to say that Einstein's STR postulates infinitely many different time series for each inertial frame, for, as we saw in Chapter 5: §IV, the inertial frames just describe differing perspectives on an underlying absolute space–time structure (the geometry of which explains, so the story goes, why space–time intervals are left invariant from frame to frame) from which differing spatial and temporal coordinates are measured.

The real issue to consider is that of the surplus content of a theory. For if all of the work can be done by the Lorentz transformations in a less structured space–time (one without absolute temporal relations), what use is this extra structure? Phrased in these terms, Einstein's version of STR is at an advantage, for STR as a successful scientific theory, i.e., one that can explain and predict certain phenomena, can do so without absolute temporal relations.

However, a point that has been missed in the literature on STR is that if the issue is one of surplus content, then it is the *presentist* who has the advantage. For, as we have seen, Einstein's STR denies the existence of an absolute plane of simultaneity and therefore, on pain of contradiction, requires the existence of the past and the future as well as the present. However, the presentist requires only the present in his temporal ontology: the past and future are the surplus content—and quite a large surplus.

Consider again the dialectical situation. The Einsteinian starts from *core* STR plus the doctrine of the relativity of simultaneity, and concludes that there is no such thing as the ontologically privileged present moment of presentism. But suppose we start from the position of presentism, then, necessarily, a more structured space–time is required to uphold this position, i.e., an absolute plane of simultaneity. Now, for the Einsteinian at this stage simply to reply that there *are* no absolute temporal relations is simply to beg the question against the presentist. Furthermore, the presentist adds, more structure is such a small price to pay for such a large gain, for the past and future can now be dispensed with. And, in any case, the presentist continues, all we need for a successful scientific theory are the *core* elements of STR, and it is this with which presentism is compatible. So it isn't just that the presentist does not have to lie down and accept defeat once special relativity is mentioned; there are *positive* benefits in adopting presentism.

Moreover, this solution can meet both of Putnam's concerns: because it invokes absolute planes of simultaneity, we never have a situation whereby it becomes true that an event existed without its having been true that it exists; nor are there any privileged observers: no-one is privileged in determining what exists—everyone is in the same boat in that respect: nobody knows!

VIII The Present Problem revisited

The presentist, then, has arrived at a position whereby nobody can know which frame is privileged. But it might be thought that this lands presentism in trouble with the Present Problem of Chapter 1. For does it not follow from this that we cannot know which time is *present*, and thus that presentism should be rejected? Or, arguing the converse claim, some might object that if this is an acceptable response to STR, then it shows that the requirements laid down by the Present Problem were too strong: it is asking too much of a theory of time for it to be able to guarantee the knowledge that I am *present* (if such a privileged time is posited), for STR shows that this cannot be had. This line of thought, however, is misguided. Knowing which frame is privileged is a quite separate issue from whether a given tense theorist can guarantee that *their own* 'now' is *present*. I do not take it as a minimal requirement that an adequate tensed theory of time should guarantee that we can know that our own now is *present* *and also know which events are absolutely simultaneous with our now*, and hence *present*. If this were the requirement, then apart from having to justify the grounds for it—something far from obvious, unlike the weaker requirement that we can guarantee that *our own* now is *present*—then the argument from STR would be a good one: STR shows that we cannot know such things, that *no* theory of time can meet such a requirement. But if we believe, with the presentists, that only the present exists, then we can conclude that we are indeed *present*. Everyone else that exists can conclude the same thing. And, as I have argued, presentists should say that there is a fact of the matter whether both observers are *present*. All that STR shows is that we cannot *know* such facts, not that there aren't any. But this is very different from saying that we cannot know that *we* are *present*, for we can certainly know *that*, if we are presentists, and nothing in STR precludes it.

IX Conclusion

Putnam rejects tense altogether; Stein rejects tense as traditionally understood; and Tooley accepts tense as traditionally understood (in the sense of adopting absolute planes of simultaneity), but rejects STR as traditionally understood. The best way for tense theorists to reconcile tense with STR is not tamper with either tense or STR as traditionally understood. But something needs to give; and that is the assumption that simultaneity needs to be defined in the way Einstein suggested.

Putnam concludes his paper with:

> the problem of the reality and determinateness of future events is now solved. Moreover, it solved by physics and not by philosophy... Indeed, I do not believe that there are any longer any *philosophical* problems about Time. (Putnam (1967: 204–5))

And Stein comments:

> ...I agree wholeheartedly with Putnam in looking to physics, rather than 'philosophy,' for decisive progress. (Stein (1968: 22))

But this is simply naïve. You get as much metaphysics out of science as you put in. As Sklar says:

> While our total world-view must, of course, be consistent with our best available scientific theories, it is a great mistake to read off a metaphysics superficially from the theory's overt appearance, and an even graver mistake to neglect the fact that metaphysical presuppositions have gone into the formulation of the theory, as it is usually framed, in the first place. (Sklar (1981: 131))

We shouldn't blindly accept physicists' pronouncements on matters which extend beyond physics. This stance allows us to place the solution to this particular problem in the *interpretation* of STR, rather than in any substantial change in the theory itself, as Tooley has proposed, or in substantially altering our conceptions of tense, as Stein has proposed. I introduced a distinction between the *core* elements of STR and the negotiable elements—those inessential aspects that can be rejected without affecting the mathematical and observational content of STR—and argued that the *core* elements of STR are compatible with presentism.

7

Becoming inflated

Some, e.g., Swinburne (1981: 202), Dorato (1995: ch. 13), Lucas (1999), have thought, and others (e.g., Savitt (2000)) have at least been open to the idea, that the process of the expansion of the universe can be used to define an absolute 'cosmic time' that then serves as the absolute time required by tensed theories of time. Indeed, this is the very reason why many tense theorists are happy to concede that special relativity (STR) is incompatible with the tensed time thesis, because they think that general relativity (GTR), which trumps STR, and on which modern cosmology rests, supplies the means of defining temporal becoming using cosmic time. But the case for defining temporal becoming in terms of cosmic time is always left at the level of suggestive remarks and is never adequately made. I shall argue that this is unsurprising since cosmic time is not up to the task, and that these tense theorists should rethink their strategy in dealing with the theories of relativity.

I The Mellor–Rees argument against tense theories

Mellor, in *Real Time II* (1998: p. xii), writes:

The main addition [to the original chapter on spatial analogues of tense and tenseless theories in *Real Time* (1981)] is a short section (for which I am indebted to Sir Martin Rees) showing that modern cosmology does not, as some [tense theorists] suppose, undermine objections to [tense theories] based on the special theory of relativity. Far from yielding a privileged reference frame and hence absolute simultaneity across space, its uniform treatment of the expansion of the universe implies that there is no such thing. (Mellor (1998: p. xii))

This argument is misguided, but, in dealing with it, we can appreciate what these tense theorists are doing, and its limitations.

Consider the argument (ARG) from the last chapter:

> ARG: Presentists state that only what is present exists; hence only things simultaneous with the present exist. STR, however, states that there is no absolute (i.e., frame-independent) simultaneity relation between events, and hence no privileged set of events that constitute the present—there is no *absolute* present. The best that can be said according to STR is that what is present (i.e., simultaneous with an event we suppose to be present) is *relative* to a frame of reference. But then, if both STR and presentism are true, it follows that what *exists* is relative to a frame of reference. But what exists is an absolute matter, not relative. Therefore, we must reject either presentism or STR. And, since STR is one of our most successful scientific theories, we should reject presentism rather than abandon STR.

Let us remind ourselves of the core features of STR:

> (i) *The Principle of Relativity*: all inertial frameworks are equivalent for the description of all physical phenomena: the same laws hold in all inertial frames.

and

> (ii) *The Law of the Propagation of Light*: light (*in vacuo*) is propagated in straight lines with a constant speed c.

By (i), (ii) must hold in every inertial reference frame, i.e., the speed of light in empty space is constant for every observer in each inertial frame. As a consequence of this, we have:

> (iii) *The Limit Principle*: no matter how fast an observer travels, they can never overtake a ray of light: however near their speed approaches that of light, light still retreats at c.

Recall that Einstein required that a definition of simultaneity should meet the following condition:

> NAT: The definition should supply us with a method by which we can decide by experiment whether given events occurred simultaneously (Einstein (1920: §VIII)),

which, for the sake of argument (i.e., setting aside the debate over whether it rests on verificationist assumptions, etc.), I shall read as a demand for a *naturalistic* basis for a definition of simultaneity; hence the change from 'VER' to 'NAT'. Now, as we saw in the last chapter, according to Einstein, all assignments of time to events involve judgements of simultaneity, and he showed how to use synchronized clocks (using the method described in Chapter 5: §II) to determine simultaneity and how to attach times to events in a single inertial reference frame when the events are separated in space. The point was that by synchronizing clocks according to this procedure, we have defined a measure of time for all points within our inertial frame of reference by means of a set of clocks at rest in this frame. Furthermore, this method is equally valid for synchronizing clocks at rest within *any* particular inertial frame of reference. This lead to the definition:

> DEF: If an observer, under the above conditions and definitions, judges some given events to occur at the same time, then they are simultaneous.

And this lead to the *doctrine of the relativity of simultaneity*: events judged to be simultaneous in one inertial frame of reference will not necessarily be judged to be simultaneous in another. This fact sets up the argument ARG.

This is the familiar story from STR. The new interest lies in what the tense theorist can gain from moving from STR to GTR, on which modern cosmology rests. Mellor says not much.

Many tense theorists think that what generates the tension in ARG is the fact that STR is tied to the universe having the structure of Minkowski space–time, i.e., that there are infinitely many possible partitions of space–time into past, present, and future, no one of which can be non-arbitrarily selected as the absolute frame required by tense theorists. Consequently, the strategy of many tense theorists has been to brush STR under the carpet and look elsewhere in physics for a naturalistic way of defining the required absolute planes of simultaneity. It seems they need not look far. For, whereas the Minkowski structure in STR is inflexible, the space–time structure according to GTR is *determined* by the density and distribution of matter in the universe. And due to the particular distribution and density of matter in the *actual* world, not all reference frames *are* equivalent for the description of reality: observers of one class *do* appear privileged, namely 'those which follow in their motion the mean motion of matter' (Gödel (1949b: 559)).

So the situation is commonly held to be this: general relativity is a better theory (of the actual world) than special relativity; so, *even if* special relativity *is* incompatible with tense theories by undermining the notion of absolute planes of simultaneity, general relativity can be invoked to trump special relativity and supply a naturalistic way of privileging a frame of reference. (Lucas (1999: 10) is a recent endorsement of this argument.) The tense theorist strategy, then, is thought to be one that undermines the idea that all frames are equivalent according to our cosmology; and that it is this that is taken to be the difference between STR and GTR, and thus the motivation for the move. But, as Mellor (1998: 57) writes:

The expansion of the universe takes remote galaxies away from us at speeds proportional to their distances, given by the so-called Hubble constant (about 0.037 m/sec per light year). We can use this fact to define unique local reference frames in which the Hubble constant is the same in all directions. (This in turn defines local velocities, like that of the earth, by how much and in which directions they make the Hubble constant vary.) And we may grant that, since the universe is expanding uniformly, such frames exist everywhere. Will they do what [tense theorists] want?

Obviously not. For as the universe *is* expanding, anything at rest in any one such frame will be moving in every other. Thus in the rest frame of a galaxy G, n light years north of us, anything at rest in our frame will be moving south at $0.037n$ metres per second. But this is just [special relativity] writ large ... [A]t any earthly date, our frame and G's will make different G-events present. And as the uniformity taken for granted by modern cosmology stops anything making any one of these frames right and the others wrong, this is bad news for [tense theorists]. Cosmology, far from saving them from special relativity, only makes matters worse. (Mellor (1998: 57))

Thus Mellor disposes of the strategy to find a privileged frame using cosmology by exploiting the fact that our universe is expanding in all directions *at every point*, and thus that everybody is in exactly the same boat: nobody is privileged and simultaneity remains relative.

This is correct. And if this were the whole strategy of those tense theorists who appeal to cosmology after conceding that STR is incompatible with their thesis, then Mellor's argument would go through. For carrying through the core features of STR *and* DEF to GTR results in relative simultaneity regardless of anything else that cosmology can offer. Of course, someone might object that this issue cannot get off the ground in the first place because the notion of an inertial frame only makes sense in STR, whereas in GTR the closest we get are approximate, local, inertial systems. But Mellor's point is that the physical system described *does* act like the inertial systems of STR, and so it is legitimate to extend the definition of simultaneity in STR to GTR, and thus extend the argument from STR against tense theories to the case of cosmology. But, in any case, Mellor's argument is impotent, for this is *not* the whole strategy of these tense theorists; the strategy is not simply to argue that cosmology supplies a privileged frame. Rather, what those who appeal to GTR rely on is the fact that a *different naturalistic definition of simultaneity is available*. That is, what is gained in the move from STR to GTR is that *cosmology offers an alternative to DEF*.

II Can expansion combat such wrinkles?

By moving to cosmology, we can exploit the process of the expansion of the universe to define an absolute 'cosmic time' that then serves as the absolute time required by tense theorists. The essentials of this strategy are as follows. Tense theorists require an order of temporal becoming, which requires absolute planes of simultaneity (on pain of being subject to ARG) that can be ordered to give a temporal sequence. Let us label these planes of absolute simultaneity, or planes of becoming, as $^B\Sigma_t$, and the order in which they come, the order of temporal becoming, as Φ^B. The suggestion is to define such absolute planes of simultaneity in terms of *planes of homogeneity*. Let $^H\Sigma_t$ be a hypersurface of homogeneity, i.e., where the distribution of matter in every region in $^H\Sigma_t$ has the same values of density and pressure. It is possible to use this as a hypersurface of simultaneity, since observer O in $^H\Sigma_t$ can set a clock to a particular time corresponding to a given value of density and pressure in his vicinity. Since other observers in different locations in the same hypersurface, $^H\Sigma_t$, can set their clocks to the same time based on the same method of correspondence used by O, every observer in $^H\Sigma_t$ will read off the same time from their respective clocks. Thus, $^H\Sigma_t$ is also a plane of simultaneity that extends across the whole of space. As the universe expands, the values of density and pressure change, defining different planes of homogeneity, $^H\Sigma_t$, $^H\Sigma_{t'}$, $^H\Sigma_{t''}$, ... It is then possible to form a sequence of all such global planes of simultaneity $^H\Sigma_t$, $^H\Sigma_{t'}$, $^H\Sigma_{t''}$, ..., ordered by an *earlier than* relation, and identify this sequence with cosmic time. Call this particular global time function Φ^H. These tense theorists then equate $^B\Sigma_t$ with $^H\Sigma_t$ and Φ^B with Φ^H. From this we can see just how different this procedure for determining the times of events is from that employed by Einstein in STR.

This is the basic strategy; but let us spell out the situation more slowly. The metric that describes a uniform isotropic expanding universe is supplied by the Robertson–Walker metric. It will be useful to visualize the discussion using Fig. 7.1. The time and position of a cluster of galaxies (at A and B, for instance) is denoted by $(t, \sigma, \theta, \phi)$, where the terms θ and ϕ are the usual spherical polar coordinates.[1] Since the galaxy clusters move radially outwards from any given point, these angles remain the same as the universe expands.

---

[1] Those who are more familiar with the Cartesian coordinates (x_{1A}, x_{2A}, x_{3A}) for point A can see from Fig. 7.1 how we can translate between them and the polar coordinates for A using the following:

$x_{1A} = R\sin\theta_A\cos\phi_A$
$x_{2A} = R\sin\theta_A\sin\phi_A$
$x_{3A} = R\cos\theta_A$,

where R is the radius of the sphere.

BECOMING INFLATED 193

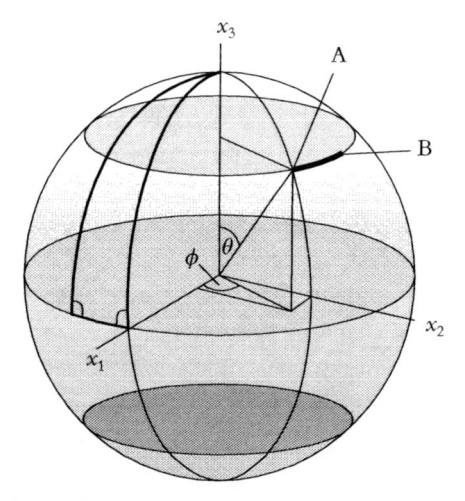

FIG. 7.1. Visualizing the Robertson–Walker metric

The time coordinate, t, is defined by assigning synchronized clocks to each galaxy cluster, and is taken to be the reading of a clock as it falls freely along the worldline of its cluster. We can think of the term σ as labelling a point on the surface of the sphere, such as at A. If we imagine the sphere as expanding, then we can see that although its radius would increase, the point on the sphere labelled by σ would remain at the same position on the surface of the sphere. Thus σ is a constant for the galaxy cluster to which it is attached. (Place a dot on a balloon, and inflate it. The dot remains at the same position on its surface.) For this reason, σ is known as a 'comoving' coordinate, since it 'moves along' with the cluster to which it is attached. To say that the universe is expanding amounts to saying that the distances between these comoving coordinates increase over time (e.g., the line AB gets longer). This is captured in the Robertson–Walker metric, which has the following form:

$$(7.1) \quad (\Delta S)^2 = c^2(\Delta t)^2 - R^2(t) \left[\frac{(\Delta \sigma)^2}{1 - k\sigma^2} + \sigma^2 (\Delta \theta)^2 + \sigma^2 \sin^2 \theta (\Delta \phi)^2 \right]$$

Here, ΔS is the Lorentz invariant interval between events with comoving coordinates $(t, \sigma, \theta, \phi)$ and $(t + \Delta t, \sigma + \Delta \sigma, \theta + \Delta \theta,$

$\phi + \Delta\phi$). $R(t)$ is the *scale factor* and has dimensions of length. k is the *spatial curvature parameter* and is dimensionless.[2] The values that k can take are $k = 0$, $k < 0$, or $k > 0$, but they can be stipulated to be $k = 0$, $k = -1$, or $k = 1$, since $R(t)$ and σ are arbitrarily scaled, and so can be suitably changed to compensate for the stipulation concerning k.

Although (7.1) may look quite complicated to those not particularly fond of mathematics, it is rather simple in form, and we can get a good feel for it by looking at two key parameters: the scale factor, $R(t)$, and the spatial curvature parameter, k.

Suppose we set $k = 0$ and $R(t) =$ constant (which we can stipulate to equal 1). (7.1) then reduces to:

$$(7.2) \quad (\Delta S)^2 = c^2(\Delta t)^2 - [(\Delta\sigma)^2 + \sigma^2(\Delta\theta)^2 + \sigma^2\sin^2\theta(\Delta\phi)^2]$$

And when the polar coordinates are re-expressed in terms of Cartesian coordinates, we get:

$$(5.2) \quad (\Delta S)^2 = c^2(\Delta t)^2 - [(\Delta x_1)^2 + (\Delta x_2)^2 + (\Delta x_3)^2]$$

which is in the form of the metric for Minkowski space–time discussed in Chapter 5. In other words, when $k = 0$ the metric reduces to a form which describes the space as being flat (i.e., Euclidean), and $R(t) =$ constant represents that the space is not expanding over time (which is what we would expect from a metric describing the flat space–time of special relativity). This is a sense in which general relativity is a generalization of special relativity, for the Robertson–Walker metric is a generalization of the metric of Minkowski space–time, since the Minkowski metric falls out as a special case.

Suppose we set $k = 0$ and $R(t) \neq$ constant. Here we have a Euclidean space, since the spatial distances at any one time are measured by the usual Euclidean formula, as in the case above. However, since $R(t)$ is not constant in this case, but varies over time, the space–*time* is not flat. Imagine a slice of bread in a bath of water. It expands over time, but the geometry of its surface at any given time is Euclidean. These

---

[2] Note that k itself does not give the value of the spatial curvature; in fact, the expression $k/R^2(t)$ measures that.

parameters can give rise to strange situations. Imagine, for instance, two people hurtling towards each other, but who never quite collide because the space is expanding at a much greater rate than their speed (see similar examples in §III below).

Suppose $k = \pm 1$, and $R(t) \neq$ constant. It can be shown, although there is no need to do it here, that both the space and space–time described by the metric are non-Euclidean. When $k = -1$, the space has negative curvature, and has a geometry where the interior angles of triangles can sum to less than 180°, and where the circumference of a circle is more than $2\pi r$. When $k = +1$, the space has positive curvature, and has a geometry where the interior angles of triangles can sum to more than 180° and where the circumference of a circle is less than $2\pi r$. This is the geometry which applies to the surface of a sphere, such as Fig. 7.1. For, as we can see on the left of Fig. 7.1, if we start at the north pole and drop a straight line down across the surface to the equator—i.e., a line of longitude—follow a straight line across the surface along the equator, and then travel up a different line of longitude back towards the north pole, we create a triangle with interior angles which sum to more than 180°. Note that these are genuine straight lines—so-called 'geodesics'—because they are the shortest distances between the points on the surface of the sphere. This, then, is the case we are interested in for our purposes.[3]

Now that we have a good grasp of the Robertson–Walker metric, its significance for the idea of cosmic time can be brought out as follows. Suppose event $e_A = (t, \sigma, \theta, \phi)$ is the emission a light pulse from a clock at A, and event $e_B = (t + \Delta t, \sigma + \Delta \sigma, \theta + \Delta \theta, \phi + \Delta \phi)$ is the reception of the pulse at clock B. As we saw in Chapter 5: §III, the interval between any two events on the worldline of a light-ray is zero, so according to (7.1), the difference in the coordinate time between e_A and e_B is

---

[3] Indeed, the Hubble parameter H, of which the Hubble constant mentioned by Mellor above is a particular value, can be expressed in terms of the scale factor $R(t)$, as $H = \dfrac{1}{R}\dfrac{dR}{dt}$, although it also requires a second-order term due to the so-called 'deceleration parameter', $q(t) = -\dfrac{R\dfrac{d^2R}{dt^2}}{\left(\dfrac{dR}{dt}\right)^2}$, which measures the slowing down of the expansion of the universe.

$$(7.3) \quad (\Delta t) = \frac{R(t)}{c} \left[\frac{(\Delta \sigma)^2}{1 - k\sigma^2} + \sigma^2 (\Delta \theta)^2 + \sigma^2 \sin^2 \theta (\Delta \phi)^2 \right]^{\frac{1}{2}}$$

What is notable here is that the expression in square brackets does not change with time, since σ, θ, and ϕ do not change with time. Thus the time interval, Δt, depends solely on the scale factor, $R(t)$, which has the same value across the entire universe. So if we measure two time intervals $(\Delta t)_1$ and $(\Delta t)_2$ at a given time t, they will be equal to each other at all times. Thus, in a universe described by the Robertson–Walker metric, the same value of the time coordinate can be used for all clusters; and so time is in this sense universal.

So whereas Mellor is absolutely correct that the expansion of the universe in all directions at every point 'only makes matters worse' if we combine this (under those conditions which allow for its application) with DEF, it is, ironically, the fact that nobody *is* privileged that *helps* tense theorists that appeal to the alternative definition that cosmology offers! For the universe being isotropic in the large implies that it is spatially homogenous, and this fact is precisely what justifies us in extending our local measurements of the density and pressure of matter in our vicinity to the rest of space. For it is the truth of the assumption that the universe is at all times homogeneous and isotropic—the so-called 'cosmological principle'—which validates the use of the Robertson–Walker metric.

The definition of simultaneity used in cosmic time, then, has an entirely different basis from DEF. It does not rely on what would be judged to be simultaneous by observers under the circumstances specified in that definition; it is neither here nor there that different observers attached to various galaxies in relative uniform motion would disagree in their observations as to which events happened 'at the same time'. For what determines simultaneity here are universe-wide facts about the distribution of matter in the universe; specifically facts about along which plane the values of density and pressure of this matter are equal. Mellor's argument, then, is not so much wrong as misconceived, for it misunderstands the point of the move from STR to cosmology. Whether or not this alternative naturalistic definition of simultaneity and the subsequent ordering of these planes is the sort of thing tense theorists should equate with the order of becoming is a matter I discuss below; but whatever difficulties there are with this tense theorist strategy, it will not be Mellor's argument that prevents it from succeeding. But are there any other difficulties for this strategy?

III Event and creation horizons

> [Light is] like a runner on an expanding track with the winning post receding faster than he can run.
>
> Arthur Eddington (1933: 73)

Let us assign observers, $O_1, \ldots, O_n$, to the various regions of the planes of homogeneity, i.e., where the observers are at rest with respect to the matter in their vicinity, ignoring 'small' variations in the motion of matter in their vicinity. (Just what 'small' means here, and its implications for the tense theorist's project, is discussed in §IV below.) Let us call these observers *fundamental observers*. In 1917 de Sitter found an interesting model of the universe whereby observers O_i and O_j could find themselves in the situation where no signal emitted by O_i could ever reach O_j, and vice versa. This situation is called an *event-horizon* and exists for any fundamental observer O_i in any expanding model where the rate of expansion increases with time so fast that eventually signals emitted by O_i will never arrive at O_j.

There are other models, however, where the rate of expansion decreases after an initial expansion that is so fast that no light emitted by O_i could reach O_j. Because of the decrease in expansion, the signal emitted by O_i eventually reaches O_j after a certain amount of time. Because it seems to O_j that matter is continually coming into existence as it becomes visible, this phenomenon is known as a *creation-horizon* (or *particle-horizon* by some writers), and exists in all models where expansion behaves in this way.

Suppose we allow the fundamental observer O_i to be detached from the region at which he is at rest and move through the universe, then the number of events that could, in principle, be observed by O_i would be increased. However, if the model contains an event-horizon before O_i moves, then wherever O_i goes he will not be able to observe every event in the universe. The horizon will change for

O_i, but cannot be eliminated. Furthermore, most of the expanding models that could possibly model the actual world have been found to have at least one of these horizons.

Dorato (1995: 200) writes that 'this must count as a limitation of the idea of cosmic time, since [it] cannot be extended beyond the horizon, ... [although horizons of either kind] do not represent a threat to its existence "within" the horizon'. But this is mistaken: since cosmic time relies on the distribution of matter in the universe and it is this that determines simultaneity relations and the successive states of the universe, the fact that it is not possible to send light signals between certain events in no way invalidates the extension of cosmic time to events outside the horizon. (Of course, horizons may raise *epistemological* problems of justifying the extension, but this is an entirely different matter from whether cosmic time *exists* beyond the horizons.) So, unlike light in Eddington's quote above, cosmic time is still in the running. But will it do?

IV Bursting the balloon

The first reason for thinking cosmic time does not quite hit the spot in capturing our notion of simultaneity and temporal becoming is *epistemological*. Callender (1997) writes:

> since cosmic time is only definable via elaborate averaging procedures over the matter distribution and is not at all the sort of thing to which we have access... [t]he passing of cosmic time is not the passing of time that [tense theorists] seek to describe. (Callender (1997: 120))

Let us fill this out, and relate it to a second, *phenomenological*, concern. For our normal everyday experience is of things—motorcycles, children, shopping trolleys—in various states of motion. And it is everyday occurrences like these from which we draw our experiences that generate our conceptions of the world. But in cosmology, it is not the average state of motion of all of these everyday objects that we take to be the average state of motion of matter 'in our vicinity'. Neither is it the average state of motion of the earth, or the sun, or even of the whole solar system. It is not even the average state of motion of our galaxy! No, it is the average state of motion of *all* of the galaxies 'in our vicinity', something that covers such a *vast* region of space that we cannot possibly be said to have any phenomenological access to it. That is, the notion of simultaneity under this definition is so divorced from our experience that it leaves us far removed from our initial intuitions about the notion of temporal becoming, and what it is for events—that is, *everyday events*—to be simultaneous.

The third reason for thinking cosmic time will not do for tense theorists is *metaphysical* and concerns the direction of dependence in the definition of simultaneity and thus of what it means for something to be present. Mellor (2005a) writes:

> The credibility of this way of defining temporal presence does not... extend to the idea that remote existence depends on it. For the continuing uniqueness of the present so defined depends on a permanent universe-wide large-scale isotropy, i.e. on the size, shape and contents of the whole of space–time. But this makes the present depend on what exists elsewhere in space–time rather than the other way round. Cosmic time, far from rescuing the idea of existence depending on temporal presence, if anything, raises the stakes against it.   (Mellor (2005a: 620))

We can add to this by noting that cosmic time is essentially a *statistical* notion. That is to say, it does not make sense to talk of the exact average state of motion of matter at a point of space–time, for 'the average state of motion of matter in our vicinity' is defined only over a *region* of space–time, namely one that comprises a sufficiently large collection of galaxies. Thus, not only does the definition of the present depend on extrinsic matters (as with all statistical concepts), there is also an element of convention in choosing how wide we should cast our nets in specifying the size of the regions when determining the distribution of matter in every region in $^H\Sigma_t$. But, for tense theorists, what is present cannot be a conventional matter; thus, cosmic time is not what tense theorists are after.

Furthermore, our nets must be cast *very* widely. For in order to regard our universe as spatially homogeneous, we must treat a vast region of space—a region which may comprise many galaxies, and involve distances that make light-years seem tiny!—as a point. To give an idea of the distances involved, consider that the diameter of the disc of our galaxy, the Milky Way, is 0.03 Mpc (i.e., 0.03 million parsecs, where a parsec is about 3 light-years). The Local Group, of which the Milky Way is a member, consists of 30 galaxies and is 2 Mpc across. Yet the Local Group cluster is relatively tiny; other clusters can include several thousand galaxies. But even at this level there are still inhomogeneities in the distribution of clusters of galaxies. In fact, the Local Group is a member of a supercluster, which is between 25 Mpc and 50 Mpc across. And yet again inhomogeneities are found at this level; and are indeed found on a scale up to several hundred Mpc. But this is still relatively small compared with the size of the observable universe, which is around 5,000 Mpc. At this scale, it does look as if the universe is isotropic and homogenous. So, in order to apply the Robertson–Walker metric, we have to treat an unspeakably big region of space as a point. Consequently, when we say of any of these 'points' that they are simultaneous, the very nature of the procedure used to define the notion of simultaneity makes it so coarse-grained that it cannot bear the weight of the metaphysical idea of temporal presence and becoming.

The fourth objection is from *physics*. As we saw in Chapter 4, there are well-known problems associated with trying to define the direction of time—let alone temporal becoming—in terms of such physical processes, such as what to say about time when the universe contracts. In the case of simultaneity, because planes of simultaneity are defined in terms of planes of homogeneity, events that lie in the planes that comprise the expanding period of the universe will be said to be simultaneous with events that lie in the planes that comprise the contracting period of the universe, since there will be (at least) two different planes where the values of density and pressure of matter are the same in every region. In the case of temporal becoming, when the universe contracts, becoming must be said to be reversing direction—either that, or such tense theorists must rule out a priori the possibility of the universe contracting.

These consequences are untenable, but perhaps not insurmountable. For what really matters in this conception of becoming is a *change* in the planes of simultaneity. Thus, we could equate the direction of time with the *change* of values at points in the planes of homogeneity. These could decrease as the universe expands, or increase as it collapses.

Essentially, all that we need to find is some kind of increasing linear function involving time associated with a given dynamic model.

This is fine so far as it goes; but it doesn't go that far. First, for all that has been said, cosmic time can, at most, be a necessary condition for temporal becoming: an extra argument is needed to show that it is also sufficient. What, after all, has expansion to do with existence? Does size really matter? But let us set this point aside for the sake of considering more profound points. Regardless of whether cosmic time tense theorists can reconcile their views with universes that contract as well as expand, there certainly are other models that are inhospitable to such views—the steady-state models, for example. Now it might be asked why we should worry about such models when they do not represent the actual world. But it is here that we can invoke an argument similar to Gödel's so-called 'modal' argument, which I shall consider in more detail in the next chapter. Gödel argues that time must be tensed in order to exist—it is an essential feature of time that it flows—and that, in order for time to exist, it must be tensed in all worlds where time exists. But since time exists in some models where it cannot be tensed—Gödel's own (1949a) pathological model being a case in point—Gödel argues that time cannot exist at all. Applying this to the current proposal: there are models in which cosmic time cannot exist, so temporal becoming is not essentially this physical process. Thus temporal becoming cannot be equated with this physical process.

One solution is to reject Gödel's modal argument and argue that the existence of temporal becoming is a contingent matter. There are two ways in which we could do this. The most obvious is to hold that temporal becoming is only possible in worlds where cosmic time is available, and so long as it is available in the actual world, that is all that matters. This is what Dorato (1995: 204) suggests. But is it plausible that the metaphysical notion of temporal becoming can be equated with a physical process that is contingent on the particular distribution of matter in the universe? A much better proposal is this: the only appealing way of viewing the matter is to invoke the notion of a functional role: specifically, we might hold that cosmic time plays the temporal-becoming-role in worlds where cosmic time is available, whereas other processes in another world might play the temporal-becoming-role in that world. This certainly bypasses chauvinism towards worlds where contingent matters of fact just happen to allow for cosmic time, over worlds that are receptive to the idea of temporal becoming but cannot deliver on cosmic time. Viewing temporal becoming as this more abstract feature of worlds should certainly appease those who say metaphysical notions should be more robust with respect to contingent features of the world and not be so world-relative.

Maybe. But neither the identity nor functional role suggestion quite hits the spot. For isn't it strange that our common sense conception of tense does not change in the slightest when we learn of the different models of how the universe may develop? On discovery that the universe is not a steady-state universe, for example, right-thinking people don't start wondering whether the world might be tensed in light of this. (Although, unfortunately, it seems that Jeans (1936) to a certain extent does.) The fact that we now suspect our universe is expanding does not lead us to think that we have better reasons now for thinking our universe is tensed than we would have done had the universe been steady. Thus it is not at all clear that cosmic time *can* be identified with, or play the role of, temporal becoming as it is conceived of in this world.

To press the point, cosmic time as used by these tense theorists only gives us an account of one of the platitudes—namely *that time flows*—that we hold about time: it tells us what time's flow amounts to. But, although it defines what it is for events to be simultaneous—setting aside for the moment the reasons above for thinking it is too coarse-grained a definition—it says *nothing* about what it is for us to be located in the present, something that, as we saw in Chapter 1, any adequate theory of time and tense must; and it does not explain our belief that the past is fixed and the future is open, for what does the relative size of the universe in a given temporal direction have to do with this? Nor does it tell us what makes past-, present- and future-tensed statements true. Compare this with the tenseless error theory account of becoming, which is intimately tied to accounting for the things we all say and believe about time. For, as explained in the Introduction, according to the tenseless theory, time does not flow, but it accounts for our *saying* that it does by showing how we can account for the illusion that it does. This typically involves causation: time appears to flow because perception works causally, and so we can only perceive past and present events, but not future, etc.; and similarly, although there is no ontological difference between earlier and later times, according to the tenseless theory, the reason why we *say* that the past is fixed and the future open is because we cannot causally affect earlier times than now, but can causally affect later times than now, and so on. Comparing all this with what the cosmic time account of becoming can offer shows just how deficient and unsuitable a candidate it is for playing the role of temporal becoming as we conceive of it in this world.[4]

Furthermore, compare identifying cosmic time and temporal becoming with other more convincing theoretical identifications, such as water = H_2O, or mental states = brain states, where the identification has explained and informed much of our pre-theoretical views, and perhaps even changed them to a certain extent after the discoveries were made.

Thus we have no compelling reason to think that cosmic time is the kind of thing tense theorists require, and every reason to reject the idea that it is. This is not to say that there can be no asymmetries in time based on these notions; it is to say that temporal becoming cannot be equated with them.

It is now time to turn in more detail to a different type of cosmological model which arises from general relativity, and which has already been mentioned above, namely that found by Gödel. Unlike the models of this chapter, which are quite kind to presentism, we shall see just how uncomfortable presentism is made to feel in Gödel's world.

---

[4] And I suspect, although this would have to be shown, that similar arguments could be constructed to show that the current fashion for appealing to certain processes in quantum mechanics in defining a physically respectable notion of becoming is at least too ambitious. For such physical theories of becoming have got to bear the weight that more traditional metaphysical theories can in order to be serious contenders as theories of becoming. At the moment, such theories are far from that.

8

All the time in the worlds: Gödel's modal moral

In recent years there has been a resurgence of interest in Gödel's philosophy of time, as given in his (1949b). Gödel arrived at his philosophical position by considering what he took to be the implications of his (1949a) solutions to Einstein's Field Equations[1] (EFE) in much the same way as his Platonism in the philosophy of mathematics is derived from his better-known technical results in mathematical logic.

---

[1] Einstein's field equations describe the relationship between the curvature of space–time and the contents of the universe, and have the form:

(8.1) $R_{\mu\nu} - \tfrac{1}{2}g_{\mu\nu}R = -8\pi G T_{\mu\nu}$

We refer to *equations*, plural, since there is one for each independent combination μ, ν. The left-hand side gives the curvature of the space–time. Twenty numbers are required to specify the curvature of four dimensions. These numbers are known as the **Riemann curvature tensor**, and for 4-dimensional space–time are denoted $R^{\lambda}{}_{\mu\nu\kappa}$ where λ, μ, ν, κ range over the values 0, 1, 2, 3 for each of the dimensions. If all of these 20 numbers are zero, for instance, the space–time is flat. The term $g_{\mu\nu}$ in (8.1) is the **metric tensor**. The term $R_{\mu\nu}$ in (8.1) is known as the **Ricci curvature tensor** and is obtained from certain sums of the Riemann tensors, and is a complicated expression involving derivatives of $g_{\mu\nu}$. The term R in (8.1) is the **curvature scalar**, which is obtained from the Ricci curvature in much the same way as the Ricci curvature is obtained from the Riemannian curvature. It is the Riemannian curvature, however, which we use when we talk about the curvature of space–time (although it is the Ricci curvature which figures in the field equations). The right-hand side term G in (8.1) is the gravitational constant familiar from the Newtonian law of gravity, and the term $T_{\mu\nu}$ in (8.1) is sometimes called the 'stress-energy tensor', but better called the 'energy-momentum tensor', since it specifies the energy and momentum densities at any point in space–time as well as the rate at which momentum flows. For the purposes of this chapter, it is not important to know the details of these components of the equations. All we need to know is that the equations systematically relate the curvature of space–time to energy and momentum. A simple way to view it is that since energy E is related to mass m, via $E = mc^2$, we could treat (8.1) as describing how much certain massive objects warp space–time.

One thing that makes Gödel's model of the universe so remarkable is that through each point in Gödelian space–time there is a closed time-like curve (CTC).[2] In light of this, some have denied that Gödel's model needs to be taken seriously because CTCs allow for all sorts of paradox, and since this is impossible, so is Gödel's model (see, e.g., Hawking and Ellis (1973)). I showed in Chapter 4, however, that, on the tenseless view, there are no good reasons for ruling out the possibility of time travel, causal loops, and the rest. Further, although I showed that presentism with a branching future is incompatible with such things, it is not clear that it is ruled out by CTCs. In other words, the type of time travel available in Gödel's model is one where the traveller moves along a smooth continuous worldline in space–time (i.e., 'external' time) into their future to arrive in their past. This is a different situation from the discontinuity in external time allowed by Lewis's (1976) kind of time travel discussed in Chapter 4. Although prima facie different, we need not go over what might end up being the same ground here. It suffices to say that CTCs are a possibility (at least on the tenseless theory), whether or not presentism can accommodate them; and so Gödel's model must be taken seriously as a possibility. But I am not interested in the possibilities it opens up for time travel. Rather, I will here centre on the much-neglected subtler implications that Gödel himself saw for his solutions, namely that time must be *ideal*. I argue that Gödel's conclusion is too strong, but that his solution is important for understanding the nature of time in our world.

I Gödel's philosophical position on the nature of time

Gödel (1949b) follows McTaggart (1908) in assuming that change is essential to time and agrees with him that 'change becomes possible

---

[2] Although Gödel's solution is perhaps the most widely known and discussed, CTCs were discovered in a different solution by Lanczos (1924), which was rediscovered by van Stockum (1937). Unlike the Gödel solution, however, the rotation in the van Stockum model is about a privileged axis (see Fig. 8.2).

only through the lapse of time' (Gödel (1949b: 588); (1990: 202)). This implies that Gödel holds:

TNT: Tense is Necessary for the existence of Time

Furthermore, Gödel's conception of what tense amounts to is a presentist conception, for he talks of 'an objective lapse of time (whose essence is that only the present really exists)' (1949b: fn. 4).[3]

Gödel lays down the following two necessary conditions for the existence of objective flow: 'The existence of an objective lapse of time ... means ... that

[∃Σ] reality consists of an infinity of layers of "now" which
[∃Φ] come into existence successively' ((1949b: 588); (1990: 202)).

But Gödel then argues not that there is a contradiction in the notion of the flow of time, as McTaggart does, but that the lapse of time is not possible according to relativity theory. And since time cannot flow, from TNT he draws the conclusion that it cannot exist: time must be ideal. Specifically, there are two parts to Gödel's argument:

Part 1: There are *some* models of the universe where conditions [∃Σ] and [∃Φ] *cannot* be satisfied.
Part 2: Conditions [∃Σ] and [∃Φ] must be satisfied in *all* models of the universe in order for time to be real in *any* of them.

Both of these steps require detailed discussion, and so this chapter falls into the two parts.

II Establishing part 1 of Gödel's argument

(a) The background dialectical situation

Although Gödel's argument primarily concerns the general theory of relativity (GTR), the story begins with the special theory of relativity (STR). Let us briefly summarize the position we have arrived at so far

---

[3] And since, as we saw in Ch. 1, presentism is the only viable tensed theory of time anyway, this is the only version of the tensed thesis on which we need to concentrate.

in the past three chapters. Gödel (1949b) was one of the first to note the tension between STR and presentism. For presentism states that only what is present exists; hence, only things simultaneous with the present exist. Presentists thus require absolute universe-wide planes of simultaneity (which I take to be Gödel's condition [∃Σ]), which can then be ordered and used to partition events into being past, present, and future (which I take to be Gödel's condition [∃Φ]). For if such planes were relative to a given frame of reference, it would follow that what *exists* is relative to a frame of reference. This would contradict the intuitive assumption that what exists is not something that can vary from frame to frame. As Gödel notes: 'The concept of existence... cannot be relativized without destroying its meaning completely' ((1949b: 589); (1990: 203)). But in Einstein's version of STR there are no absolute simultaneity relations between spatially separated events; rather, in Einstein's version of STR, simultaneity is relativized to a frame of reference, the various planes of simultaneity being those orthogonal to the worldline of an observer considered at rest within that frame. Now because in STR no set of such worldlines is privileged, this allows for infinitely many different yet legitimate partitions of the space-time into past, present, and future, which consequently, for presentists, renders existence a relative notion. STR, then, appears to be a hostile environment for presentism, for it does not have the machinery available to satisfy in a non-arbitrary way the tense theorist's requirement for an absolute partitioning of events.

At this point, many tense theorists, as we saw in the last chapter, are tempted to brush STR under the carpet and look elsewhere in physics for the required absolute planes of simultaneity—the 'layers of "now"' of condition [∃Σ]. For although STR is inhospitable to presentism, a shift to GTR appears at first sight to be much more welcoming: unlike STR, which offers no non-arbitrary way of partitioning events, GTR has resources available for doing just that. For one set of worldlines *does* appear privileged, namely 'those which follow in their motion the mean motion of matter' (Gödel (1949b: 559); (1990: 204)). Gödel writes further:

[I]n all cosmological solutions of the gravitational equations... the local times of all *these* observers fit together into one world time, so that apparently it becomes possible to consider this time as the 'true' one, which lapses objectively... [And so] there is no reason to abandon the intuitive idea of an absolute time lapsing objectively. (Gödel (1949b: 559); (1990: 204)).

It seems, then, that we have naturalistic and non-arbitrary reasons for holding that conditions [∃Σ] and [∃Φ] are met in such models. The move to GTR seems to do presentism the world of good.

However, as we saw in the last chapter, such a cosmic time is not the sort of thing that tensed theorists are after. But, in any case, Gödel's objection to cosmic time is different from the main arguments put forward against it there. He writes:

[I]t has even been said by the physicist Jeans that this circumstance justifies the retention of the old intuitive concept of an absolute time. So one is led to investigate whether or not this is a necessary property of all possible cosmological solutions. (Gödel (1949c: 12); (1995: 274))

Gödel argues that it is not; so we need to discuss why.

(b) A sketch of Gödel's model

In Gödel's (1949a) model, universe-wide planes of simultaneity cannot be found. This is, first, because it is not an expanding model, and so it is not possible to use the method suggested by tensed theorists who appeal to modern cosmology of equating planes of simultaneity with planes of homogeneity, where the distribution of matter in every region of the plane has the same values of density and pressure. And, given this is not possible, it is not possible to then go on to order such planes in a temporal sequence, as it is when these values change as the universe expands. Nevertheless, we might still think we can use the planes orthogonal to the congruence of worldlines of the major mass-points to define planes of simultaneity. But the reason why this cannot work is due to a second feature of Gödel's model: it is a model where matter is everywhere rotating. For in such models it is not possible to find planes orthogonal to the congruence of worldlines of the major mass-points.[4] As Malament (1995: 263) points out, it is

---

[4] It is interesting to note, however, that Gödel (1952) describes a class of rotating universes which, unlike (1949a), do expand. Universes of this class (with sufficiently small rotational velocity) are not isotropic, but are spatially homogeneous. These do not contain

rather like taking the worldlines of the major mass-points to be the fibres of a rope: where the fibres are in an untwisted state, it is possible to find planes orthogonal to every fibre at every point, whereas when the fibres are twisted, it is not possible, using this method, to find any plane orthogonal to all fibres.

Let us spell out the situation more slowly. Hermann Weyl in 1918 was one of the first to point out that GTR might allow for a person's worldline to loop back and intersect itself. Anticipating by around thirty years Gödel's published discovery, Weyl writes:

> it is possible to experience events now that will in part be an effect of my future resolves and actions. Moreover, it is not impossible for a world-line (in particular, that of my body), although it has a time-like direction at every point, to return to the neighbourhood of a point which it has already once passed through. (Weyl (1918: 274))

We can appreciate how this could happen by contrasting GTR with STR. As we saw in Chapter 5, associated with each space–time point is a light-cone, which can be thought of as the bounds of the possible worldlines of a particle through a given space–time point. For all worldlines of particles passing through point N must fall on or within N's light-cone, otherwise that particle would be travelling faster than the speed of light, which is not possible according to the limit principle. But then, in STR, it seems that it is not possible for a worldline of a person to double back and intersect itself, since this would require those worldlines to fall outside the light-cones. We can see this in Fig. 8.1. The worldline on the left conforms to the limit principle of relativity theory, whereas the worldline on the right does not. But in order for the worldline to intersect itself in this space–time, the worldline must violate the limit principle (in the absence of a more complex topology). The scenario envisaged by Weyl, then, is not possible in this space–time—we need GTR for that.

The significance of GTR is that gravitational effects are explained by a distortion of the geometry of space–time; and a distorted space–time

CTCs, and present no obstacle to the use of subspaces of constant mass-density to define successive planes of simultaneity. They therefore show that the class of universes to which the criteria of the cosmic tense theorists can be applied is larger than the class of isotropic universes.

210 GÖDEL'S MODAL MORAL

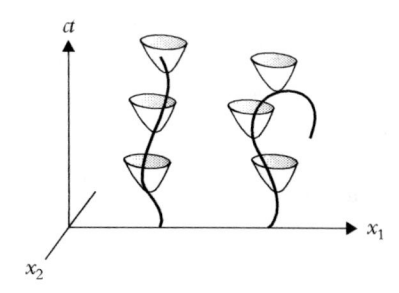

FIG. 8.1. Two worldlines: the left worldline conforms to the limit principle; the right worldline does not

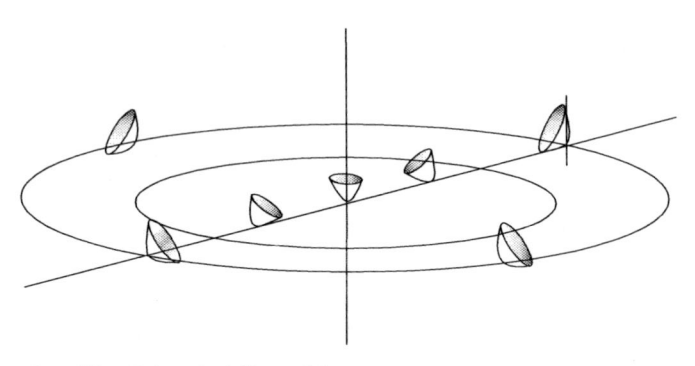

FIG. 8.2. Visualizing Gödel's model

will, in turn, affect the paths of light-rays such that the light-cones themselves can tip over in its presence. This is what happens in Gödel's model, depicted in Fig. 8.2 (see also Malament (1984)). I have drawn this such that we only see the future light-cones of various arbitrary points in the horizontal plane. Matter in this universe is rotating anticlockwise about the vertical axis; so as we move radially outwards, the future light-cones gradually start to tip in the direction of rotation, due to the relationship in GTR between rotation and gravity. (Note that the cones also get wider; so the vertical axis and worldlines remain time-like, as can be seen by the vertical worldline in the light-cone in the top right-hand corner.[5] Note also that this universe is

---

[5] In their discussion of Gödel's universe, Hawking and Ellis (1973: §5.7, Fig. 31) misrepresent the situation by not widening the light-cones such that the vertical lines remain time-like.

homogeneous: there is nothing special about the origin of these axes; there is no privileged point around which the rest of the universe rotates: the universe would look like this wherever the origin were placed; it is *everywhere* rotating.) There comes a point on this journey outwards at which the cones open up so much such that *locally* an observer can travel into his future (i.e., along a worldline within the future light-cone, i.e., without travelling faster than the speed of light) but *globally* be travelling into his past. That is, there are closed time-like curves (CTCs) in this model. But we can see that this does not just affect those travelling on the outer ring of the diagram: *every* point can be reached from *any* point in this model. To see this, take the point that is the origin of the axes. We can spiral upwards and outwards until we reach the critical point where the cones tip. We may then make our descent around this critical radius, such that we end up below the horizontal plane from where we began, gradually spiralling inwards and upwards to our starting-point at the origin.

However, this journey is more theoretical than practical, for the Gödel universe is infinite in size and non-expanding, so it must rotate at a speed great enough to counteract its tendency to collapse under gravitational attraction. More matter, then, requires greater rotation. As Nahin (1993: 337–8) points out, a universe like ours would have a rotational period of one cycle every 70 billion years, with the critical radius being 16 billion light-years. So a human hoping to achieve this in a lifetime would require a good cryonics advisor and a rather fast ship! But whether or not this is a physically realistic option for travelling into our own past is not the important issue. The philosophically significant point for presentism is that, unlike in STR where the problem arose from there being an *infinite* number of ways to partition space–time into past, present, and future, in the Gödel universe there is *no* consistent way of partitioning space–time into past, present, and future; there are no universe-wide planes of simultaneity.[6] Gödel thus establishes Part 1 of his argument. Further,

---

[6] Thus, the problem posed by Gödel's model has nothing to do with whether presentism is compatible with circular time, as some seem to think. For the notion of circular time, in itself, creates no difficulty for presentism at all. For take the case where the time-like curves form a complete circle. We could use topological means to order events, such as the relation of pair-separation proposed by Newton-Smith (1980: ch. 4, §2). Or, and my preferred way,

this is a rather powerful tactical move, since it bypasses the debate over the status of the present in STR. For even if presentists claim that out of the infinite array of reference frames available in STR there just *is* a metaphysically privileged frame, even though we cannot know which one it is, it is not a strategy that could work in the case of Gödel's model. So, given that CTCs are genuinely possible, Gödel was right to concentrate on a model which cannot be made compatible with the presentist ontology, rather than deal with the weaker argument from STR. But we now need to explore the implications of such a model.

III Part 2 of Gödel's argument

This step is known as Gödel's 'modal' argument (Yourgrau (1991)). As Earman (1995: 197) notes, Gödel's own formulation requires some

we could use metrical means by invoking metric tense operators that specify when certain facts were the case. For example, if the basic unit of time is a year, and p is the proposition that Friedrich is doing a dance, 'Friedrich did a dance 100 years ago' can be written '$\mathbf{P}^{100}p$'. These metric operators are sufficient to order events, even when the past tense *100 years ago*, and the future tense *one cycle minus 100 years hence* denote the same time. That is, we should merely conclude that, in the environment of circular time, metric tense operators act like periodic functions, e.g., for some period with value T, $\mathbf{P}^{n+T}p = \mathbf{P}^n p$. Two objections spring to mind. First, presentism asserts that neither the past nor the future exists, but only what is present exists; that is, in the standard case, presentism asserts that there are no (concrete) times either earlier or later than the present. However, in the circular setting, there is at least one time that exists later than the present, and at least one time that is earlier than the present, namely the present itself. So where does this leave presentism in this setting? The correct inference to draw, the presentist should argue, is that we should not assume that what is earlier than or later than the present does not concretely exist. For, in this context, some things do exist later than and earlier than the present, namely, present things *but only present things*. The second objection is that according to presentism in this circular context, a time t_1 comes into existence when it is present, goes out of existence when it is past, and then comes (back) into existence when it becomes present (again). But, given that times are particulars and so can only occur once, it does not make sense to say that the present can forever circle time, returning to the same time t_1. For to say that the same time occurs again and again is to say that the same time occurs at different times, which is a contradiction. But this argument is confused. For, in this context, there is only ever one token time of a certain type, and so it can never be the case that the same time can occur at any other time: a given time occurs at that time and no other. This confusion stems from trying to fit circular time into a linear context. The burden is on the opposition to find an incoherence in the thesis of presentism in the circular context taken on its own terms, i.e., without assuming linearity; for otherwise objections amount to no more than accusing time in this context of being something that it is not, namely linear, and this will not do.

interpretation in order to constitute a valid argument. But, unlike the impression given in the literature, this does not mean it is a mystery how to make the inference from 'time is unreal in Gödel's universe' to 'time is unreal in all universes'. For, as mentioned above, there is a quite natural way of understanding the argument, namely: if what we propose to *identify* time with cannot be applied to all models where time exists, then it cannot be what we take time to be in *this* universe. The following formulation captures Gödel's thought:

(IIIa) Tense is necessary for the existence of time (TNT)
(IIIb) If A is necessary for B, A exists in every possible world where B exists
(IIIc) For time to exist it must flow in every possible world where time exists [from (IIIa) and (IIIb)]
(IIId) There is a world where time in that world cannot be said to flow
∴ (IIIe) Time cannot exist [from (IIIc) and (IIId)]

This is a valid argument, and some, for example Yourgrau (1991; 1999), and Savitt (1994) (discussed below: §V), agree with Gödel that it establishes that time is ideal. I claim, however, that this argument fails. My first argument against Gödel uses TNT as ammunition.

IV Using TNT as ammunition against Gödel's conclusion

The inference from (IIIa) and (IIIb) to (IIIc) is unproblematic, as is the inference from (IIIc) and (IIId) to (IIIe). The bone of contention lies in the acceptability of asserting premises (IIIa) and (IIId) simultaneously. The argument is not simply one of *reductio ad absurdum*, for Gödel argues for both premises (IIIa) and (IIId) and does not reject either. But, in order for it to work, the premises must be suppositions essential to the position of the realist about time. Yet realists who hold TNT need not grant (IIId): it is quite contrary to their position. Tense theorists who hold TNT can, then, respond that (IIId) begs the question against them.

Replacing (IIId) with its nearest non-question-begging equivalent, however, leaves us with:

> (IIId*) There is a model, Gödel's, in which the variable 't' occurs in the solutions to EFE, but where what 't' denotes cannot be said to flow.

But this will not give Gödel his desired conclusion. For those who hold TNT could deny that there is any meaningful sense in which there can be said to be *time* in these models: '*whatever "t" is, it ain't time*'.

Thus, this is one of the ways in which (IIId) can be rejected. However, it is not satisfactory for tense theorists to leave things like this, for we are left wondering how 't' *is* to be interpreted in Gödel's model according to them. It certainly looks as if it should be interpreted as time. After all, Gödel's solutions are solutions to *equations* where 't' *is* time; so it is hardly plausible to deny that 't' is time in the *solutions* to those equations just because it is inconvenient for tense theorists. Those, e.g., Lucas (1999: 11), wishing to play the game of 'one man's *modus ponens*...' should not forget this point. We need better arguments than this, then, if we are to think 't' cannot be interpreted as time. I believe it is only by accepting that it *is* time in Gödel's model and engaging with time as presented in Gödel's model that a more satisfactory response to Gödel's argument can be given. And only then can the full implications of Gödel's argument be appreciated.

V Tenseless time: one way to dispose of TNT safely

We have here a situation much like the one reached after considering McTaggart's argument against the reality of time. And, as with McTaggart, there is the tenseless theory option open to resist Gödel's strong conclusion that *time* is unreal; for given that there is a plausible account of change available to the tenseless theorist, the most that

Gödel's argument can achieve, according to them, is that *tense* is unreal.

This is essentially the view that Savitt (1994) takes.[7] He agrees with Gödel and Yourgrau (1991) that the argument shows that time in the sense of our 'intuitive' conception, i.e., as a one-dimensional, flowing time-series in its own right, cannot exist. However, he argues that the argument is not wholly negative, for he uses it to show that it vindicates the notion of *space–time* as the fundamental structure of the universe—that is, instead of time and space considered separately—and that we should replace our old notions with the new one. His strategy can be captured as follows:

Step 1: Gödel's argument shows that time is ideal
Step 2: Therefore, we should replace the old notion with the (tenseless) temporal component of space–time.

But Step 1 is subject to the argument of §IV, and so Savitt's strategy fails. Specifically, in order for the ideality of time to be established, 't' in Gödel's model must be interpreted as time. But we have seen that in order to avoid question begging, Savitt must replace (IIId) in Gödel's argument with (IIId*). But then he must interpret 't' in Gödel's model as standing for the tenseless temporal component of space–time. And, as noted above, realists holding TNT need not grant that 't' *is* time in (IIId*). But this is precisely what is required for the argument to go through.

This is not to say that 't' cannot be interpreted as one of the components of space–time or as tenseless time in general. Of course it can. Indeed, the advantage of this kind of option is that at least it gives an interpretation of 't' in Gödel's model. But the point is that nothing has been said to rule out the reality of tense in the first place, from which the tenseless time or space–time moral is drawn. Realism about tense in our world is still viable.

---

[7] Although, strictly speaking, there is a difference in that Savitt *grants* the premiss that time essentially flows (i.e., *grants* TNT), but argues that Gödel shows time cannot exist and that it should be replaced by the temporal component of space–time, whereas with the tenseless option, time itself can still exist, but due to Gödel's argument, tense cannot (so in this respect TNT is *rejected*).

VI The essential properties of time

It is apparent from this discussion that the central assumption in the Gödelian argument (including Savitt's version) is that if time cannot be tensed in *all* worlds, then it cannot be tensed in *any*, which amounts to saying that if tense is a feature of time, it is an essential feature of time. But can we find any basis for this unargued for claim? And if we can, does it necessarily work in the Gödelian's favour? Perhaps tense theorists can *appeal* to the essential features of time in order to ground their dismissal of Gödel's model being a problem for them? Suppose we run an argument along the following lines: water is actually H_2O; therefore, water is necessarily H_2O. For what we mean by our use of the term 'water' is the stuff that we have interaction with in the actual world, the stuff that we actually use for drinking, washing, and swimming, etc. This stuff happens to be H_2O, and not, say, XYZ. Thus what we *mean* by our term 'water' is H_2O; thus 'water' rigidly designates H_2O, i.e., designates H_2O in all possible worlds. In other worlds, water is necessarily H_2O.

In a similar vein we could argue as follows: time is actually linear; therefore, time is necessarily linear. For consider two worlds: the actual world and the Gödelian world. What we in the actual world mean by our use of the term 'time' cannot be what is meant by inhabitants of the Gödelian world. For the time with which we have acquaintance in the actual world is linear, whereas those in the Gödelian world have acquaintance with something incorporating CTCs. Thus what we mean by the term 'time' is something that is linear; thus 'time' rigidly designates something linear, i.e., is linear in all possible worlds. In other words, time is necessarily linear. It follows that when we talk of Gödelian 'time', however much it looks like we're talking about *time*, we're not; so it's not something tense theorists need to be concerned about.

This is initially attractive, but the problem remains of specifying which are the essential properties of time and which contingent. We would not want this argument to be so strong as to make all actual facts about time necessarily the case. But how to decide? According to those that hold TNT, tense is essential. But tenseless theorists would ask why we should buy that. And it is even more controversial to think that a given topology is essential.

Suppose we try to ground the claim that certain features of time are essential. We come across a fundamental problem. For we as inhabitants of this world are acquainted only with a certain (relatively small) interval of time. Granted: this is a small part of something that globally is not linear. But, nevertheless, we are not acquainted with the *whole* thing that has it. That being so, is it really plausible to say that what we understand by 'time' cannot be what those in a Gödelian world understand by that term? For suppose that it is true that what we mean and understand by 'time' is that with which we have acquaintance. Given that *locally* time is linear in both worlds, it is not at all clear that we do mean different things by 'time' in the two worlds, since *both* sets of inhabitants experience time as linear. In other words, it seems more in the spirit of this kind of position to argue that 'time' rigidly designates something that is *locally* linear. Yet this says nothing about its *global* features. For the *global* features are something that extend beyond our acquaintance, and so it is indeterminate whether these features fall under our term 'time'; and thus our understanding of *time* leaves it open whether globally it is linear or not. Thus '*t*' in the Gödel solutions could still represent something that matches our conception of time, even though globally the solutions contain CTCs.

Gödelians require the TNT premiss for their argument to go through. But, without being able to find any grounds for thinking tense is an essential feature of time, perhaps tense theorists should reject that assumption, and in that way undermine Gödel's argument? How can this be done?

VII Another way to dispose of TNT— although taking great care to do it safely

According to this proposed strategy, Gödel's argument is not sufficient to establish the *unreality* of tense, but merely the *contingency* of tense:

some worlds are tensed, whereas others are not. Stein (1970: 593), Savitt (1994: 466), Earman (1995: 198), and Torretti (1999: 78) have all mentioned this option, but none of them expands sufficiently on what it could mean for tense to be contingent; so I shall. As we shall see, most of the possibilities are unsatisfactory for tense theorists. One option, however, is quite attractive. If it is satisfactory, we could save tense by denying the TNT premiss in Gödel's argument. So how do we make sense of the idea that tense could be a contingent feature of the world? Some options:

(a) Is tense an empirical matter?

(i) Is tense to be settled solely by de facto features of each world? We have seen that tense is not ruled out by GTR *per se*, but ruled out in some models by particular matters of fact. But we cannot simply argue that presentism holds when it is shown to be consistent with matters of fact, since consistency with matters of fact is only a necessary, not a sufficient, condition for asserting the tensed thesis: further empirical support is required to favour the tensed thesis over the tenseless. But there simply are no convincing cases of empirical facts or tests which can be conducted to support either tensed or tenseless theses in such worlds once the question of consistency with matters of fact in those worlds has been settled. So although claiming that tense is a contingent feature of the world does undermine TNT, which, in turn, undermines Gödel's argument, in the absence of any convincing examples to support the tensed thesis, they have left themselves with no good empirical grounds for asserting it for the actual world, and thus have shot themselves in the foot.

(ii) An argument from experience Some argue that we can *directly perceive* the lapse of time, or that the lapse of time gives the best explanation of our perceptions. But this brings us on to another of Gödel's arguments, something that can be used as an objection to tense being a contingent feature of time. Gödel writes:

[T]o assume an objective lapse of time would lose every justification in these worlds. For, in whatever way one may assume time to be lapsing, there will always exist possible observers to whose experienced lapse of time no objective lapse corresponds...But, if the experience of the lapse of time can exist without an objective lapse of time, no reason can be given why an objective lapse of time should be assumed at all.   (Gödel (1949b: 561); (1990: 205–6))

This argument is meant to undermine those reasons that we may have for believing in the existence of an objective lapse of time that are grounded in the way we experience the world. For, if the inhabitants of the Gödel universe have the same experiences as we do, then, given that the Gödel world cannot be tensed, what justification have *we* for taking our experience as a good reason for believing that our world is tensed?

This is a slightly stronger claim than the mere fact that the tenseless theory can account for our experience of time's apparent flow without having to postulate time's flow (see the Introduction: §III), for in this standard case it is not necessarily ruled out that it is possible for the universe either to be tensed or tenseless. Gödel's epistemic argument, however, shows that there is a universe where time *cannot* be tensed and yet we experience the same apparent flow of time. So it is not possible to argue *from experience* that we experience the objective flow of time, since we cannot know simply from experience that we are, in fact, experiencing the objective flow of time; we would need independent reasons for thinking that time did flow. And Gödel's position is that nothing can supply this.

The epistemic argument is much weaker than the standard modal argument, and the tense theorist simply need say that it is only strong enough to establish the fallibility of our intuitions about the passage of time than whether tense is real. But the point still stands: if tense theorists concede that tense is contingent in the empirical sense, then it does not seem as though they have any good empirical grounds (whether scientific or from experience) for asserting their thesis.

(b) There are no reasons: it is a brute fact that some worlds are tensed and others are not, and that's that

Maybe there is nothing about the empirical features of a world that determines whether it is tensed or tenseless, but it is simply a metaphysical fact about a world that it is either one or the other? This response certainly allows us to reject Gödel's modal argument, and it is close to the position I wish to adopt. However, although it is one way of saving tense in light of Gödel's argument, those who require more certainty in their metaphysics should look elsewhere. I shall first sketch the bad news for those wanting certainty, and then I shall place this view in a context which makes it more palatable.

The bad news is that this view leads to scepticism about the ontological make-up of our world. For if it is just a brute matter of fact what the ontological make-up of a world is, how can we know whether the actual world is one which is tensed or tenseless, contains universals or only particulars, or Cartesian minds as well as bodies, etc? We have conceded that there is no role for tense to play in physics, and there are no other reasons why one world is tensed and another tenseless, for what right have we to think that the world is the way it is for some good reason, such as simplicity, say? Our world could just be a shoddy heap of junk containing all sorts of superfluous entities.

Anyone who adopted this view in its bald form would be a curious character. It began as a genuine way of saving a seemingly substantial metaphysical thesis (that the actual world could be tensed) only to go on to draw the conclusion that metaphysics is a positively disreputable enterprise. For speculations on how the world is, and the reasons for it being that way, become entirely futile. It would be a mistake for tense theorists to think that they can derive any real comfort from appealing to this sort of contingency. Sure, Gödel's argument fails; but it completely undermines any reason for thinking that any world is tensed.

There is, however, a more sophisticated and plausible sense in which tense could be contingent which allows for the idea that it is a brute fact what the ontological make-up of a world is, whilst saving metaphysics.

(c) Time as a functional concept

Suppose that 'time' is a functional, or theoretical, term along the lines of Ramsey–Carnap–Lewis: time is that which plays a certain role in our thinking, and which plays a certain role in explaining certain phenomena (cf. Lewis (1970)). So we might gather together a collection of platitudes that contain the word 'time', and perhaps also a number of scientific truths involving 'time', and say that time is whatever best fits the role defined by these sentences. Now, just as a pain state might be c-fibres firing in me, but, say, salt-solution leakages in Martians (in other words, a question of mind–brain identity as opposed to mind–brine identity), time might be tensed at one world but tenseless at another. Of course, this contingency happens because of our semantics rather than something metaphysical. When we say that pain could have been a brine leakage, we do not mean: take pain to be c-fibres firing, and then try to imagine that those very c-fibres firing might have really been brine leakages. (After all, is it possible for a c-fibre to have been brine?) Rather, brine leakages might have played the role that c-fibres firing actually play in us. Similarly with time. Perhaps, in some worlds, tensed facts fit our definitional theory of time. But perhaps in other worlds, tenseless facts do. It is not that we are to imagine that *those very tensed facts* might not have been tensed—which would be very odd!—but just that tenseless facts might fit the time role.

This 'fitting the role' idea is most likely what prompts scientists and mathematicians to interpret their functions as temporal. They may say something like: 'anything that moves along a curve defined by this function will experience change, etc., and this is enough for us to say that, in this model, this *is* time.' It may be that *nothing* perfectly fits the role defined by our common sense and scientific hypotheses about time, but nevertheless, their function fits the role closely enough, and maybe that is enough for it to deserve the name 'time'.

This approach certainly undermines Gödel's argument against the tense thesis being true of any worlds without our having to reconcile tense with his model. But is it a strategy that tense theorists could use? How is it any better than the position we arrived at in (b) above? It may be thought that it is difficult to see how this contingency thesis could help tense theorists assert their thesis for the actual world. For, if they concede that the tenseless time could adequately play the role of time, then it is hard to see any reason for thinking that the actual world is tensed rather than tenseless.

I think this is true, but that we are in a better position with this view to save metaphysics. For it is misleading to say that 'anything goes' once we admit that tense is a contingent feature of the world: good metaphysics constrains what the possibilities are; and in the case of time, it constrains them quite nicely. For any adequate theory has to accommodate the platitudes about time, and explain how such truths can be true. This itself rules out a whole host of possibilities for how time could contingently be, and so we are immediately better off than the position we arrived at in section (b). For instance, just from considering the problem of how our metaphysical account of time can account for the knowledge that we have that we are present, we saw in Chapter 1 that time must be either tenseless or presentist in nature. The very possibility that arises with some theories that we could be located anywhere other than the present does not show that we should seriously consider it as a genuine possibility. Rather, it shows that this was the wrong way to think about how time *could be*. Similarly, any adequate theory of time must explain and accommodate the so-called 'truth-value links' which hold across time; that is, that if a proposition *p* is presently true, it must be true in the future that *p was* true. The fact that this systematic truth-value link cannot be guaranteed according to some theories (as we saw in Chapter 2) should not lead us seriously to worry that present truths may not be tomorrow's past truths: that some theories have this consequence shows that they are conceptually misguided and not ways that time itself could be. In these cases, it is not that we reject the theories because there is a more elegant theory which does it better. Rather, they are rejected because they do not do the job *at all*. This is the sense in which good metaphysics leaves open the genuine possibilities and filters out the dross.

Despite this, however, it seems to me that metaphysics cannot quite give us a determinate answer, in the case of time, on how the actual world is. Of course, if tensed statements have tenseless truthmakers, then they do not also have tensed truthmakers (Mellor (1981)), and vice versa (Priest (1986)). But this only establishes what any particular world can be like and does not touch the issue whether tensed statements can have tensed truthmakers in one world and tenseless truthmakers in another. Still less does it tell us which of the two the actual world has.

Perhaps we could make an appeal to philosophical methodology? Aren't there, after all, widely accepted conditions for good theory construction and acceptability, such as initial plausibility, simplicity, parsimony, and a good weighting of benefits to costs? The problem here is establishing in what sense these virtues can, in a metaphysical theory, lead us to the truth. As we saw in Chapter 2: §VII(c), one reason for preferring presentism over the tenseless theory is the fact that presentists can do all of the work on the cheap: the tenseless theory invokes the existence of equally real concrete times, past, present, and future, whereas presentism invokes only one concrete time (which is a saving so long as abstract objects are required in any case by all). Here, it is simply an issue of quantitative parsimony, and if we thought that this was a factor in determining the truth of a theory, then we would be able to make much progress. For not only would it lead us to think that presentism is true of the actual world, it would also give us a reason for thinking it is true of many worlds. For in *every* world containing time, presentism is more quantitatively parsimonious than the tenseless theory. But this, of course, is not to say that presentism is *available* to the inhabitants of every world. Ideally, we might think that the presentist world is the world at which to be seen, the theory that any rational person in any world would adopt, given the choice. But the conditions obtaining in a given world might just take that choice away from us; we might just have to settle for the best theory that flies in that world; we might have to settle for the tenseless theory in worlds such as Gödel's, even though presentism, because more parsimonious, is the preferred option.

Nevertheless, there will still be reservations about whether we can go even this far. Suppose we think that parsimony is truth-conducive. We still have to weigh that against the other supposedly truth-conducive virtues: perhaps the simpler, more elegant, theory would be the one where you could apply the same interpretation of '*t*' across the board (as, it seems, the tenseless theory can), and thus rule out the 'tense as contingent' theory as being the most elegant, even if it is the most parsimonious. It is difficult to see how the issue could be resolved.

The best we can do, then, is to be honest about what can be shown. I think it is this: there are two theories (presentism and the tenseless theory) which can do everything we want a theory of time to do, and in those worlds where particular matters of fact do not rule either out, we have to say that either could be true and that it is a brute matter of fact which is.

This seems to me to be the most attractive way to interpret the idea that tense is a contingent feature of time, and it is certainly a strategy that presentists could use to fend off Gödel's argument without shooting themselves in the foot. For the arguments for their position remain, and even though they may not be decisive, in this regard they are no worse off than their tenseless opposition. This is a nice position for presentism to be in, since, even if we reject models like Gödel's as worthy of serious attention, there may still be other models of the universe that cause trouble for presentism.[8] And if such models exist, Gödel's modal argument threatens. But whatever models are found, Gödel's own conclusion based on his modal argument—namely, that time is unreal—is too strong: both the tenseless theory and presentism can survive his argument.

[8] Indeed, as Earman (2002) points out, GTR looks rather inhospitable to presentism. It would be premature, however, to draw strong conclusions from current physics. There are always new discoveries being made and we are not short of ingenuity. But when all of the dust has settled and all of the facts are in about our world, it may well be that presentism is ruled out by matters of empirical fact. Presentism would then be actually false. But it would still remain as the only possible alternative to the tenseless theory.

Bibliography

Adams, R. M. (1974), 'Theories of Actuality', Noûs, 8, 211–31.
—— (1986), 'Time and Thisness', in P. French, T. Uehling, and H. Wettstein (eds.), *Midwest Studies in Philosophy*, II (Minneapolis: University of Minnesota Press), 315–29.
Aristotle, *De interpretatione*, trans. E. M. Edghill from *The Works of Aristotle*, ed. W. D. Ross (Chicago: Encyclopædia Britannica, Inc., 1952).
Armstrong, D. M. (1983), *What is a Law of Nature?* (Cambridge: Cambridge University Press).
—— (1997), *A World of States of Affairs* (Cambridge: Cambridge University Press).
Ayer, A. J. (1954), 'Statements about the Past', in his *Philosophical Essays* (London: Macmillan), 167–90.
—— (1956), *The Problem of Knowledge* (London: Penguin).
—— (1973), *The Central Questions of Philosophy* (London: Penguin).
Bacon, J. (1995), *Universals and Property-Instances: The Alphabet of Being* (Oxford: Basil Blackwell).
Bigelow, J. (1996), 'Presentism and Properties', in J. E. Tomberlin (ed.), *Philosophical Perspectives 10: Metaphysics* (Cambridge, Mass. and Oxford: Blackwell), 35–52.
Bochvar, D. A. (1938), 'Ob odnom tréhznacnom iscislénii i égo priménénii k analizu paradosov klassičéskogo rassirennogo funkcjonal'noga iscislénia (On a Three-Valued Calculus and its Application to Analysis of Paradoxes of Classical Extended Functional Calculus)', *Matématicéskij Sbornik*, 4, 287–308.
Bourne, C. P. (2002), 'When am I? A Tense Time for Some Tense Theorists?', *Australasian Journal of Philosophy*, 80, 359–71.
—— (2004a), 'Becoming Inflated', *British Journal for the Philosophy of Science*, 55, 107–19.
—— (2004b), 'Future Contingents, Non-contradiction and the Law of Excluded Middle Muddle', *Analysis*, 64, 122–8.
—— (2005), 'Review of *Time, Tense and Reference*, ed. Q. Smith and A. Jokić', *Mind*, 114, 747–50.
—— (2006), 'A Theory of Presentism', *Canadian Journal of Philosophy*, 36, 1–24.

Broad, C. D. (1921), 'Time', in J. Hastings (ed.), *Encyclopaedia of Religion and Ethics* (New York: Scribner), 334–45.
—— (1923), *Scientific Thought* (London: Routledge).
—— (1938), *An Examination of McTaggart's Philosophy* (Cambridge: Cambridge University Press).
Butterfield, J. N. (1984a), 'Relationism and Possible Worlds', *British Journal for the Philosophy of Science*, 35, 101–13.
—— (1984b), 'Prior's Conception of Time', *Proceedings of the Aristotelian Society*, 84, 193–209.
—— (1984c), 'Seeing the Present', *Mind*, 93, 161–76.
—— (ed.) (1999), *The Arguments of Time* (Oxford: Oxford University Press for The British Academy).
—— and Isham, C. (1999), 'On the Emergence of Time in Quantum Gravity', in J. Butterfield (ed.), *The Arguments of Time* (Oxford: Oxford University Press for The British Academy), 111–68.
Callender, C. (1997), 'Review of Dorato, *Time and Reality*', *British Journal for the Philosophy of Science*, 48, 117–20.
—— (2000) 'Shedding Light on Time', *Philosophy of Science (Proceedings)*, 67, 589–99.
—— (ed.) (2002), *Time, Reality and Experience* (Cambridge, Cambridge University Press).
Casati, R., and Varzi, A. C. (1996), *Events* (Aldershot: Dartmouth).
Christensen, F. (1976), 'The Source of the River of Time', *Ratio*, 18, 131–43.
—— (1981), 'Special Relativity and Space-Like Time', *British Journal for the Philosophy of Science*, 32, 37–53.
Cockburn, D. (1997), *Other Times* (Cambridge: Cambridge University Press).
—— (1998), 'Tense and Emotion', in R. Le Poidevin (ed.), *Questions of Time and Tense* (Oxford: Oxford University Press), 77–92.
Craig, W. L. (1997), 'Is Presentness a Property?', *American Philosophical Quarterly*, 34, 27–40.
—— (2000a), *The Tensed Theory of Time: A Critical Examination* (Dordrecht: Kluwer).
—— (2000b), *The Tenselesss Theory of Time: A Critical Examination* (Dordrecht: Kluwer).
—— (2003), 'In Defense of Presentism', in A. Jokić and Q. Smith (eds.), *Time, Tense, and Reference* (London: MIT Press), 391–408.
Crisp, T. (2003), 'Presentism', in M. J. Loux, and D. W. Zimmerman (eds.), *The Oxford Handbook of Metaphysics* (Oxford: Oxford University Press), 211–45.

Crystal, D. (2002), 'Talking about Time', in K. Ridderbos (ed.), *Time* (Cambridge: Cambridge University Press), 105–25.
Davidson, D. (1967a), 'The Logical Form of Action Sentences', in N. Rescher (ed.), *The Logic of Decision and Action* (University of Pittsburgh Press); also in his *Essays on Actions and Events* (Oxford: Oxford University Press, 1980), 105–48.
—— (1967b), 'Causal Relations', *Journal of Philosophy*, 64; also in his *Essays on Actions and Events* (Oxford: Oxford University Press, 1980), 149–62.
—— (1969), 'The Individuation of Events', in N. Rescher (ed.), *Essays in Honor of Carl G. Hempel* (Dordrecht: D. Reidel), 216–34; also in his *Essays on Actions and Events* (Oxford: Oxford University Press, 1980), 163–80.
Dieks, D. (1988), 'Special Relativity and the Flow of Time', *Philosophy of Science*, 55, 456–60.
Divers, J. (2002), *Possible Worlds* (London: Routledge).
Dorato, M. (1995), *Time and Reality* (Bologna: CLUEB).
—— (2002), 'On Becoming, Cosmic Time and Rotating Universe', in C. Callender (ed.), *Time, Reality and Experience* (Cambridge, Cambridge University Press), 253–76.
Dorling, J. (1983), 'Reply to Mackie', in R. Swinburne (ed.), *Space, Time and Causality* (Dordrecht: D. Reidel), 23–35.
Dummett, M. (1960), 'A Defence of McTaggart's Proof of the Unreality of Time', *Philosophical Review*, 69, 497–504; also his *Truth and Other Enigmas* (London: Duckworth, 1978), 351–7.
—— (1963), 'Realism', in his *Truth and Other Enigmas* (London: Duckworth, 1978), 145–65.
—— (1969), 'The Reality of the Past', *Philosophical Review*, 78, 239–58; also in his *Truth and Other Enigmas* (London: Duckworth, 1978), 358–74.
—— (1982), 'Realism', *Synthese*, 52, 55–112; also in his *The Seas of Language* (Oxford: Oxford University Press, 1993), 230–76.
—— (1992), 'The Metaphysics of Verificationism', in L. E. Hahn (ed.), *The Philosophy of A. J. Ayer* (La Salle, Ill.: Open Court), 128–48.
—— (1993), 'Realism and Anti-Realism', in his *The Seas of Language* (Oxford: Oxford University Press), 462–78.
—— (2003), *Truth and the Past* (Columbia University Press).
Earman, J. (1989), *World Enough and Space–Time* (Cambridge, Mass.; London: MIT Press).
—— (1995), *Bangs, Crunches, Whimpers, and Shrieks* (Oxford: Oxford University Press).
—— (2002), 'Thoroughly Modern McTaggart, or What McTaggart Would Have Said if he had Read the General Theory of Relativity', *Philosophers'*

Imprint, 2 (which can be found at <www.umich.edu/~philos/Imprint/frameset.html?browse>).

Eddington, A. (1933), *The Expanding Universe* (Cambridge: Cambridge University Press).

Eells, E. (1982), *Rational Decision and Causality* (Cambridge: Cambridge University Press).

Einstein, A. (1905), 'Zur Elektrodynamik bewegter Körper (On the Electrodynamics of Moving Bodies)', *Annalen der Physik*, 17, 891–921.

—— (1920), *Relativity: The Special and General Theory* (London: Methuen & Co.)

—— (1924), 'Zwei Tondokumente Einsteins zur Relativitätstheorie', recording, transcribed in Friedrich Herneck, *Forschungen und Fortschritte*, 40 (1966), 134.

Evans, G. (1973), 'The Causal Theory of Names', *Proceedings of the Aristotelian Society Supplementary Volume*, 47, 187–208.

—— (1982), *The Varieties of Reference* (Oxford: Clarendon Press).

Falk, A. (2003), 'Time Plus the Whoosh and Whiz', in A. Jokić and Q. Smith (eds.), *Time, Tense, and Reference* (London: MIT Press), 211–50.

Findlay, J. N. (1941), 'Time: A Treatment of Some Puzzles', *Australasian Journal of Psychology and Philosophy*, 19, 216–35.

Fitzgerald, P. (1969), 'The Truth About Tomorrow's Sea Fight', *Journal of Philosophy*, 66, 307–29.

Frege, G. (1892), 'Über Sinn und Bedeutung (On Sense and Reference)', *Zeitschrift für Philosophie und philosophische Kritik*, 100, 25–50.

French, A. P. (1968), *Special Relativity* (London: Thomas Nelson & Sons).

Gale, R. M. (1968), *The Language of Time* (London: Routledge & Kegan Paul).

—— (ed.) (1967), *The Philosophy of Time* (New York: Doubleday).

Geach, P. (1969), 'The Perils of Pauline', *Review of Metaphysics*, 23, 287–300.

Gibbard, A., and Harper, W. L. (1978), 'Counterfactuals and Two Kinds of Expected Utility', in W. L. Harper *et al.*, *Ifs* (Reidel: Dordrecht-Holland), 153–90.

Gödel, K. (1949a), 'An Example of a New Type of Cosmological Solutions of Einstein's Field Equations of Gravitation', *Review of Modern Physics*, 21, 447–50; also in S. Feferman *et al.* (eds.), *Kurt Gödel, Collected Works, Volume II* (Oxford: Oxford University Press, 1990), 190–8.

—— (1949b), 'A Remark about the Relationship between Relativity Theory and Idealistic philosophy', in P. A. Schlipp (ed.), *Albert Einstein: Philosopher-Scientist* (La Salle: Open Court Press), 555–62; also in S. Feferman *et al.*

(eds.), *Kurt Gödel, Collected Works, Volume II* (Oxford: Oxford University Press, 1990), 202–7.

―― (1949c), 'Lecture on Rotating Universes', in S. Feferman et al. (eds.), *Kurt Gödel, Collected Works, Volume III* (Oxford: Oxford University Press, 1995), 261–9.

―― (1952), 'Rotating Universes in General Relativity', *Proceedings of the International Congress of Mathematicians: Cambridge, Massachusetts, USA August 30–September 6, 1950*, I (Providence, R.I.: American Mathematical Society, 1952), 175–81. Also in S. Feferman et al. (eds.), *Kurt Gödel, Collected Works, Volume II* (Oxford: Oxford University Press, 1990), 208–16.

Goodman, N. (1951), *The Structure of Appearance* (Indianapolis, Ind.: Bobbs Merrill).

Grice, P. (1989), *Studies in the Way of Words* (Cambridge, Mass., London: Harvard University Press).

Grünbaum, A. (1967), 'The Status of Temporal Becoming', in his *Modern Science and Zeno's Paradoxes* (Middleton, Conn.: Wesleyan University Press), 7–36.

Halldén, S. (1949), *The Logic of Nonsense* (Uppsala: Uppsala Universitets Arsskrift).

Hawking, S. W. (1969), 'The Existence of Cosmic Time Functions', *Proceedings of the Royal Society*, 308, 433–5.

―― and Ellis, G. F. R. (1973), *The Large Scale Structure of Space–Time* (Cambridge: Cambridge University Press).

Horgan, T. (1978), 'The Case Against Events', *Philosophical Review*, 87, 28–47.

Hume, D., *An Enquiry Concerning Human Understanding*, 3rd edn., repr. from the posthumous edition of 1777, ed. L. A. Selby-Bigge, text revised and notes P. H. Nidditch (Oxford: Clarendon Press, 1975).

Jeans, J. (1936), 'Man and the Universe', Sir Stewart Alley Lecture, in his *Scientific Progress* (London: Allen and Unwin), 13–38.

Jeffrey, R. (1980), 'Coming True', in C. Diamond and J. Teichman (eds.), *Intention and Intentionality* (London: Harvester), 251–60.

Jokić, A., and Smith, Q. (eds.), (2003) *Time, Tense, and Reference* (London: MIT Press).

Kamp, H. (1971), 'Formal Properties of "Now" ', *Theoria*, 37, 179–87.

Keller, S., and Nelson, M. (2001), 'Presentists Should Believe in Time-Travel', *Australasian Journal of Philosophy*, 79, 333–45.

Kneale, W., and Kneale, M. (1962), *The Development of Logic* (Oxford: Clarendon Press).

Kripke, S. (1963), 'Semantical Considerations on Modal Logic', *Acta Philosophica Fennica*, 16, 83–94.

Kripke, S. (1972), 'Naming and Necessity', in D. Davidson and G. Harman (eds.), *Semantics of Natural Languages* (Dordrecht: D. Reidel), 253–355; also as his *Naming and Necessity* (Oxford: Blackwell, 1980).

Lanczos, C. (1924), 'Über eine stationäre kosmologie im sinne der Einsteinischen Gravitationstheories', *Zeitschr. f. Phys.*, 21, 73.

von Laue, M. (1912), 'Zwei Einwände gegen die Relativitätstheorie und ihre Widerlegung', *Phys.Z*, 13, 118–20.

Le Poidevin, R. (1991), *Change, Cause and Contradiction* (Basingstoke: Macmillan).

—— (1998), 'The Past, Present, and Future of the Debate about Tense', in R. Le Poidevin (ed.), *Questions of Time and Tense* (Oxford: Oxford University Press), 13–42.

—— (2002), 'Zeno's Arrow and the Significance of the Present', in C. Callender (ed.), *Time, Reality and Experience* (Cambridge: Cambridge University Press), 57–72.

—— and MacBeath, M. (eds.) (1993), *The Philosophy of Time* (Oxford: Oxford University Press).

Lepore, E., and Ludwig, K. (2003), 'Outline of a Truth-Conditional Semantics for Tense', in A. Jokić and Q. Smith (eds.), *Time, Tense, and Reference* (London: MIT Press), 49–105.

Levison, A. B. (1987), 'Events and Time's Flow', *Mind*, 96, 341–53.

Lewis, D. K. (1970), 'How to Define Theoretical Terms', *Journal of Philosophy*, 67, 427–46; also in his *Philosophical Papers, Volume I* (Oxford: Oxford University Press, 1986), 78–95.

—— (1973a), 'Causation', *Journal of Philosophy*, 70, 556–67; also in his *Philosophical Papers, Volume II* (Oxford: Oxford University Press, 1986), 159–213.

—— (1973b), *Counterfactuals* (Oxford: Basil Blackwell).

—— (1976), 'The Paradoxes of Time Travel', *American Philosophical Quarterly*, 13, 145–52; also in his *Philosophical Papers, Volume II* (Oxford: Oxford University Press, 1986), 67–80.

—— (1979a), 'Counterfactual Dependence and Time's Arrow', *Noûs*, 13, 455–76; also in his *Philosophical Papers, Volume II* (Oxford: Oxford University Press, 1986), 32–66.

—— (1979b), 'Prisoners' Dilemma is a Newcomb Problem', *Philosophy and Public Affairs*, 8, 235–40. Also in his *Philosophical Papers, Volume II* (Oxford: Oxford University Press), 299–302.

—— (1979c), 'Attitudes *De Dicto* and *De Se*', *Philosophical Review*, 88, 513–43; also in his *Philosophical Papers, Volume I* (Oxford: Oxford University Press), 133–56.

—— (1980), 'A Subjectivist's Guide to Objective Chance', in R. C. Jeffery (ed.), *Studies in Inductive Logic and Probability, Volume II* (University of California Press); also in his *Philosophical Papers, Volume II* (Oxford University Press, 1986), 83–132.

—— (1981), 'Causal Decision Theory', *Australasian Journal of Philosophy*, 59, 5–30; also in his *Philosophical Papers, Volume II* (Oxford University Press, 1986), 305–37.

—— (1986), *On the Plurality of Worlds* (Oxford: Basil Blackwell).

—— (1991), *Parts of Classes* (Oxford: Blackwell).

—— (2001), 'Forget About the "Correspondence Theory of Truth"', *Analysis*, 61, 275–80.

—— (2003), 'Things qua Truthmakers', in H. Lillehammer and G. Rodriguez-Pereyra (eds.), *Real Metaphysics: Essays in Honour of D. H. Mellor* (London: Routledge), 25–38.

Lorentz, H. A. (1916), *The Theory of Electrons* (Leiden: Brill, 1909; rev. edn., 1916; New York: Dover, 1952).

Lowe, E. J. (1987), 'The Indexical Fallacy in McTaggart's Argument for the Unreality of Time', *Mind*, 96, 539–42.

—— (1998), 'Tense and Persistence', in R. Le Poidevin (ed.), *Questions of Time and Tense* (Oxford: Oxford University Press), 43–60.

Lucas, J. R. (1999), 'A Century of Time', in J. N. Butterfield (ed.), *The Arguments of Time* (Oxford: Oxford University Press for The British Academy), 1–20.

Ludlow, P. (1999), *Semantics, Tense, and Time* (Cambridge, Mass.: MIT Press).

Łukasiewicz, J. (1920), 'On Three-Valued Logic', in S. McCall (ed.), *Polish Logic 1920–1939* (Oxford: Clarendon Press, 1967), 16–18; also in *Selected Works*, ed. L. Borkowski (Amsterdam: North Holland, 1970), 87–8.

—— (1930), 'Philosophical Remarks on Many-Valued Systems of Propositional Logic', in S. McCall (ed.), *Polish Logic 1920–1939* (Oxford: Clarendon Press, 1967), 40–65.

—— (1951), *Aristotle's Syllogistic from the Standpoint of Modern Formal Logic* (Oxford: Oxford University Press).

—— (1970), *Selected Works*, ed. L. Borkowski (Amsterdam: North Holland).

McArthur, R. P. (1976), *Tense Logic* (Dordrecht: Reidel).

MacBeath, M. (1983), 'Mellor's Emeritus Headache', *Ratio*, 25, 81–8.

McCall, S. (1976), 'Objective Time Flow', *Philosophy of Science*, 43, 337–62.

—— (1994), *A Model of the Universe* (Oxford: Clarendon Press).

—— (ed.) (1967), *Polish Logic* (Oxford: Oxford University Press).

McCulloch, G. (1989), *The Game of the Name* (Oxford: Clarendon Press).

McDowell, J. (1977), 'On the Sense and Reference of a Proper Name', *Mind*, 86, 159–85.
Mackie, J. L. (1974), *The Cement of the Universe* (Oxford: Clarendon Press).
—— (1983), 'Three Steps Towards Absolutism', in R. Swinburne (ed.), *Space, Time and Causality* (Dordrecht: Reidel), 3–22.
Mackintosh, R. et al. (1997), *General Relativity and Cosmology* (Milton Keynes: Open University).
McTaggart, J. McT. E. (1908), 'The Unreality of Time', *Mind*, 17, 457–84.
—— (1927), *The Nature of Existence, Volume II*, ed. C. D. Broad (Cambridge: Cambridge University Press).
Malament, D. (1984), '"Time Travel" in the Gödel Universe', *PSA: Proceedings of the Biennial Meeting of the Philosophy of Science Association, 1984, Volume Two: Symposia and Invited Papers*, 91–100.
—— (1995), 'Introductory note for 1949b', in S. Feferman et al. (eds.), *Kurt Gödel, Collected Works, Volume III* (Oxford: Oxford University Press), 261–9.
Markosian, N. (2004), 'A Defense of Presentism', in D. W. Zimmerman (ed.), *Oxford Studies in Metaphysics, Volume I* (Oxford: Oxford University Press), 47–82.
Maxwell, N. (1988), 'Are Probabilism and Special Relativity Incompatible?', *Philosophy of Science*, 55, 640–5.
Mellor, D. H. (1974), 'Special Relativity and Present Truth', *Analysis*, 34, 74–8.
—— (1980), 'Necessities and Universals in Natural Laws', in D. H. Mellor (ed.), *Science, Belief and Behaviour* (Cambridge: Cambridge University Press), 105–25.
—— (1981), *Real Time* (Cambridge: Cambridge University Press).
—— (1995), *The Facts of Causation* (London: Routledge).
—— (1998), *Real Time II* (London: Routledge).
—— (2003), 'Replies: Change and Time', in H. Lillehammer and G. Rodriguez-Pereyra (eds.), *Real Metaphysics: Essays in Honour of D. H. Mellor* (London: Routledge), 235–7.
—— (2005a), 'Time', in F. Jackson and M. Smith (eds.), *The Oxford Handbook of Contemporary Philosophy* (Oxford: Oxford University Press), ch. 21.
—— (2005b), *Probability: A Philosophical Introduction* (London: Routledge).
Mill, J. S. (1843), *A System of Logic* (London: Routledge).
Miller, A. I. (1998), *Albert Einstein's Special Theory of Relativity: Emergence (1905) and Early Interpretation (1905–1911)* (New York: Springer-Verlag).
Minkowski, H. (1908), 'Space and Time', in J. J. C. Smart (ed.), *Problems of Space and Time* (London: Macmillan, 1964), 297–312.

Nahin, P. J. (1993), *Time Machines* (New York: American Institute of Physics).
Newton-Smith, W. H. (1980), *The Structure of Time* (London: Routledge & Kegan Paul).
Nozick, R. (1969), 'Newcomb's Problem and Two Principles of Choice', in N. Rescher (ed.), *Essays in Honour of Carl G. Hempel* (Dordrecht-Holland: D. Reidel), 114–46.
Oaklander, L. N. (1984), *Temporal Relations and Temporal Becoming* (Lanham: University Press of America).
—— (1987), 'McTaggart's Paradox and the Infinite Regress of Temporal Attributions: A Reply to Smith', *Southern Journal of Philosophy*, 25, 425–31.
—— (2002), 'Presentism, Ontology and Temporal Experience', in C. Callender (ed.), *Time, Reality and Experience* (Cambridge: Cambridge University Press), 73–90.
—— (2003a), 'Presentism: A Critique', in H. Lillehammer and G. Rodriguez-Pereyra (eds.), *Real Metaphysics: Essays in Honour of D. H. Mellor* (London: Routledge), 196–211.
—— (2003b), 'Two Versions of the New B-Theory of Language', in A. Jokić and Q. Smith (eds.), *Time, Tense, and Reference* (London: MIT Press), 271–303.
Perry, J. (1977), 'Frege on Demonstratives', *Philosophical Review*, 86, 474–97.
—— (1979), 'The Problem of the Essential Indexical', *Noûs*, 13, 3–21.
Plantinga, A. (1974), *The Nature of Necessity* (Oxford: Clarendon Press).
Poincaré, H. (1902), *La science et l'hypothèse* (Paris: E. Flammarion); English trans., W. J. Greenstreet, *Science and Hypothesis* (London: Walter Scott, 1905).
—— (1904), 'L'état actuel et l'avenir de la Physique mathématique', in *La valeur de la science* (Paris: E. Flammarion); in English as *The Value of Science* (New York: Dover, 1958), 91–111.
Priest, G. (1986), 'Tense and Truth-Conditions', *Analysis*, 46, 162–6.
Price, H. (1996), *Time's Arrow and Archimedes' Point* (Oxford: Oxford University Press).
Prior, A. N. (1953), 'Three-Valued Logic and Future Contingents', *Philosophical Quarterly*, 3, 317–26.
—— (1957), *Time and Modality* (Oxford: Oxford University Press).
—— (1959), 'Thank Goodness That's Over', *Philosophy*, 34, 12–17.
—— (1967), *Past, Present and Future* (Oxford: Oxford University Press).
—— (1968a), 'Changes in Events and Changes in Things', in his *Papers on Time and Tense* (new edn., Oxford: Clarendon Press, 2003), 7–19.
—— (1968b), 'On Spurious Egocentricity', in his *Papers on Time and Tense* (new edn., Oxford: Clarendon Press, 2003), 27–37.

Prior, A. N. (1968c), 'Tense Logic and the Logic of Earlier and Later', in his *Papers on Time and Tense* (new edn., Oxford: Oxford University Press, 2003), 117–38.

—— (1968d), 'Stratified Metric Tense Logic', in his *Papers on Time and Tense* (new edn., Oxford: Clarendon Press, 2003), 159–70.

—— (1968e), 'Now', in his *Papers on Time and Tense* (new edn., Oxford: Clarendon Press, 2003), 171–93.

—— (1968f), 'Tense Logic for Non-Permanent Existents', in his *Papers on Time and Tense* (new edn., Oxford: Oxford University Press, 2003), 257–75.

—— (1970), 'The Notion of the Present', *Studium Generale*, 23, 245–8.

—— (1971), *Objects of Thought*, ed. P. T. Geach and A. J. P. Kenny (Oxford: Clarendon Press).

—— (1996a), 'A Statement of Temporal Realism', in J. Copeland (ed.), *Logic and Reality: Essays on the Legacy of Arthur Prior* (Oxford: Oxford University Press), 45–6.

—— (1996b), 'Some Free Thinking about Time', in J. Copeland (ed.), *Logic and Reality: Essays on the Legacy of Arthur Prior* (Oxford: Oxford University Press), 47–51.

Putnam, H. (1957), 'Three-Valued Logic', *Philosophical Studies*, 8, 73–80; also in his *Philosophical Papers, Volume I* (Cambridge: Cambridge University Press, 1975), 166–73.

—— (1967), 'Time and Physical Geometry', *Journal of Philosophy*, 64, 240–7; also in his *Philosophical Papers, Volume I* (Cambridge: Cambridge University Press, 1975), 198–205.

—— (1981), *Reason, Truth and History* (Cambridge: Cambridge University Press).

Quine, W. v. O. (1960), *Word and Object* (Cambridge, Mass.: MIT Press).

Ramsey, F. P. (1927), 'Facts and Propositions', *Proceedings of the Aristotelian Society Supplementary Volume* 7, 153–70; also in his *Philosophical Papers*, ed. D. H. Mellor (Cambridge: Cambridge University Press, 1990), 34–51.

Reichenbach, H. (1928), *Philosophie der Raum-Zeit-Lehre* (Berlin: W. de Gruyter); English trans. M. Reichenbach and J. Freund, *The Philosophy of Space and Time* (New York: Dover, 1958).

Russell, B. (1903), *The Principles of Mathematics* (London: Routledge).

—— (1905), 'On Denoting', *Mind*, 14, 479–93.

—— (1911), 'Knowledge by Acquaintance and Knowledge by Description', *Proceedings of the Aristotelian Society*, 11, 108–28.

—— (1915), 'On the Experience of Time', in *Monist*, 25, 212–33.

____ (1918–19), 'Lectures on the Philosophy of Logical Atomism', in his *Logic and Knowledge*, ed. R. C. Marsh (London: Routledge, 1956), 175–281.

____ (1919), *Introduction to Mathematical Philosophy* (London: Routledge).

____ (1921), *The Analysis of Mind* (London: Allen & Unwin).

Saunders, S. (2002), 'How Relativity Contradicts Presentism', in C. Callender (ed.), *Time, Reality and Experience* (Cambridge, Cambridge University Press), 277–92.

Savitt, S. F. (1994), 'The Replacement of Time', *Australasian Journal of Philosophy*, 72, 463–74.

____ (2000), 'There's No Time Like the Present (in Minkowski Spacetime)', *Philosophy of Science (Proceedings)*, 67, 563–74.

____ (2002), 'On Absolute Becoming and the Myth of Passage', in C. Callender (ed.), *Time, Reality and Experience* (Cambridge, Cambridge University Press), 153–68.

Schlesinger, G. (1980), 'Temporal Becoming', in his *Aspects of Time* (Indianapolis: Hackett), 23–40.

____ (1982), 'How Time Flies', *Mind*, 91, 501–23.

Shimony, A. (1993), 'The Transient Now', in his *Search for a Naturalistic World View, Volume 2* (Cambridge: Cambridge University Press), 271–90.

Shoemaker, S. (1969), 'Time Without Change', *Journal of Philosophy*, 66, 363–81.

de Sitter, W. (1917), 'Einstein's Theory of Gravitation and its Astronomical Consequences. Third paper', *Monthly Notices of the Royal Astronomical Society*, 78, 3–28.

Sklar, L. (1981), 'Time, Reality and Relativity', in R. Healey (ed.), *Reduction, Time and Reality* (Cambridge, Cambridge University Press), 129–42.

Skyrms, B. (1980), *Causal Necessity: A Pragmatic Investigation of the Necessity of Laws* (New Haven: Yale University Press).

Słupecki, J. (1936), 'Der Volle Dreiwertige Aussagenkalkül', *Comptes Rendus des Séances de la Société des Sciences et des Lettres de Varsovie Cl. III*, 29, 9–11; English trans. 'The Full Many-Valued Propositional Calculus', in S. McCall (ed.), *Polish Logic 1920–1939* (Oxford: Clarendon Press, 1967), 335–7.

Smart, J. J. C. (1949), 'The River of Time', *Mind*, 58, 483–94.

____ (1963), *Philosophy and Scientific Realism* (London: Routledge & Kegan Paul).

____ (1980), 'Time and Becoming', in P. van Inwagen (ed.), *Time and Cause: Essays Presented to Richard Taylor* (Dordrecht: D. Reidel), 3–16.

____ (ed.) (1964), *Problems of Space and Time* (London: Macmillan).

Smith, P. (2003), 'Deflationism: The Facts', in H. Lillehammer and G. Rodriguez-Pereyra (eds.), *Real Metaphysics* (London: Routledge), 43–53.

Smith, Q. (1986), 'The Infinite Regress of Temporal Attributions', *Southern Journal of Philosophy*, 24, 383–96.

—— (1987), 'Problems with the New Tenseless Theory of Time', *Philosophical Studies*, 52, 371–92.

—— (1993), *Language and Time* (New York; Oxford: Oxford University Press).

—— (1998a), 'Absolute Simultaneity and the Infinity of Time', in R. Le Poidevin (ed.), *Questions of Time and Tense* (Oxford: Oxford University Press), 135–84.

—— (1998b), 'Tense and Temporal Logic', in E. Craig (ed.), *Routledge Encylopaedia of Philosophy* (London: Routledge).

—— (2002), 'Time and Degrees of Existence: A Theory of "Degree Presentism"', in C. Callender (ed.), *Time, Reality and Experience* (Cambridge: Cambridge University Press), 119–36.

Stalnaker, R. C. (1976), 'Possible Worlds', *Noûs*, 10, 65–75.

Stein, H. (1968), 'On Einstein–Minkowski Space–Time', *Journal of Philosophy*, 65, 5–23.

—— (1970), 'On the Paradoxical Time-Structures of Gödel', *Philosophy of Science*, 37, 589–601.

—— (1990), 'Introductory note to *1946/9', in S. Feferman *et al.* (eds.), *Kurt Gödel, Collected Works, Volume II* (Oxford: Oxford University Press), 202–30.

—— (1991), 'On Relativity Theory and Openness of the Future', *Philosophy of Science*, 58, 147–67.

van Stockum, W. J. (1937), 'The Gravitational Field of a Distribution of Particles Rotating Around an Axis of Symmetry', *Proc. Roy. Soc. Edinburgh A*, 57, 135.

Swinburne, R. (1981), *Space and Time* (2nd edn., London: Macmillan).

—— (ed.) (1983), *Space, Time and Causality* (Dordrecht: Reidel).

Tomberlin, J. E. (2003), 'Actualism and Presentism', in A. Jokić and Q. Smith (eds.), *Time, Tense, and Reference* (London: MIT Press), 449–64.

Tooley, M. (1977), 'The Nature of Laws', *Canadian Journal of Philosophy*, 7, 667–98.

—— (1997), *Time, Tense, and Causation* (Oxford: Oxford University Press).

Torretti, R. (1999), 'On Relativity, Time Reckoning, and the Topology of Time Series', in J. Butterfield (ed.), *The Arguments of Time* (Oxford: Oxford University Press for The British Academy), 65–82.

Van Inwagen, P. (1986), 'Two Concepts of Possible Worlds', *Midwest Studies in Philosophy*, 11, 185–213.
―― (ed.) (1980), *Time and Cause: Essays Presented to Richard Taylor* (Dordrecht: D. Reidel).
Weingard, R. (1972), '"Relativity" and the Reality of Past and Future Events', *British Journal for the Philosophy of Science*, 23, 119–21.
Weyl, H. (1918), *Raum Zeit Materie* (Berlin: J. Springer); English trans. H. L. Brose, *Space–Time–Matter* (London: Methuen, 1922).
Wheeler, J. A. (1978), 'The "Past" and the "Delayed Choice" Double-slit Experiment', in A. Marlow (ed.), *Mathematical Foundations of Quantum Theory* (New York: Academic Press), 9–48.
Williams, D. C. (1951), 'The Myth of Passage', *Journal of Philosophy*, 48, 457–72.
Winnie, J. A. (1970), 'Special Relativity Without One-Way Velocity Assumptions', *Philosophy of Science*, 32, 223–38; 37, 81–99.
Yourgrau, P. (1991), *The Disappearance of Time* (Cambridge: Cambridge University Press).
―― (1999), *Gödel Meets Einstein: Time Travel in the Gödel Universe* (Chicago: Open Court).
Zahar, E. (1983), 'Absoluteness and Conspiracy', in R. Swinburne (ed.), *Space, Time and Causality* (Dordrecht: Reidel), 37–41.
―― (1989), *Einstein's Revolution* (Cambridge: Cambridge University Press).
Zimmer, R. S. (1993), *Getting the Picture in Special Relativity* (Milton Keynes: Open University).

Index

absolute
  becoming 75
  elsewhere 153
  frame of reference, *see* frame of reference, absolute
  future 153
  past 153
acceleration 142-4
actualism 79
actuality
  absolute theory of 23
  indexical theory of 22
Adams, R. M. 23, 95
æther 176-8
Aristotle 82-6, 95
Armstrong, D. M. 40, 49
A-scale 4, 9
A-series 4, 8, 71-5
Ayer, A. J. 71-2

bivalence 40, 47, 82-9, 95
Bochvar, D. A. 88, 94
Broad, C. D. 12, 40, 75
B-scale 4, 9
B-series 3-4, 8-9, 16-17, 71-5
Butterfield, J. N. 66

Callender, C. 198
causal connectibity 153
causation 16-18, 47, 59, 109-35
  and Newcomb's problem 122-31
  and physical processes 119-21
  causal loops 131-4
  chance raising theory 114-15
  counterfactual connotation of 115-21
  counterfactual theory 113-14
  direction of 117-35
  means-end connotation 121-31
  presentism and backwards causation 134-5
  regularity theory 110-13
  relata of 109-10

  see also reference, causal theory of
change 2, 4-5, 7, 9, 11, 13, 17, 25, 29-32, 34, 58, 66-8, 70-7, 81-2, 109, 205, 214
closed time-like curves 205, 208, 211-12, 216-17
comoving coordinates 193
cosmic time 190-203, 207-8
  problems with 198-203
counterparts 106
Craig, W. L. 44, 46, 105
Crystal, D. 1

decision theory
  causal 127-8, 130-1
  non-causal 127-9
  principle of dominance 122, 124
  principle of maximizing expected utility 122, 124
  see also probability
determinism 47-50, 61, 81, 83, 116, 134-5
Dorato, M. 164, 187, 198, 201

Earman, J. 212, 224
Eddington, A. 197
Eells, E. 129
Einstein, A. 141, 146, 148-50, 172-8, 180, 185, 189, 192, 207
Einstein's field equations 204
ersatzer presentism 52-69
  accessibility relation 55, 57, 62-65
  advantages of 65-9, 135
  dates 54-5, 63-4, 67-8, 78
  e-proposition 53
  E-relation 53-5
  u-proposition 53
events 5-8, 75, 81, 109-10
existence, relativity of 168-70
expanding universe, *see* cosmic time
externalism 108

240　INDEX

Falk, A. 16
fatalism 84
Fitzgerald, G. 176
frame of reference 141
　absolute 144–5, 157, 176–82, 189
Frege, G. 104
future contingents 40, 61, 82–95

Galilean transformations 144–6
geometry 159, 183, 194–5, 209
Gibbard, A. 127–9
Gödel, K. 139, 190, 201–15
　epistemic argument 218–19
　modal argument 201, 212–24
Gödel's model 205, 208–15

Halldén, S. 89
Harper, W. L. 127–9
here-now 170–2
homogeneity 192, 196–200, 208, 210
horizon, event and creation 197–8
Hubble constant 190, 195
Hubble parameter 195
Hume, D. 110, 113

identity over time 59
inertia, law of 141
inertial force 142–4
invariant quantities 146, 149–50, 153, 156–7, 159, 163, 165, 183, 193
isotropy 192, 196, 200, 208

Jeans, J. 202, 208

Kamp, H. 42
Kripke, S. 102–3

von Laue, M. 178–9
law of excluded middle 70, 82, 85–7, 89, 91, 95
law of non-contradiction 70, 82, 85–7, 89
laws of nature 48–51, 83, 116–19, 146
length contraction 150, 156, 177
Le Poidevin, R. 34, 36, 43, 47, 66, 76, 80–1, 103
Lepore, E. 79

Lewis, D. 22–3, 40, 43, 52, 54, 60–1, 68, 113, 116–21, 127–8, 132–4, 205
light
　Law of the Propagation of 146, 188
　one-way speed of 180–1
　speed of 146–7, 149–54, 158, 180–1, 188, 209–11
light-like separation 152–3
limit principle 147, 188, 209
logical truth 86–9, 92
Lorentz, H. A. 150, 176–7
Lorentz transformations 149–51, 176–80
Lowe, E. J. 14, 36
Lucas, J. R. 187, 190
Ludlow, P. 48
Ludwig, K. 79
Łukasiewicz, J. 47–8, 82, 84–9, 94–5

MacBeath, M. 17
McArthur, R. P. 42
McCall, S. 12, 25, 30–3, 37
Mackie, J. L. 179–82
McTaggart, J. McT. E. 27, 70–7, 205–6, 214
McTaggart's argument 70–8
Malament, D. 208
Mellor, D. H. 16, 22–3, 33–6, 50, 70–1, 114, 121–2, 126, 131–4, 158, 187–91, 195–6, 199
Mellor-Rees argument 187–91
Michelson-Morley experiment 176–8
Mill, J. S. 104
Minkowski, H. 157–9
Minkowski space-time 142, 151–9, 161–5, 174, 189, 194
motion, dynamic and static accounts of 80–1

Nahin, P. J. 211
neo-Newtonian space-time 144–6
Newton, I. 145
Newtonian mechanics 141–6, 150, 177, 204
Newton-Smith, W. H. 67
Nozick, R. 124, 130

Oaklander, L. N. 46, 74

INDEX 241

parsimony 182–4, 222–3
Plantinga, A. 44
Poincaré, H. 177–8
possible worlds 51–2
  similarity 116–17
  transworld relations 114
  see also actualism; actuality
present
  indexical theory of 21–4, 165–6, 170
  redundancy theory of 42, 95
  referential use of 22
Present Problem 21–38, 184–5
Price, H. 119–21
Prior, A. N. 17, 42–4, 52, 67, 75, 82, 95, 99–100
probability 114, 122, 126–31
Putnam, H. 86, 139, 162–3, 166–7, 169, 174, 184, 185
Putnam's thesis 160–2

quantification 10, 57–60
  substitutional vs objectual 100–101
quantum mechanics 31, 48, 112, 203

reference 44–5
  causal theory of 103–8
  descriptive theory of 99–103
  Millian theory of 104
  rigidity 102–3, 216
relativity
  general theory of 187–224
  special theory of 139–191
  Principle of Relativity 146, 179, 188
Robertson-Walker metric 192–6, 200
rotating universe 205, 208–11
Russell, B. 71, 100–3
Russell's hypothesis 51, 57

Savitt, S. F. 164, 215
scale factor 194–6
Shoemaker, S. 68
simplicity 182–4, 220, 222–3
simultaneity 96–7
  absolute 153, 160–2, 173–6, 184, 187–91, 207, 211
  'conspiracy of silence' 179–82
  defined using cosmology 191–6
  relativity of 147–9, 155, 160, 171–3, 176, 181, 183, 189

naturalistic basis for 174, 189–91, 196, 208
  and the present 160–2
de Sitter, W. 197
Sklar, L. 170–2, 185
Skyrms, B. 127–8
Smart, J. J. C. 31–2
Smith, Q. 12, 24, 58–9, 74, 172, 182
space
  curvature of 194
  differences with time 71–2, 109, 157–9, 172
space-like separation 152–4, 171
space-time conjunction 153
space-time interval 151–2, 156, 159
steady state universe 201–2
Stein, H. 48, 73, 139, 162–70, 174–5, 185–6
Stein's antithesis 162–72
Swinburne, R. 187

tense operators 5–10, 42–3, 46, 97
  de re 58–9, 103
tense theories 10–14
  branching-futurism 12, 30–3
  degree presentism 12, 24–5
  no-futurism 12–13, 25–30, 167
  past, present, and futurism 11
  Priorian presentism 41–6, 53
  reductive presentism 47–51
  see also ersatzer presentism
tensed beliefs 25–6, 33
tenseless theory 2–5, 8–11, 13, 16–18, 21, 24–30, 33, 38–9, 42, 46–7, 53, 58, 65–6, 68–70, 72, 79, 81–3, 109, 112, 134–5, 139, 164–9, 202–3, 205, 214, 216, 219, 223, 224
tenses 5–11, 71–5
  higher-order 73–4
  minimalism concerning 163–6
  relativity of 166–70
Thomas, D. 1
time
  and emotion 17–18
  and perception 16–18, 29–33, 218–19
  as a functional concept 220–4
  as opposed to space, *see* space
  as opposed to space-time 214–15

time (cont.)
  branching 12–14, 25, 30–3, 45, 55, 57, 60–5, 86, 93, 112–13, 134, 205
  circular 55, 211–12
  contiguity 111
  contingent features of 217–24
  continuous 55, 64
  deontic need for 78–9
  dilation 150, 156
  direction of See causation, direction of; cosmic time, problems with
  discrete 55, 64
  essential properties of 201, 216–17
  infinite 55
  linear 11, 45, 55, 112–13, 134, 212, 216–17
  metaphors concerning 1–2
  paradoxical need for 80–1
  platitudes concerning 2, 15–18, 37, 55, 61, 65–6, 202–3, 220, 222
  semantic need for 79–80
  tensed-tenseless differences 8–10, 66
  unreality of 71, 76, 205–6, 213–15, 224
  without change 66–8
time-like separation 152–3, 210
time travel 132–4, 205
Tomberlin, J. E. 78–9
Tooley, M. 9–10, 13, 25–33, 37, 43, 50, 68, 86–9, 180, 185–6

transtemporal relations
  determinables 98
  earlier than 95–7
  qualitative 98–9
  reference 99–108
  see also causation
truth
  redundancy theory of 42, 95
  simpliciter 34–5, 42, 53, 56–8, 60, 62–3, 76, 78
truth-at-a-time 34–5, 56, 58, 60
truth-conditions 4, 8–10, 26, 33–7, 56–60, 94
truth-functionality 86–7
truthmakers 5, 10, 37–47, 50, 53, 55–9, 63, 68, 78, 87, 222
truth-value links 39–41, 45–6, 50–1, 53, 61–3, 65, 92–3

velocity 142–5, 149–51
verificationism 11, 171–3, 176, 189

Weyl, H. 209
Wheeler, J. A. 48

Yourgrau, P. 215

Zahar, E. 179–80
Zeno's Arrow 80